The Sign of The Cross

Colm Tóibín was born in Enniscorthy, Co. Wexford in 1955. A former editor of *Magill*, Ireland's leading current affairs monthly, he has published five books. *Walking Along the Border* was republished by Vintage in 1994 in the form the author intended for it, as *Bad Blood*. *The Sign of the Cross* was shortlisted for the Esquire/Volvo/Waterstones Non-Fiction Award. Tóibín's first novel, *The South*, won the *Irish Times* Prize and was an acclaimed fictional debut; his second, *The Heather Blazing*, received the Encore Award. Both novels have been translated into several European languages and published in the USA. Tóibín, who lives in Dublin, has also published a book about Barcelona.

BY COLM TÓIBÍN

Fiction

The South
The Heather Blazing

Non-Fiction

Dubliners
(with photographs by Tony O'Shea)
Homage To Barcelona
Bad Blood
The Sign Of The Cross

Colm Tóibín

THE SIGN OF THE CROSS

Travels in Catholic Europe

VINTAGE

Published by Vintage 1995

2 4 6 8 10 9 7 5 3 1

Acknowledgement is made to Faber and Faber for permission to reproduce lines from 'Snow' from the *Collected Poems of Louis MacNeice*. The quotation from 'Church Going' by Philip Larkin is reprinted from *The Less Deceived* by permission of The Marvell Press, England and Australia

First published in Great Britain by Jonathan Cape Ltd, 1994

Vintage
Random House, 20 Vauxhall Bridge Road, London SW1V 2SA

Random House Australia (Pty) Limited
20 Alfred Street, Milsons Point, Sydney
New South Wales 2061, Australia

Random House New Zealand Limited
18 Poland Road, Glenfield,
Auckland 10, New Zealand

Random House South Africa (Pty) Limited
PO Box 337, Bergvlei, South Africa

Random House UK Limited Reg. No. 954009

A CIP catalogue record for this book is available from the British Library

ISBN 0 09 988300 7

Papers used by Random House UK Ltd are natural, recyclable products made from wood grown in sustainable forests. The manufacturing processes conform to the environmental regulations of the country of origin

Printed and bound in Great Britain by
The Guernsey Press Co. Ltd., Guernsey, Channel Islands

for
Padraig Tóibín, Kathleen Tóibín and
Harriet O'Connell

Contents

I

A Native Son

I HAVE A MEMORY of a train arriving in Enniscorthy station in the early morning. My mother and my aunt were coming back from Lourdes. I must have been five or six, which would make the year 1960 or 1961. I remember getting on the train and finding that the blinds were drawn on the windows. My mother and my aunt had just been sleeping; they were tired. They had travelled overland to Lourdes.

'Overland': that was one of the new words that suddenly became commonplace as the story of the journey was told. 'Basilica', 'Courier', 'Down through France'. There was no fizzy orange to be had in France, and the heat was terrible in the bus, and everybody was dying of thirst. A bottle of orange juice cost a lot of money, but still it was worth it. It was so hot in France.

Postcards came of torchlit processions, or of Saint Bernadette, or of the statue of Our Lady of Lourdes. There were large plastic bottles of Lourdes water with shoulder straps, or smaller bottles in the shape of Our Lady of Lourdes with a blue screw-cap top. These were my first intimations of the world outside Ireland. My parents and aunts and uncles went to Lourdes, sometimes venturing over the border to San Sebastian in Spain. One aunt, my father's sister, went on pilgrimages to Rome and Santiago de Compostela. All along the mantelpiece of the back room at home there were souvenirs from these journeys – an ashtray of Toledo gold, a small, ornamental sword in a leather scabbard, a holy statue.

And stories of the strangeness of continental Europe continued to be told. In the morning, in Lourdes, you would hear the adults say, they just had coffee and a 'roll' for breakfast. They didn't have tea in France. I can still see myself sitting quietly watching the adults discussing this. You'd love a cup of tea, someone would say, and the rest would nod, remembering their ordeal, exotic and frightening at the same time, and so oddly memorable. And maybe then there would be a moment's silence and someone would say that there was nothing like Lourdes all the same, nothing like the procession, the torches at night, and the invalids being led down to the basilica. And they all would agree, all nod in a thoughtful, melancholy and distant way. If you believed that you had problems, they'd say, you'd always meet someone worse.

In the cathedral in Enniscorthy the names of the bishops from the beginning of time were written on a painted scroll which stretched down the high walls on each side of the altar. There was benediction after the boys' confraternity when the priest's voice would boom down the huge, half empty, almost dark church: death comes soon, he would say, judgement will follow, so now dear children, examine your conscience and find out your sins.

This was the centre of power, our neo-gothic cathedral at the top of Main Street. Designed by Pugin, towering over us all, much grander than the town's Protestant church, it was a sign of the great, rich might of the Catholic Church in nineteenth-century

Ireland. But if I forget about its grandeur and majesty for a few minutes and if I concentrate on what it was like to be a child in that place – at children's Mass on Holy Thursday, for example, or at ten o'clock Mass any Sunday – I remember hours of unsettled boredom.

None the less, it was where you could see everybody, you could notice that people who owned shops tended to walk confidently up the centre aisle at the last minute. It was where you could see the merchants in their new clothes. I was an altar boy there and I accompanied the priest with a patten as he gave out communion to the faithful. And thus I got to see everyone's tongue at close range. Some stuck it out with great force as though it was a leather strap; others were timid about sticking it out as though it was an intimate part of their body which they preferred to keep hidden. Some had broad flat tongues, the shape of a piece of sole or plaice; others had narrow, thick tongues. And each tongue had a different texture – small wrinkles and indentations filled the surface – and each person had a different colour tongue, pink, for example (some were pure pink), with eddies of brown and grey. Some people had trouble keeping their tongue stuck out, despite their best intentions, and would draw it back in, as though someone was going to commit some offence against it, and the priest would stand and wait until it ventured out again. And I would stand there too, watching.

In a book, published in 1946 to celebrate the centenary of the cathedral, an essay drily entitled 'Analysis of Some Cathedral Records' looks at the donations to the cathedral's building fund in the 1840s. 'Lists of names, with sometimes the trade or profession and the address of the donor, the amount which he had contributed – nothing more . . . At the time when these entries were made the Great Famine was sweeping through the land.

Many of those whose small subscriptions helped to build Enniscorthy Cathedral must soon have known bitter hunger, starvation and death, or a long exile made more lonely by memories of a silvered river flowing between green fields; by the thought of a still churchyard looking across the valley where their bones would never lie.'

The essay lists the names in the old records, and they are the names of the people I was brought up with: Byrne, Bolger, Clifford, Dempsey, Hendrick, Kehoe, Roche, Walsh, Stafford, Sinnott, Cullen. And in 1946, despite the displacements of the past century, the author can place some of the donors' relatives in the town: 'The two sisters of David Byrne, victualler, Slaney Street, Miss Byrne and Mrs Kennedy, died not so many years ago in Enniscorthy. Denis Byrne, who was evicted from Ballyorril, was a brother of Mrs M. Ennis, Oulartard. His eviction caused much ill-feeling in the district. Paul Bolger, who lived in the Shannon, was the grandfather of Mr Dan Bolger, Market Square. Patrick Clifford, who was a carpenter, had a house in New Street which his son now occupies . . . The descendants of Mrs Harris, Brownswood, still live in the same place, as do those of Moses Harpur, Brownswood . . .'

The past is recent, alive, easy to get in touch with. I have a feeling that the ease with which the list of subscribers connects with the town one hundred years later is because there are hardly any surviving buildings in Enniscorthy before the cathedral, and hardly any documents. History can be vivid once the Catholic classes are rising and the new class of merchant is prepared to build a cathedral, a monument to its power, in spite of the famine raging among the lower orders. But before this time – 1846 in Enniscorthy – the Catholics are mainly silent. I know that one of my great-grandfathers owned a public house on the Island Road in this town – I have a glass with the name of the pub inscribed on it. Another had a stone-cutting business near the cathedral. Another had a smallholding outside the town. Another came from a farm thirty miles away. There are certain things I know about them, or can imagine, but before them I can imagine nothing and I know nothing. The cathedral is the beginning of real, imaginable time.

In the evening at home we knelt down to say the Rosary, and each adult had a different way of giving out the Mysteries, as each had a differently shaped handwriting: some recited the Hail Mary slowly, in a dreamy sort of way, others were brisk, making it clear that they meant business. Sometimes I could let myself go with it, forget myself and say the prayers, but most of the time it was, like being in the cathedral, pure boredom, broken only by the possibility that my father would be discovered shaking with laughter while continuing to kneel there with his hands joined and his beads in his hands. It did not happen often but when it did he would leave the room. When he came back and the Rosary resumed there would be a really good chance that the solemnity of the family praying together would be too much for him once more and he would convulse again with nervous laughter while the family continued to pray. After the Rosary there was the Hail Holy Queen and odd prayers known as trimmings, including a call on God to spare us from a sudden and unprovided-for death. Then it was over and you could put your beads back in the first press in the kitchen.

If you wanted to pass an exam you prayed to St Joseph of Cupertino, but you had to study as well. If you lost something you prayed to St Anthony, but you had to look as well. My mother had a prayer which had a note at the bottom reminding you that it was so efficacious you must be sure you really wanted what you were asking for. I was a child when my father became ill, and I can remember vigils of prayer, I can remember a nun telling my mother that she was going to go that very night and, literally, knock on the tabernacle and ask Jesus to make my father better. It was something she had done very few times, but it had always worked, she said. When my father went to Lourdes now it was not part of an exotic journey to the European mainland, it was to take the waters, to pray, to get better. Suddenly, it was serious.

When my father died his body lay overnight in the cathedral and I remember watching an altar boy with a large cross which he held with his two hands, as he led the coffin down the centre aisle of the church.

My father was dead now and there was a greater need to study and try and do well for myself. I kept a mass card in my missal with his photograph on it and special prayers which my mother had chosen printed on it. In all the advice given to me there was a mixture of worldliness and unworldliness: the need to save your soul was coupled with a need to get on in the world. The need to find and keep a good job and the need to please God and save your soul at the same time were intrinsic parts of the same dream on which I was brought up, after my father's death, in that small town.

I was about fourteen when a friend a couple of years older announced with certainty that this religion, this Catholic stuff was all nonsense, every bit of it – not just the rituals, not just the saints and the holy pictures, the relics and the days of obligation, but the fundamentals. There was no God, he assured me, not with bravado or a desire to shock, but as if it was something he had always known. So who made the world? I asked. It's just there, he said. And what about Jesus Christ? He saw the break-up of the Roman Empire, my friend told me with absolute and quiet authority, and he sought to replace it with a notion of treating thy neighbour as thyself, but it never caught on. Instead, we have all those priests and sermons and silly rules.

I still walked up the cathedral aisle and took communion, and walked back to my seat with my eyes cast down. I still prayed, but slowly my faith was fading. I attended a seminar on vocations when I was sixteen and a theologian spoke about 'the paradox of faith', the idea that to believe you must first 'believe', that faith required a blind leap and then a more rational approach. In certain (and, indeed, uncertain) ways I came to realise that I had never believed. I had always known that the interest all around me in security, money, power and status was greater than any love of God or belief in his mercy. Religion was consolation, like listening to music after a long day's work; it was pure theatre, it was a way of holding people together. By this time I was in a school where most of the priests spent their summers in America, and debate was allowed on every issue relating to faith and morals. I drifted away, I read Kafka and D.H. Lawrence, and by the time I reached university I had other things to think about.

At university I knew no one who believed. Thus it was always a shock on Ash Wednesday when a majority of students walked the campus sporting ashes on their foreheads. I looked at them in wonder, wanting to ask if no one had told them, as my friend had told me, that it was all nonsense. Could they not wake up? How could they still believe? Those were the early 1970s, the days of the Women's Movement, the Divorce Action Group, the beginning of Gay Rights, and I, with many others, believed that Ireland was well on the way to becoming a secular republic. I attended meetings of the League of Decency to laugh and heckle. I did not know that the students wearing ashes would become part of the moral majority in Ireland in the 1980s. All change when I was a student seemed a form of progress. In 1975 I went to Barcelona to live and I did not think about Catholicism again for some years. It did not cost me a thought.

In the autumn of 1979 I was back in Dublin, however, looking for work as a journalist. I convinced a magazine for which I had written a few pieces to let me apply for press accreditation for the Pope's visit to Ireland.

The first day of the Pope's visit was one of those remarkable sunny days in Dublin, a pure blue sky all day. I remember him descending from the aeroplane, dressed in white, a half-watchful smile, a half-pained look on his face. He was attentive to people, it was easy to see that, while he remained distant, a fatherly prelate and a figurehead at the same time. As he went to his helicopter I watched a woman approaching him who desperately wanted to touch him, or have him bless her. She was an ordinary woman, not one of the dignitaries the Pope had been greeting. I tried at the time to describe this moment as though it was important, because the Pope was not on show, there were no television cameras or photographers. I saw that the Pope noticed the woman, but he was determined now to continue. She followed and there was a sort of panic in her eyes as she called out to him. And then I saw his face change from that soft warmth to something else, something tougher. He was not going to pay any attention to the woman. I don't know why I thought this was so important; maybe because he had seemed so kind and spontaneous during his time at the airport. But now his face hardened completely. It was a strange, funny moment. It hardly mattered. And yet it stayed with me for the rest of his visit. At that time we knew almost nothing about him.

Because I had a press pass I had a front seat in the Phoenix Park in Dublin where a million Irish Catholics congregated for the Papal Mass. It was pure drama. It was Fellini's *Roma* mixed with an elaborate tableau from the Inca period. There was a high silver cross on a mound, and it glinted in the sun; the Pope was dressed in white and yellow, utterly glamorous against the blue sky. It was like something out of a dream as he spoke in his broken English. The priests in front of me were so excited that they took photographs of each other.

At first he spoke about the liturgy, and then later about peace; but as the days of his visit went by he started to talk about sex and sexual morality. He began by winning the crowd over in a display of complete theatricality and ended by hectoring us. At least that was how I saw it. He displayed the full paradox of the Christian message which begins with 'Suffer the little children to come unto me' and ends with 'Thou art Peter, and upon this rock I will build my Church'. Mysticism and mystery followed by authority and power. No one else saw it like this, however. For most Irish people his visit was a glorious episode, and the newspapers reflected that. Needless to say, no one was interested in publishing my version of events.

On the last day of his visit I met an old school friend walking along St Stephen's Green with his girlfriend. I told them proudly that I had been in the front row at the Phoenix Park and I had seen priests talking right through the consecration. It was all theatre, I said, until he started to tell us what to do about our laws and our sex lives. My friend and his girlfriend remained silent. And then my friend said quietly that they had been deeply inspired by the visit and they did not like me speaking with such disrespect about the Pope. I walked away, unable to understand.

The following year I wanted to go back to Barcelona on a visit and I discovered that the cheapest way of getting there was by flying to Lourdes and taking the train from there to Barcelona. In the summer there were several direct flights from Dublin to Lourdes every weekend. So I booked a ticket.

I was certainly the youngest person on the flight that Friday night, and the only passenger, I was sure, intent on holidays rather than spiritual renewal. I think the other passengers believed I was a priest.

At the hotel it soon became clear that the tour operators had overbooked, and an enormous comedy began as the owner – a large and determined elderly Frenchwoman – read out names of people who would have to share rooms. The pilgrims could not at first understand her pronunciation, but when their names were finally translated for them they went crazy because they did not want to share rooms with people they did not know. They sat tight. They refused to go to the rooms appointed to them. They were most indignant. They made clear that they had nothing personal against the people with whom they would not share. They were Dublin lower middle-class and working-class people and they were used to getting value for money, and they did not take kindly to being pushed around by this woman who could not even speak English. The Frenchwoman shrugged, and told the porter to take their bags to the designated rooms. A few of them began to shout and demand their rights, but still she shrugged. The Dublin pilgrims were tired; they had consumed a great deal of energy refusing to share with each other. Now they set about organising who would share with whom, how many beds were available in how many rooms. They did not notice the owner beckoning me over, handing me a key and instructing the porter to show me to my room. She, too, thought that I was a priest. This worked well and it struck me as I lay in my comfortable bed that it was something I must try again.

A week later I arrived back in Lourdes from Barcelona early in the evening. I was travelling on a night flight so I left my bags at the hotel and wandered into the street. I noticed that people were moving towards the grotto with unlit torches, and, casually at first, I followed them since there was really nowhere else to go.

It was dark now and some of the ceremonies seemed to be over as people passed on their way back towards the town. The grotto was in a dip in the ground and as I walked in through the gates I was aware of having entered another atmosphere. I was expecting stalls with statues and rosary beads for sale but there was nothing except small groups of pilgrims carrying torches towards the basilica in the distance, their faces calm, serene. Everything was quiet and low-key. Some people were singing the simple 'Ave Maria' I knew from processions at home. I stood close to a German group who had formed a circle, each pilgrim holding a lighted torch. They sang a hymn I had never heard before, the men's and the women's voices forming strange harmonies. I was sure now that the evening's devotions were over and these were people who had lingered on.

A few pilgrims were still moving towards the rock where the apparition was said to have occurred and where the statue now was. I followed them slowly. I still had time, the flight was not for another few hours, but I was worried that the lights below us would be turned off and we would be motioned to leave. In some way, without realising it, I wanted to see this, I did not want to go home without experiencing it, whatever it was. I did not feel that the pull towards this place was anything supernatural, or came from outside myself, it was perhaps simply the pull of curiosity. People were kneeling staring up at the lit statue of Our Lady of Lourdes, and others were queuing to touch the rock. I sat and watched them, trying to fathom this: these people around me here in the night believed that the Virgin had come down from heaven and appeared here, that her body had flown through the air to be in this place. I watched them all as I tried to imagine, or remember, what it would be like to believe that.

I stood up and joined the queue to touch the rock.

Most people had gone, and there were just a few pilgrims waiting in line. The woman in front of me touched the rock below the statue with care and concentration as though its power were live and real and she could extract something from it, something miraculous and vital. She stayed there, tracing her hand over the stone. When it came to my turn I bowed my head for a moment, but I did not touch the stone. I went back to my seat and stayed there watching, trying not to think at all.

Soon, it was time to leave, they were going to turn off the lights. I went back to the hotel to find my pilgrims singing songs in unison, full of good humour, waiting for the bus which would take us to the airport and home to Dublin.

Lourdes stayed in my mind. I wrote a piece for radio about it which was never broadcast, and in my first novel I had the main character go to Lourdes and experience what I experienced, but I took it out. It didn't work. I had felt a sense of wonder that was new and unexpected. It was something that often came into my mind. And in 1987 when I was in Spain again I had an opportunity to go back to Lourdes and I took it. This time I would spend a few days there with friends, one of whom was interested in the shrine. I was interested too, but not sure in what way.

This time I took the train from San Sebastian, the city the Basques call Donostia, and found a small hotel. It was early September, and it was hot in Lourdes, even at night. In the morning I went on my own to look at the basilica and found the street where every type of religious object is sold. Postcards that change their image when you move them about, as though to mock the notion of the apparition, enormous statues of the Virgin, holy pictures, every type of rosary beads imaginable, containers for holy water. Shop after shop full of religious objects, all with stalls outside and colourful decorations. In conversations about Lourdes, people had said that this was what really put them off, this commercialisation, this marketing of religion as a product. But that morning as I wandered up and down the street examining this enormous display of religious objects, it all seemed to me quite normal – similar objects had been in our house when I was growing up, had been brought home as presents and souvenirs.

That night I saw the torch-light procession for the first time. It was dark. Hundreds of old-fashioned wheelchairs, like small carriages, were being pushed along towards the basilica. Men were standing by. And they were in charge. They reminded me of the men in my home town who controlled the annual Blessed Sacrament Procession, who stood with their hands behind their backs looking strict and solemn, as though they had suddenly joined the army, and were taking their new duties very seriously. These men in Lourdes wore special belts and insignia to make their rank and importance clear rather than the ordinary red sash worn by the men in Enniscorthy. There was something odd and old-fashioned about it, it looked like something from the 1930s, this half-military get-up. They came here for a week or two from small towns in Ireland or France or Germany, and now they had power to put out their hands and stop the flow of pilgrims towards the basilica. We allowed ourselves to be regimented as we moved towards the place of the apparition holding lighted candles.

The following day I went to take the waters and I joined in a long queue of men, overseen by another of the middle-aged men who exuded watchfulness and authority. Priests did not have to join the queue, I discovered, but I decided to remain a lay person for the moment, realising that I would probably be found out by the man at the door and sent home. No one was carrying a towel, and I wondered how we would dry ourselves. When I was a child and heard my elders talking about taking the baths in Lourdes I always imagined them in bathing costumes. Now no one seemed to have bathing costumes. It seemed impossible that people would take off all their clothes, and make the baths of Lourdes into one big locker-room. To Irish Catholics, at least, modesty was one of the cardinal virtues. I waited in the hot sun, wondering what was going to happen. The man in front of me was very old and was finding it difficult to wait for so long.

Once inside, we were told to take off all our clothes down to our underpants. In a moment of panic I wondered if I was wearing underpants, and when I realised that I was, I panicked once more, wondering if they were clean. I followed the others and stripped slowly down to my briefs, ordinary Y-fronts, like most of the other men taking the water, and reasonably presentable. What would happen now? Would we wear our underpants in the baths? Also, how deep was the water? Was it cold? We had always been told that even if the person before you had an infectious disease, it would not matter, the water was powerful and blessed and you could not catch a disease from it. I found as I stood there that I still believed this, and that even though the old man who was in front of me had scabs on his legs, I, none the less, had no fear that I would develop a horrible skin ailment from taking the same water as him.

We were herded into the room where the baths were. I was instructed to stand in the corner and face the wall. I obeyed orders, although I could see no logic to this. A man then took a towel and spread it out behind me, shielding my bottom from sight, as he told me to take off my underpants and hang them on the nail above. And when I had done this he tied the towel around me without touching me. He was fast and skilful as though he had been doing this all his life. I turned around and faced the baths. Three men were waiting there, and they motioned me towards them.

'English?' one of them asked.

'No, Irish,' I said.

'Paidreacha as Gaeilge?' he asked. I was surprised by this. I did not know anyone here was Irish, and I realised that I had probably forgotten my prayers in Irish, and had to say no, in English please. And then they got ready. The previous day someone had talked about an Irishwoman with cancer who was so overwhelmed in the baths and believed so fervently in the power of the water that she was sure she must be cured, and was in no doubt when she went home that she would live. Thus her dying was more difficult, because she could not believe that her cancer did not disappear in Lourdes.

The men held me down, said the prayers over me and made me say the refrain, and then they poured the cold water over me while I lay in the bath, which was more like a drain.

When I got out and went back to retrieve my underpants I was shaking. I hated being held down. I had expected to be allowed to lower myself into a tub of cold water in my own time. But I had also felt something of the power of the place, the amount of hope and spirit which had been let loose within these walls over all the years. I was confused by this mixture of hatred and fear of the Church's authority with my susceptibility to its rituals and its sheer force. I wanted to go away on my own and curl up in the dark. And in my confusion as the man unloosed my towel and held it so that no one could see me in my nakedness and told me to put on my underpants without drying myself, I put them on the wrong way around. He noticed then as I was about to go back and put on my clothes, and suggested that I come back and do it right. There was all the time in the world, he said. He held up the towel to protect my modesty once more. I went out, then, and like everybody else, put on my clothes without drying myself, still shaken by taking the waters. Outside, the light seemed blindingly sharp and intense as I walked back to my hotel to meet my friends.

2

The Memory of War

AN HOUR BEFORE the train from Prague to Warsaw was due to leave there was an atmosphere of frenzy on the platform as Polish men bought beer from a shop, filling bags with bottles, shouting to each other about prices and money, and pushing and shoving their way to the counter. Prague had been sedate and calm, no one had raised their voices in the street; there was a sense that people had learned to live at some distance from the material world. These Polish men in the railway station were different. They elbowed each other out of the way; they seemed excited at the prospect of going home.

The train was crowded; most of the passengers were men. In my compartment, however, there was a Polish family who seemed upset at a stranger joining them; they were silent and suspicious as I put my luggage on the overhead rack. But they soon resumed what had been an animated conversation. They were very cheerful: they talked, laughed and giggled without stop. Even before we left the station they seemed to get used to me, and when they found out that I was not going all the way to Warsaw but getting out at Katowice, they laughed again and told me that the train would be stopping there at five o'clock in the morning. So, they mimed, I had better not sleep too soundly.

As soon as the train started, various officials came

to visit us, looking for tickets and visas. My Polish companions laughed heartily each time an official left our compartment; they seemed to view authority with immense amusement and disrespect. After a while one of them went out into the corridor to have a smoke. There was no sign anywhere saying that you could not do this, and the smoker seemed genuinely surprised when a Czech official told him to put it out and began to interview him, then took a few notes and confiscated his ticket.

His family watched this scene with great attention, it had a sobering effect on them, but as soon as the smoker came back and sat down they rocked with laughter at the pomposity of the official. The official, however, was taking his duties seriously and between Prague and the Polish border the Polish smoker was interviewed several times more, and eventually fined the equivalent of one dollar, big money. He was handed back his ticket and sat there silently for a while, suitably chastened by the Czechs, before returning to his normal self, giggling at the good of it all in the company of his family.

At the border in the early hours a woman in uniform opened the compartment door and woke me to ask how much money I had. The Poles woke as well, and watched uneasily as I showed her my dollars and my travellers' cheques. For them, I knew, this would amount to a fortune, they could probably live for a year on it, and they averted their eyes as she left, and remained silent.

Between four and five in the morning the train arrived at Katowice. Even though it was still pitch dark outside, the station was busy with people going to work. I needed zlotys, but had not wanted to ask the Polish family on the train to change money for me. I realised that nothing would be open in the station this early and I wandered out into the dark city, which was bleak and cold, in the hour before dawn until I found a big hotel which changed my money. Back at the station I looked at the list of times and destinations, but could see no mention of where I wanted to go. People seemed pale and tired as they hurried past. Eventually, I stopped a man in his early twenties and showed him the name of the place: Oswiecim. He was clearly on his way to work, but motioned me over to the ticket window, took some money, and bought a ticket for me, indicating which platform I should go to.

The train, just a few carriages, was old and moved slowly through a sullen landscape dotted with chimney-stacks and sidings with wagons full of coal. Everything was untidy; the machinery looked old and in the dim light of the early morning the place seemed worn out, an industrial world at the end of its tether. The station, I knew, was some distance from the camp, but these were the same train lines along which the condemned had been ferried. I got off at Oswiecim, and took a taxi to the camp.

As soon as I stood at the door of the reception centre I felt that I was wrong to be here. There was already controversy over the presence of Carmelite nuns who had moved into a building on the site. It was not a Catholic shrine. Most of those murdered here were Jews. I thought of turning and going on to Warsaw. In Prague the previous day, in the museum beside the old Jewish cemetery, I had seen an exhibition of drawings by Jewish children who had been held in a concentration camp. The drawings had the frail colouring and naive perspectives of other children's drawings. If you did not examine them too carefully, you might not notice that all of them dealt with the camp. Just as other children might depict innocent scenes, these children drew hangings, barbed wire, armed guards, guard dogs. There was no sense of fear in the work, no dark colours used to express horror. A note explained that most of the children were later transported to Poland and died here at Oswiecim – Auschwitz.

Beside the reception centre there was a small, modest hotel. I hadn't slept all night, and had put no thought into what it would be like to arrive here, just like that, as though this was an art museum or a seaside resort. I went into the hotel and rang the bell. The woman who came could have been a nun. She was quiet-spoken and reserved; the atmosphere was that of a convent. She took my passport and a small amount of money and gave me a room-key.

I thought that probably relatives of those who were murdered here would find it unbearable to visit the site of the camp and leave immediately. But maybe the hotel was a good idea: they could sleep for a night close to the ashes of those who were slaughtered. The floors were covered in polished lino, and my room was bare except for a bed and a table. There was nothing on the walls; it was like a cell. I slept for a while, awoken later by the sounds of a school tour, young people's voices breaking the stillness. I got up and went downstairs. In the building next door I bought a ticket for the camp museum and another ticket to see a film on the liberation of Auschwitz.

I went inside the gates. Maybe it was important simply to come here, I thought; to remember. Most people that day were quiet and subdued; there was a note asking visitors to remain silent. I passed the office where prisoners coming from the trains were taken first. I wandered among the brick buildings at least half of which were closed up. I saw the gallows built for Rudolf Hoss, who ran this camp. He was tried at Nuremberg, brought back here and hanged. I looked at the map which explained which buildings were used for extermination. I walked into one which housed an expressionist exhibition about the horrors of what had happened, but it was too distant, too artificial and I wandered out again, still wondering if it was right to be here, if the whole place should not be closed, given back to nature, fenced off in honour of those who died here or had their lives destroyed.

Outside, I found a tour guide talking to his group in English. 'And now,' he said, 'we're going to go to gas chamber and crematorium number one, follow me.' I walked away, back towards the gate. I decided to look at the film and leave. At least I had been silent; but nothing anyone could do here could be right.

The film did not help; it was a piece of propaganda made after the war by the Allied forces which focused more on the successes of the Soviet Army than the plight of the inmates of Auschwitz. Some of the scenes were affecting, but the old-fashioned newsreel voice-over was too full of the joys of victory. The film ended with Roosevelt, Churchill and Stalin coming together to talk about world peace.

I went into the camp again. In one of the brick houses I met another tour. 'Six hundred people lived where we now are,' a man was saying. We stood looking at the long, bare room. I walked away and went alone into the next house, where there was a whole wall made of glass, as in a zoo, and behind it were all the basins and pots the prisoners had used, lying together at random. In the corridor there was another glass case from floor to ceiling, this time full of their shoes; another case showed wooden legs; another was full of children's clothes; another was full of hair; another was full of gas canisters.

A few daffodils were left at the door of the block where the standing cells had been built. The same guide was explaining how prisoners would be made to work all day, and then in the evening would be locked in here in a space where they could only stand, and left until the morning. Eventually, they would die, but it could take up to eleven days. Everyone on the tour seemed cowed into silence. Why didn't they just shoot them? Or gas them? Instead, they led them out to work every morning, and back every evening, for the long night's torture until they died. People walked quietly out into the open, not speaking, not looking at each other.

Of all the exhibits the starkest were the suitcases, with the prisoners' names and addresses written on labels stuck to them. All now piled up. But worse, for me, was the pile of discarded glasses and lenses, mashed together. I stood there thinking of the Jews in Europe who sent their children to study music, who became writers, philosophers and art connoisseurs. Imagine the books they read, the lamp-lit rooms they inhabited, the things they had seen in their lives, the warm light in their eyes. And then the moment when their glasses were taken from them, when their glasses would be no use anymore. Each lens so carefully constructed to suit each person's sight.

Along the corridors of some of the houses there were photographs of the prisoners which were taken with that precision which interested the Nazis so much: each head was shaved and in exactly the same position as the next. The photographer was clearly an artist because there is a peculiar and direct beauty in each face. Not one seemed disfigured or diminished by the suffering they must have been going through. The way the head was tilted back and lit by the photographer gave each prisoner a gaunt and fearless dignity. The world must have missed these people. The photographs of the children, like the case of children's clothes, were almost unbearable to look at, but none of the children appeared frightened. All of them, like their parents, met the camera with a doomed equanimity. Below each photograph were details of the prisoner's date of birth and date of arrival and date of death.

These were the dead, then, and this was the last place they had inhabited. But there was nothing about where they came from, or who they were. There was a large bunch of flowers and a notice at the spot where the Catholic priest, Father Kolbe, who had heroically allowed himself to be starved to death in place of another, had died. But there was no mention of Jews, or homosexuals, or gypsies.

I went back outside the gates and sat in the restaurant where I met the taxi driver who had ferried me from the railway station earlier that morning. We talked for a while in English and I told him that I did not intend to spend the night here. I thought of going back to Katowice and maybe on to Warsaw the next day. He told me that he would drive me to Krakow, less than a hundred kilometres away, for twenty dollars. He could start right away. I decided to leave and went into the hotel to check out. I stood in the room for a while with my eyes closed, not sure whether I was trying to get what I saw out of my mind or preserve it there.

When we reached the main road I asked the driver to stop in front of the camp. This was where the Carmelite nuns had their convent. There was a huge cross facing the road and a nun was walking up and down along a path. It looked as though the whole Auschwitz complex was a Catholic institution, as though it had been taken over by the Catholic Church. And this completely undermined its purpose as a memorial to those who had been transported here and murdered. I wondered now that Poland was about to become a Catholic state how the camp would be treated in the future.

The driver asked if I wanted to see Birkenau, which was close by. This was a huge site, much bigger than Auschwitz, but all the buildings were mere shells. I stood and looked at it for a while, as the driver waited in the car. During the war years four million people were murdered in these two camps.

The driver did not want to talk about the camps, and was surprised that I had come here. We went first to his house, a new house built from the brick I had seen all around, the same brick which was used to build the camps. It was large and comfortable, with plate glass windows and varnished floors. The driver told me that he had gone to America and worked there for several years to raise the money for the house and the taxi. You could not make that sort of money in Poland, he said. As we drove along the straight, flat roads between Oswiecim and Krakow he told me that the rate for the dollar on the black market had been high, but was now more or less the same as the official rate, which had put all the speculators out of business. It was good to have the communists out, he said, but prices had begun to rise. Some prices had increased as much as fifteenfold.

He left me at the edge of the medieval quarter of Krakow. It was the Tuesday evening of Holy Week 1990. The streets were full of shops and shoppers; the city seemed bright and busy in the twilight. It was easy to find an hotel room in the old city. I had not expected to come to Krakow; I had caught a glimpse of Katowice that morning in the darkness before dawn and had imagined myself sleeping in a dingy modern hotel there. Now, suddenly, I was excited at being in this untouched medieval city which had escaped the ravages of the Second World War, over which John Paul II had presided as Archbishop and Cardinal before he became Pope. The main square was like a small, flat city in itself, housing a cathedral, an old, squat basilica and a café and covered market. Now, as darkness fell, there were flower sellers everywhere. In the café, the trendy local youth had gathered, wearing western-style clothes and long hair. One had a cigarette holder which held his cigarette at right angles and he puffed on this to the amusement and delight of his colleagues.

There was a casino in my hotel, and after dinner I wandered in to find it full of Poles playing for dollars, some of them playing for a great deal of money indeed. A young blonde Polish woman was placing dollars on the table as though they were zlotys. My dinner had just cost two dollars. I could not understand how she had this money and was prepared to lose it in the casino.

At midnight I went out into the dark city and stood again in the vastness of the square. Joseph Conrad was brought up in Krakow. He wrote about the square 'immense in its solitude . . . full to the brim of moonlight. The garland of lights at the foot of the houses seemed to burn at the bottom of a bluish pool.' Towards the edges of the square I caught a glimpse of a woman overburdened with bags and parcels as she flitted into the shadows of a side street. For a moment she seemed like a ghost, something I had imagined as much as seen. Then I realised that she was a baglady, the only figure still wandering the streets of Krakow at this hour.

In the morning the city was splendid in the raked light of spring. The flower sellers were out again. I found an English-speaking taxi driver – who had been to America – and asked him to take me to what used to be the Jewish quarter. It was still on my mind, the remnants of the camps, and I wanted to go to the part of Krakow from where some of those murdered had been taken. He explained that there wasn't much. He did not think that there were any Jews left in Krakow. He drove me across the city and pointed at a few street names which were Jewish, and a disused synagogue. He showed me the Jewish quarter where there will never be Jews again. He looked at me, wondering what he should do now; this was it, he said. I asked him to take me back to the main square.

As each hour came round, a trumpeter appeared in one of the openings in the spire of the cathedral and heralded in the new hour. I noticed a queue outside the cathedral. Thinking perhaps it was a special tour, I paid no attention to it, browsing instead in second-hand bookshops and print-shops. But later in the morning when I saw that there still was a queue I realised what it was: a queue for confession. People were preparing to do their Easter duties. The priest was sitting in an open confession box in the church, and he could be heard whispering to each penitent.

Most of those in the queue were teenagers, or in their early twenties. Most of them had a devout and deeply serious look on their faces. The clothes, the hairstyles and the lack of make-up made the women look like figures from old photographs of the 1940s or early 1950s. This was some dream-world from the Catholic past, the last thing I had expected to find, something which no longer happened in Ireland in Holy Week. These were so different from the kids I had seen in the café the previous night, they were so well-behaved, so mild and obedient-looking I wondered what sins they could possibly have committed.

In Krakow that Wednesday the kiosks were blaring out pop music from cheap cassettes: Simon & Garfunkel, The Police, The Rolling Stones. There were stalls selling decorated eggs. The shops were full of bread and fruit, vegetables and clothes. Only meat seemed to be in short supply; there were queues outside the butchers' shops. Nobody seemed underfed or hungry. The city seemed prosperous, thriving. One restaurant, overlooking the old square, was very popular and there was a queue for lunch, but because I was alone, or spoke English, or because she liked the look of me, the haughty, impeccably-dressed woman in charge gave me a table at the window. The menu and the service were elaborate, the décor was plush, the view over the square magnificent and the waiter's self-importance beyond belief. The bill came to less than three dollars.

That evening I took the train to Warsaw. The station was busy with people going home for Easter. The train was comfortable. Two people in my compartment read paperback novels and a teenage boy a textbook. It was all easy and quiet and exciting going to a city where I had never been before. But the image was there all the time, none the less, of the standing cells at Auschwitz, the slow, gratuitous cruelty of it, a man working all day and coming back to be forced to stand all night, not being able to sleep, having nowhere to fall. Who thought of this? I could not get it out of my mind.

I stayed that night in Warsaw in a modern hotel near the railway station which had several restaurants and a casino. In the morning I moved to the older Hotel Europecski. The streets and squares around the hotel were wide and airy, having been rebuilt from rubble after the war. It was Holy Thursday and there were queues outside the cake shops. I wanted to find the Jewish Museum, which my guide-book said was not far away. I passed elegant clothes shops and some jewellery shops and a few restaurants, and eventually I found the Jewish Museum down a side street. When I opened the door a porter seemed surprised and motioned me to wait while he summoned a woman from a nearby room. The hallway was dingy and run-down, though the high ceilings and stairway made it clear that the building had once been very grand. The woman asked me in English what I wanted. I told her that I wanted to see the museum. I said that I was interested in the Jewish ghetto in Warsaw. She told me that I could go upstairs and look around and come back down if I needed anything else.

There was hardly anything in the room upstairs, a few blown-up photographs of distressed people being led away, some mementos, but nothing else. I didn't know what I was looking for. When I went back downstairs the woman told me that she was busy but that if I waited she would find me someone else.

After a while, a younger woman came and immediately asked if I wanted to speak in Hebrew. I told her I wasn't Jewish. I asked if this was the only museum and if there were monuments to the Jews in the city. I also wanted to know where the ghetto began and ended and if it was marked now.

She smiled; she was young and pleased that someone had come here asking questions. There was one monument a good distance away, she said, and there was one other room in the museum which she would open for me if I wanted, but there was nothing exceptional in it. She did not know why it was locked. No one came here much, she said. At one time there had been half a million Jews in the Warsaw ghetto; now there were only three hundred religious Jews in the city. For a long time there had been no rabbi. Anti-semitism was still alive in Poland, she said; in the late 1960s the communists had purged the government of Jews. But in general there was very little interest in the subject, and there was certainly no line marking where the ghetto had begun.

Changes were coming fast in the city. There were two Writers' Unions now. One from communist times had a big building close to my hotel where a few men who could have been writers sat around talking to each other. At the office, they refused to tell me where the other Writers' Union was, but said they thought that it might be closed, since it was Holy Week. Instead, I found the institution which paid royalties to writers, and waited in an office while they got someone who spoke English. As I sat there I noticed that every object in the room – the drum-shaped filing system, the blinds on the windows, the lamps on the desks, the make of the desks and the typewriters – was completely different from anything I knew. They had an odd, old-fashioned elegance.

There was a Polish woman in her twenties visiting the offices. She had just returned from London, and had developed a rather superior English accent which she mixed with her Polish one. She agreed to wander around with me for a while, insisting, however, that it was all as strange to her as it was to me. She had a sharp answer to every question and an opinion on most matters. Her clothes were good, and she walked fast. She explained that I hadn't seen any poor or hungry people in Warsaw simply because I was living in a posh hotel in the centre of town. Most people had not got the money to come into the centre. Even the price of a bus ticket now had gone up to what was, for most Poles, an unbelievable sum. I told her about the queues for the cake shops, and about the casino and the brand new taxis in Krakow. Money was moving, she explained: the rising prices and the opening up to the West meant that some people now had money, just as in the West, but, in general, people's spending power had decreased.

As we walked along we passed crowds on their way to Holy Thursday devotions. I suggested to her that we go into one of the many churches in the city centre and see what was going on. She was having none of it. She refused even to look at the people going into the churches.

Poland, she said, was bad under the communists, but under the Catholics it was much worse. Now, you turned on the television and instead of having to listen to party members extolling the party, you had Catholic priests telling married people that if they had a dog they should get rid of the dog and have another child. It took forty-five years to remove the communists, she said, and it was going to take another half century to get rid of the Church.

'Look,' she said, 'look at their Solidarnosc eyes', as we passed another bunch of church-goers. I had been looking at the faces and I thought I understood what she meant. There was about each person who passed us, and indeed those in the queues for confession, a sort of mildness, a quietness, a sense of a guarded and cautious nature hidden behind each face.

I dined alone in the hotel that night; the service was as ceremonious as it had been in Krakow. A band came and played for a while, offering old songs in English. Several waiters offered me Russian caviar in exchange for dollars. After dinner a waiter told me that there was a cabaret downstairs which guests in the hotel could attend free of charge. I went down some time after eleven and had a drink. The place was full, most of the clientele was Polish, but there were some tourists as well. Two men came on to the small stage dressed as women and sang a song, then did a cabaret act with vaguely sexual overtones. A woman came on and did a half strip-tease, then the two men returned and the sexual overtones of their act became more obvious. I had to remind myself that this was Poland in the early days of Solidarnosc rule as the lady began to strip rather than tease, hanging around the place topless at first and then removing her underwear so that she was completely naked, finishing with a tour of the joint so that everybody could see her properly. It was after midnight. This was not the Good Friday I had expected in Poland.

In the morning I walked out again into the city. There was a pale warmth in the sunshine. I wandered into the old quarter which had been restored from rubble after the war, using photographs and recollection, but it still bore the marks of its reconstruction, with nothing out of place, no sense of random detail or small flourish, everything at right angles, like a film set – or something built for tourists, or something built, indeed, to hide and obliterate the memory of what happened in the war. There was an attempt to give this artificial city life, but even at night when it was dimly lit it never seemed real, it always seemed a city of absences and empty, open spaces.

A few weeks previously the Russians had finally admitted the murder of the entire Polish officer class at Katyn in 1940. In the British and Irish newspapers it had been a minor news item, another aspect of the dramatic changes which were going on in the former Soviet Empire. But in Warsaw on this Good Friday, fifty years after the massacre, some of the city centre churches exhibited photographs of Katyn, above the dates 1940–1990, as an announcement of a pilgrimage or a novena would be pinned up on a noticeboard in an Irish church.

That afternoon as the Good Friday devotions took place I walked from church to church in the centre, visiting more than a dozen. They were all packed, the congregation full of that mild, obedient demeanour which I had noticed first in the queue for confession at Krakow. Even the children were solemn. The streets were deserted.

After darkness fell they opened the tabernacles in the churches and displayed the Host from the altar. But there was another display on most of the altars beside the monstrance with the Host: the crowned eagle, symbol of the resurrected Poland. Those who came to pray knelt in front of the martyred and risen Poland as well as the martyred and risen Christ. These churches served as vast public spaces, offering not simply religion, but centres for a whole nation to congregate, to witness itself in motion, from occupation to deliverance.

I went that night in search of the monument to the Warsaw ghetto. They had rebuilt the city centre, but there was no sign of where the ghetto had been, no buildings lovingly reconstructed in the place which had housed half a million Jews. In the old days before the war this would have been the Sabbath: the sights in the street, the smells, the noises, the sense of an ancient culture at prayer would have been welcome now. But it was all gone and it would never come back. In its place were leafy, suburban streets with low, rationalist, well-kept blocks of flats on each side instead of Jewish houses, shops and synagogues. There was life here too; lights in the windows, families having supper and a few people walking in the badly-lit streets, unafraid when accosted by a stranger looking for directions in a foreign language. Eventually, I found the monument in a grassy square: the only memorial in Warsaw to the Jews.

On Saturday all roads still led to the churches. There were three reasons to go to church. In the morning the children had to be taken to have their Easter eggs blessed. I walked through the old city to find children all dressed up leaving the churches with parents or grandparents, smiling, delighted with their hoard of Easter eggs. Then the Blessed Sacrament and the crowned eagle, faith and fatherland, could still be visited. And there were still queues for confession. If you did not go to church that Saturday, it seemed hard to think of much else to do.

In the early afternoon I went to a suburban railway station and stood on the platform waiting for the train to Gdansk, the old German port of Danzig. When the train arrived it was clear that there would not be room for all of us. People began to push, shove and elbow their way on. Some of the men had a rough determination about them which meant that I kept out of their path. Whole families joined forces in taking over compartments, shouting to each other, blocking the way so that others could not pass. I was lucky to get on to the train at all and spent the journey standing in the corridor.

I was booked into a modern high-rise hotel, just beside the old city. There were German tour buses in the car park. From my window I could see the cranes and gantries of the great shipyards, stretching out for miles against the sky, beautiful now in the early evening. I took a taxi up the coast to Gdynia to buy a train ticket to Berlin. The coast road was lined with old houses and hotels, like a nineteenth-century seaside resort. I had expected Gdansk to be completely industrial, but this was much gentler and more domestic.

On the journey back I asked the taxi driver to stop at the pier and I got out and walked down to the huge stone statue of Joseph Conrad, which had been erected in 1976; his customary signature was carved into the stone. The sky was tossed with layers of blue-grey cloud; the Baltic was mild green in the late afternoon light, the waves were calm as they hit the stone of the pier, but the sea was choppy for as far as the eye could make out. And here at the very edge of things Joseph Conrad sat, his stately, plump shape captured in stone. He stared out to sea, having left Poland, he said, 'as a man gets into a dream'.

Later, when it was dark, I found the dream-city – not the Gdansk of Solidarnosc, but the Danzig of Günter Grass's *The Tin Drum*, the city of narrow streets, and tall, severe-looking brick houses, facing each other across the gloom of dim street lights, the city which had been lovingly re-assembled after the war. (I met Günter Grass in Dublin after I had been in Danzig, and he told me how relieved the architects and builders had been after the war to work on this restoration rather than rationalist buildings for the new regime. Grass himself had become part of the displaced Europe after the war; but when he returned, he said, most people understood what he had lost and what he felt at seeing his old city, because most of the new citizens of Gdansk had not been born there but had been moved from elsewhere.)

It was Easter Saturday night as I walked through this world of old merchant families, Protestant ethics, guilds, this dark, strange Hanseatic city full of images of early bourgeois opulence and wealth. Each street ended in a gateway to a quay and the waterfront. The streets were empty; I looked for a bar or a restaurant in the old city but could find nothing.

But all the churches were open, and again there were photographs of Katyn and the graves being exhumed, as though the massacre at Katyn had been part of the Passion itself, and its memory a part of the Easter liturgy. In Enniscorthy Cathedral the Irish tricolour had flown, and there was always a sense that the Church and the nation were closely intertwined, but the altar was sacred;

nothing from the state or the nation could go beyond the altar rails. Here it was different; as I wandered about the cathedral before the evening Mass I noticed that on a side altar around the consecrated Host were images not of the crucified or the risen Christ but of Poland itself. Poland was so insistent on its martyrdom, so self-conscious about its status as a risen victim that, as in Warsaw, the priests had put a statue of a risen eagle and a Polish flag beside the monstrance with the consecrated Host.

The church was packed for Mass. The faces again were serious and intent; no one looked around, or allowed themselves to be distracted. And afterwards they all approached the side altar, which was now guarded by two stern-faced youths dressed in military uniform who stood to attention. And then they went to look at the Katyn exhibition. I began to understand why the churches and the ceremonies were so important: there was nowhere else to go and nothing else to do. Once the churches closed that night in Gdansk at around eleven o'clock there was nobody wandering in the shadowy streets, and there was no sign of life from any of the merchants' houses. The city was dead.

In the morning there was nothing open either, no newspaper kiosks or cafés, no bread-shops nor bars. The city remained austere and dull as its citizens made their way to the churches. The main morning Mass in the cathedral was even more packed than it had been the night before.

I was taking a train to Berlin that evening so I left my luggage at the station and took a taxi to the Grand Hotel at Sopot, the resort between Gdansk and Gdynia. The bar was closed; they were serving only coffee and cakes. Most of the clientele was foreign. The Grand Hotel was still splendid; built in the early years of the century, it was full of airy, high-ceilinged rooms and had maintained a shabby luxury. It backed on to the beach and the Baltic. To the side of the hotel was a long pier, and all afternoon families walked up and down here. In the bright stillness of the early afternoon the waves broke in small curls without much energy. It could have been Easter Sunday in any seaside town in the north of Europe.

But there was something different about this scene. Something was missing. There was nothing for sale. Once I was outside the hotel I could buy nothing. There was no bar or restaurant, but what I missed more was the lack of any stall or small shop selling soft drinks, ice-cream or sweets. The Poles seemed happy enough idling up and down the pier without the flush and excitement of exercising their purchasing power. They seemed mild and easy-going, as we all would, perhaps, in a world where there was nothing for sale.

The café in the station at Gdynia was dreary and underlit. A number of badly dressed men were queuing for stew. There was a real sense of misery here, as though it were a soup kitchen, and the stew looked as if it had been there for days. The men in the café had that glazed, watchful expression of people who live on charity, and it struck me that if you had no food at home, then this was the only place you could come; this was the only place outside the churches where there was some warmth and the possibility of company.

I took the night train to Berlin, paying the cheerful, tubby ticket collector ten dollars for a sleeper. For a few hours after the train started he went around trying to sell Coca-Cola for foreign currency and then he fell asleep in a chair in his own little compartment. At nine in the morning we arrived in East Berlin, and I caught a metro to the West and found a hotel off the Ku'damm.

Suddenly, although I spoke no German, I was back

in a world I understood. I could make sense of the vast shopping centre at the end of the street and the crowds in the city aimlessly window-shopping on a bank holiday Monday. The clothes, the manners, the public life of the street were all familiar and reassuring. I felt at ease here, back in my own world where the currency was hard. I could have stayed in East Berlin, it would have been cheaper, but I realised as I wandered around the bars of West Berlin that I had been looking forward to this. It was a relief.

I met a friend, an Irish painter, and we went around the trendy places where everyone was carefully dressed, and everything from hairstyle to facial expression was carefully chosen. It was all cool and sexual. Have another drink, someone said, this place is open late, and there's a new place open even later. And getting back to the hotel won't be a problem. The taxis are on all night. I was out of Poland now, and could consume and choose, I could find out what was fashionable and what was old-hat. I could rest my head against the wall and run my eyes along the rows of bottles and the crowds of people. I could relax, feel at home.

3

Blood in the Sand

IT BEGAN with the sound of drums in the side streets off Avenida de la Constitution. By now all the chairs that had lain for days piled up with chains around them had been spread out. You could buy tickets and rent a chair from a man in a booth beside the cathedral. You paid more for a front seat. It was the early afternoon of Palm Sunday in Seville: nine slow processions were about to make their way through the city. Some would take twelve hours to go from their local church to the cathedral and back again.

When I heard the drums I headed towards the parade, edging my way through crowds of spectators. The procession was being led along a main street by men wearing cream-coloured tunics and black conical hats, with slits for eyes, like the Ku-Klux Klan; each was holding a huge yellow candle. There were hundreds of them marching along. People looked on in wonder and lifted their children up to see them better. The drums echoed loudly in the street to a marching beat, announcing the real spectacle: a life-size tableau of Jesus having his tunic removed, on a float carried by thirty-two men, and a second platform with a life-size Virgin. The floats were carried slowly and with some difficulty along the street, followed by a band. Both were decorated with enormous quantities of fresh flowers and expensive and colourful cloth.

People stared at the statues and the platforms as though they had never seen anything like it in their lives, as though one of the wonders of the world had just passed in front of them. All afternoon and well into the night I stood in the streets around the cathedral in Seville as the eight other parades went by. Some were accompanied by brass bands; one had more than a thousand cowled figures marching in front and behind the platform, some of them in bare feet; all of the processions had huge floats as their centrepieces, bearing life-size statues of Jesus or the Virgin; the floats, which seemed incredibly heavy, were all decked out with lamps and flowers. Some of the statues and scenes dated from the sixteenth century. The Virgin was always young and white and often in tears, standing under a golden, swaying canopy, or wearing a long gilded robe. The figure of Jesus was taken from a moment in the story of his Passion and Crucifixion. Often, the figures wearing the black pointed cowls carried crucifixes too.

The processions kept stopping and starting, like Catholic processions all over the world. And each time they started, the men had to hoist the float up, making sure the statues did not topple over, and carry it as gently as possible. People stood and watched. And when the Virgin came past or a statue of Jesus there was a silence filled with wonder and admiration. The faces watching were as interesting as the tableaux on the platforms; each face was utterly absorbed in the scene, and if the face of the Virgin was sad, or had tears rolling down her sculpted cheeks then there would be tears in the eyes of some spectators.

The city was beautiful beyond belief. Away from all these processions, up behind the cathedral, was the Barrio de Santa Cruz, built like a small and intimate

Andalucian village in the middle of the city. Most of the buildings in the narrow winding streets or the small squares were painted white, there were fountains, and flowers growing in boxes on the balconies. And there were Moorish remains, including the magnificent Giralda, the massive tower which dominated the square near the cathedral. Seville was busy. There were long shopping streets full of traffic, and bars and restaurants everywhere. Even now, when the weather was still cold, there were tables and chairs outside. Across the river, in the district known as Triana, there were streets full of bars where the glamorous young congregated. There were sixty churches, each of which would have to send a procession through the streets during Holy Week. Each had its own traditions, and there was great competition between churches.

On Monday I stood around watching more parades. Judas appeared life-size, as did Mary Magdalen and St John the Evangelist, all surrounded by fresh flowers. Each statue of the Virgin seemed like a real person to the crowd. They looked at her as though she were real, as though the face could talk to them, men and women the same. I stood on a street corner in the evening watching the men hoist up a float and carry it slowly towards us. The street lights were turned off. The Virgin, dressed in a rich robe, was lit by candles. A priest carried incense, and there was soft music from a band. I watched the people opposite me and around me. They believed in this, they stared at her face in awe. They blessed themselves and they broke into applause, but they did not once take their eyes off the statue.

I was puzzled. I had never seen people in Ireland stare at a statue being carried through the streets in the way people in Seville stared. But I was puzzled also by the politics. In Catalonia no one on the left had anything to do with the Church. It went much deeper than the Civil War. The Church was for the middle classes, the young and the old, but men and women who voted socialist and communist would not carry the banners in the religious procession, even in the villages. There was a strong anti-clerical strain in the society, a profound loathing for the Church. Here, I sensed that the entire community was involved with these processions, and yet Seville voted overwhelmingly socialist and communist. It was the home of Felipe Gonzalez, the socialist prime minister, and his deputy, Alfonso Guerra. I walked to the churches from which the processions emerged and some of them were in poor districts of the city.

Had something changed? Had anti-clericalism among the Spanish working class faded? On Tuesday evening I stood outside the church of San Lorenzo waiting for the Virgin to be carried out. The people around me were ordinary working-class citizens, and they were all watching for the procession to begin. Five hundred men were going to accompany it through the streets between now, eight o'clock in the evening, and three o'clock in the morning. As the canopy came out the door of the church, it was clear that it could barely fit. The Virgin was wearing a crown and an embroidered robe. Trumpets began to play and drums to roll and there was applause from the crowd. Gold cloth dangled from the canopy with tassels and pink carnations. There were tall candles and lamps alight at the back of the platform. It was lifted high above the crowd, triumphant, and carried through the streets.

Inside the church, people now queued to kiss the hand of a wooden life-size carving of Jesus, his face all contorted in pain. Two young girls stood back and looked at his face, marvelling at the expression, the artistry. There were computer print-outs on the wall of names of people working on the procession. As I headed back to have a drink in the Barrio de Santa Cruz, it struck me that it would be very hard to live in Seville during this week and take no part in all these festivities. But it was impossible to get back to the Barrio de Santa Cruz; for more than an hour I stood at a junction watching more processions, dreaming of an L-shaped bar in the heart of the old quarter for which I had developed a very special devotion. The streets were thronged even more than on Sunday. There was the constant sound of drums and the smell of incense. Things moved very slowly. People blessed themselves when an enormous gilded chariot appeared followed by the three wise men, life size like all the rest, on a platform. But there was less interest when there was no Virgin. Even a gruesome crucified Christ surrounded by flowers did not get the same attention as a Virgin. You could not move as she went by, people crushed forward to see her. There were moments of pure and strange beauty as the face passed slowly in front of us. People turned to follow her.

Avenida de la Constitución was becoming more crowded now and noisier and more festive. There was the sound of drums in the distance as another procession came into sight and made its way to the cathedral. This one stopped right in front of me. There must have been forty carriers under the platform. They sat down on their hunkers and waited for the sound of a stick hitting the ground and then they all rose at the same time and carried the massive platform to the cathedral, to the accompaniment of triumphant music. I followed in a desperate effort to make it to the bar in the Barrio de Santa Cruz.

In the morning I telephoned the Communist Party and asked them if they had a member who had lived in Seville for many years and might be free to talk to me. I was still amazed at the city's fierce addiction to the Virgin and the Church. I wanted a dissident or someone who could explain why the entire working class of the city gathered around their churches during Holy Week, or spent all night carrying heavy platforms for the church. When I rang back as arranged they gave me the name of Arturo Cabo and said he would be expecting me that afternoon.

He was in his late seventies, perhaps, living with his wife on the fourth floor of a bright building near the city centre. He sat beside a table with family photographs on display and he told me the story of his life as the afternoon wore on. His father was from Madrid, his mother from Malaga. They split up when he was in his teens; he stayed with his father and learned the trade of printing. It was a good way, he said, to learn about politics: the old trade unionists around him included people who had been in Barcelona and there was a great deal of talk about syndicalism. He joined the Communist Party, and was moved to work in a right-wing newspaper. He went drinking with his fellow workers and gained their trust and after a few months he began to talk about wages and conditions. The owner of the newspaper became deeply antagonistic and tried to hire an assassin to shoot him.

In 1931 he was sent to Moscow and he spent a year there, with comrades from all over the world, studying the theory of revolutionary Marxism. In October 1932 he was sent back to Spain; first he worked in Madrid and then he travelled the country, organising the party. The left-wing movement was strongest, he said, in Andalucia, and especially in Seville. In 1934 there was a general strike there and great divisions within the city.

What he could not believe was the relationship between the most diehard communist in the city and the

Church. No matter what happened they would still go out and carry the thrones and the statues. Men who wouldn't dream of going to church, men of the left, when Easter came would go with their confraternity through the streets of the city in traditional dress. And on the way home from meetings they would discuss whose band had played the best at last year's Holy Week, whose Virgin was the most beautiful and whose confraternity was the most dedicated. He thought they were mad, but he learned something about them: that their involvement in these religious ceremonies had very little to do with religion and more to do with Seville. But, really, he explained, he did not understand it.

He fought the Civil War in Seville against the forces of Quipo de Llano, and afterwards spent eighteen months hiding in a cupboard, before escaping. He spent the years after the war first in Moscow and then in France, but he entered Spain a few times on a false passport to organise various missions for the party. On the day Franco died he took the train from Paris to Madrid. The police were waiting for him there, they questioned him for a while and then let him go, and he went to Seville, where he became involved with politics once more. He was not going to take part in a procession, he said, he did not have a local confraternity, he felt nothing about Holy Week. But he was still an outsider. Anyone with roots in the city, no matter what their politics, felt differently. It was strange.

The processions continued as the week went on. Every time I ventured out I got caught up in the spectacle. On Wednesday evening I made my way to Bar Gonzalo near the cathedral. There were more tourists in the city now and everywhere I went there were crowds. As the Virgin and her crucified Son passed the bar on a platform the people at the outside tables stood up. The cross had two ladders reaching to the arms. It was all graphic and detailed, down to the red paint for blood on the wood of the cross. Then a man began to sing to the Virgin from a window. It sounded like a traditional Andalucian love song. His voice was high and strong, his hands outstretched, his tone full of longing and the sorrow of love.

Later, there was more singing. When another crying Virgin went by, her hands in front of her in a gesture of pain, a man and a woman sang to her from a window as well. The singing was passionate, notes rising to express infinite despair, as both singers gestured at the statue, and the crowds in the street stayed silent. 'Brava!' a woman roared as the bearers hoisted up the platform once more and carried it towards the cathedral. Just then forty guardia civiles, complete with machine-guns, marched by full of pomp and circumstance.

I went back to my L-shaped bar in the Barrio de Santa Cruz and started to ask the locals – they were mainly men – what they felt about the processions. No one could be exact or precise. They all agreed that they felt emotion – they pointed to their hearts – when they saw the statues and the flowers, especially if it was from their parish, but really no matter whose parish it was from they liked to see it done well: the flowers fresh, the cloth rich, the figures life-like. It was hard to describe the emotion you felt when you saw it going by, it wasn't exactly religious, it had more to do with who you were and your roots and your pride in Seville and your grand-parents and your memories of childhood . . . it was hard to define. People shook their heads and narrowed their eyes and thought for a moment. No, they couldn't say what it was, but it existed and it was very powerful.

But you have not seen the *real* Holy Week, they

said. Wait until midnight on Thursday. Then the *real* parade takes place. As midnight strikes, the gates of the church of the Virgin of the Macarena will open and the Virgin will appear and two thousand one hundred local men in traditional costume will accompany the Virgin through the streets; they will walk all night and all the next morning and they will not return to the church until one o'clock in the afternoon of the following day. And the people of Seville will stay up too, this is part of the tradition, and everybody must see the Virgin at least once as she is carried through the streets.

On Thursday night the sky was clear; the moon was almost full. At twelve o'clock the huge square in front of the Basilica of the Macarena held its breath as the doors of the church opened. It was like a medieval version of the gates of heaven, bright and golden. There were drums and a brass band. The people were spell-bound, children were lifted up to see, as this enormous platform, twelve feet by six, began to edge its way out of the doors of the church carrying nine life-size figures, led by more than a thousand men in uniforms and hoods, with another thousand waiting inside.

A woman sang from a window: she paid tribute to the Virgin and lamented her sorrow. As the platform moved through the square people began to shout out to the Virgin: '*Guapa*! *Guapa*!', meaning beautiful, beautiful. They whistled and cheered as though the statue could hear them. '*Parece pálida*,' a woman behind me said, 'she looks pale.' It took hours for the procession to make its way to the crowded centre. At four in the morning there were still crowds in the streets, women wearing fur coats to keep out the cold. The procession spent an hour getting from the Corte Ingles to Plaza de San Francisco, at most a five-minute walk. A good number of the two thousand one-hundred strong confraternity were in bare feet. All along the route people sang to her from windows, telling of her beauty, her innocence and the cross she had to bear. At six in the morning the streets around the cathedral were full of the smell of incense. The procession was still moving slowly towards the cathedral – so slowly, indeed, that some of the confraternity could stop at a nearby bar, take their hoods off and have a beer, chatting and laughing.

They had another seven hours to go.

On Good Friday afternoon I took a look inside the Basilica of the Macarena. There were hundreds of people milling around the platform and the statues which had been returned to the church after their long sojourn in the streets. To the left of the entrance I noticed two graves. I went over to read the names of the people buried there. One was the grave of General Quipo de Llano; the other that of his wife. Quipo de Llano took Seville for the Fascists in 1937; he commanded the Nationalist forces in the south during the Civil War. He was responsible for the execution of many thousands of prisoners. In his famous broadcasts he threatened the Republicans in the most graphic terms. He probably ordered the execution of Lorca and, in one broadcast, he warned Casals that when the Nationalists took Barcelona his arms would be cut off at the elbow to stop him playing the 'cello. For me, this was like coming across the grave of Goebbels. No one in the church, however, took the slightest interest in these graves.

The following day I arranged to meet a group of Socialist Party activists in an old sherry bar near the cathedral. None of them would call himself a practising Catholic. Their relationship with the Church was complex, nevertheless. They agreed that the Church had some progressive priests and that in the 1960s and 1970s it was the only place you could meet. In those years the Church made facilities available to the illegal opposition, even though it at an official level stayed close and loyal to Franco's regime.

Had they seen the Macarena procession on Thursday night and Friday morning? Yes, they said, they had. And had they toured the churches to look at the statues and the flowers? Yes, they said, and they had gone to a bar afterwards. Did they believe in God? No, they said. Why, then, had they gone to see the statues?

And again the inarticulate litany began: your roots, your pride in Seville, your grandparents and some notion of the past's legacy and your heritage that was impossible to define. One of them said that it was a way for everyone to go out on to the streets, and possess them, no matter who they were, just as the weather was beginning to turn. It was a popular festival as much as a religious one, he said. They started to tell stories. Did I know that the Virgin of the Macarena was in fact a general in the Spanish army, and wears a general's belt, having been so decorated under the old regime? Another described how she was dressed in black each year on the anniversary of the tragic death in the ring of a famous bullfighter. The area around the basilica, they said, was solid working class, voting communist and socialist, and taking part in the confraternity as well.

I asked them about Quipo de Llano's grave. How could so many left-wing people take part in a procession from the church where he is buried? That was the war, they said, that is over. They shrugged. It was not that long ago, I said. They shook their heads: it was a trauma that no one wants to repeat, and no one thinks about it. Should he be buried there? I asked. They looked at the ground, remained silent and shrugged again. It bothers no one, one of them said.

This feeling that the past was over and traditional enemies were to be included was part of the new Spain, whose main architects, Felipe Gonzalez and Alfonso Guerra, came from this city where the Church was not the enemy, but an aspect of the rich fabric of things, and the past was not a haunting and dangerous presence but something to be forgotten, or shrugged off. But I was still puzzled and amazed at how people could be so moved by the appearance of a statue. I loved their willingness to be impressed and taken in. There was a brightness about these processions and the attitude of the citizens in the street; I did not know that it had an opposite side. Perhaps I should have guessed as I bought a ticket for the first bull-fight of the season to be held on Easter Sunday.

The Catalans don't like bull-fights. Although there are two bull-rings in Barcelona, they are for tourists and people from the south. If you want to see proper bull-fights in a proper atmosphere, go south, everyone said. I had gone once in Barcelona but left after a short time; I could not see beyond the cruelty and the blood. This now, I was told, the first bull-fight of the season would be an example of bull-fighting at its best.

It began at six-thirty in the evening; the hour had changed overnight so it was still bright. The place was packed. There were a few tourists, and perhaps as many as one third of the spectators were women. And there were three matadors who would kill two bulls each. First, bugles played and the horses and picadors did a lap of the ring. Soon the first bull appeared. He darted around the ring, as though puzzled and disconcerted by the crowd. I thought that something else would happen before the picador stuck the pics into his back: it was all very sudden, without any sense of conflict or drama.

He was injured now, we could see the dark blood ooze from the wounds on his back. There was a feeling of silent excitement from the crowd, followed by loud applause as the bull began to run blindly at nothing. You could see now how heavy and powerful the animal was. The matador let him come close in; the crowd seemed to understand and appreciate the skill as he stuck the sword in between his shoulders. He then played with him and walked away before returning for the real kill. All around me people shouted wildly as the horses dragged the bull away.

The second bull was fiercer than the first, he ran at the side of the horse, but caused it no injury. Instead, he was pierced with a pic and I could see the raw flesh on his back and the blood spilling on to the sand. The horses withdrew then. I watched this injured and bewildered animal standing there as the matador killed him, the crowd cheering and whistling and waving white handkerchiefs.

I could see no drama in this, I shared none of the excitement that was all around me. The third bull came out and the matador played with him to the crowd's delight, shouting 'Hi! Hup!' to attract him, and then striding away, having let the bull run at his cape. The colours were brilliant in the soft evening light: the ochre sand, the gold uniform and pink stockings of the matador, the red cape, the black weight of the bull with the raw pink flesh and the red blood on his back, the red and yellow *banderillas* sticking out of him.

The matador started showing off. To huge applause, he put his sword flat on the bull's head, demonstrating that he could kill the bull now if he wanted to, and then he walked proudly away. For a second as he started to play with the bull again, the cheering and shouting all stopped; everybody watched in silence and awe. I could not understand it. Then he ran at the bull with his sword, as in a scene from a dance, and, full of grace and purpose, he stuck his sword in and completed the act. For the people around me it was a moment of truth. He strutted around the ring, puffed up with pride as the dead bull was dragged away. I wanted to leave.

The crowd loved it when the matador enticed the injured bull around his body with a flourish of the cape. The colours were becoming more sombre as the light began to give. There were swifts darting and circling in the sky. They killed a fourth bull and then a fifth. The drama seemed to me momentary and not very intense. It was all over so quickly; there was so little conflict. The last bull ran frantically around the ring, banging his horns against the wood of the sides. And then he stood utterly still. The lights had come on now in the stadium which made all the colours deeper. The bull ran at the horse and tried to get under it and lift it up. The picador put the pic into his back. He bellowed in temper and ran at the horse a few times, locking into its side and then getting free again, the blood pouring down his flanks. The coloured *banderillas* were sticking out of him now, they swung from his back as he ran at the horse, they hung out of his flesh, clearly driving him mad with pain. He tried to arch his back to get rid of them, as the horse withdrew and the matador came towards him. He managed to shake one of the *banderillas* off.

Once more there was silence, a strange, watchful stillness among the crowd, as they waited for the kill. The matador shouted 'Hi! Ih!' and when the bull approached him he strolled nonchalantly away. Afterwards, I thought, I would walk across the city to the Barrio de Santa Cruz, I would find one of the beautiful squares with the walls painted white and with flowers hanging from the balconies and subtle lights. Maybe the depression I felt would lift if I could sit in a square like that for a while.

The matador stuck the sword straight between the bull's shoulder blades. The bull howled in pain but would not go down. The two figures ranged against each other, the matador stuck a second sword in but still the bull held on to life, as the crowd roared. It would not go down, and when it did, it seemed to give up for a moment and then get more courage and stand up again. The sky was dark now; night had fallen. Some people around me were leaving to avoid the crush at the end, as though this was casual and routine, this horribly injured animal standing in a ring, its back a mass of raw flesh and oozing blood, slowly dying in front of us while the matador dressed in bright colours looked on.

4

The Magic Mountain

IT STARTED TO RAIN as soon as I drove out of Galway, and after a while it came pouring down, relentless and hard as though it was never going to end. I was going to Westport in County Mayo on the last Saturday in July. The following day pilgrims from all over Ireland traditionally climbed Croagh Patrick, the holy mountain outside the town overlooking Clew Bay. If this rain kept up, and if there was a wind, the climb would be even more difficult.

And then the rain lifted as I got closer to Westport as though I had entered a new climate or a new season. Suddenly, it was a summer's evening in a busy Irish town, with cars badly parked, slowly moving traffic and people wandering around, some on the way to early evening Mass. I had arranged to meet two friends; we discovered that all the hotels were booked, and we had to drive out of town to a bed and breakfast house.

When we went back into Westport the shoppers and the Mass-goers had gone home; the place was now full of young people and the evening was still warm. They stood outside the pubs, with pints of Guinness, talking and laughing, or they roamed the streets. The young men and women were well dressed and in good humour. In some of the pubs there was traditional music playing. Everywhere there was a sense of plenty, of security, of ease. You could make the mistake of thinking that it was prosperous here; you could mistake the atmosphere in a market town on a summer's night if you did not know that emigration had decimated Ireland in the previous five years, that in 1989 alone as many as fifty thousand young people had left the Republic of Ireland, which has a population of three and a half million. Whole villages had lost all their young people; there were countless stories of entire football teams leaving in one or two years, ending up in Boston or New York.

It had happened in Ireland before, not just after the Famine in the nineteenth century, but again after independence. Four out of every five children born in the Republic of Ireland between 1931 and 1941 emigrated in the 1950s. I was born in 1955: two years before Ireland was admitted into the World Bank and the International Monetary Fund, three years before the government published its First Programme for Economic Expansion, which abandoned the failed protectionist policies and opened the country to foreign capital and investment. In the seven years after the Programme's publication industrial exports rose by one hundred and fifty per cent.

I came from that climate of hope; a world of free education, returned emigrants, television, reduced censorship. Even when unemployment began to rise again in the late 1970s, I did not think that people would emigrate, I thought they would believe enough in the future of the country to wait. But by the mid-1980s it had begun again, and it was hard, on nights like this in Westport, not to look around and know that things were less comfortable than they seemed, that many of these young people would leave too, that some were just home on holiday, that there was not much chance of things improving.

But you could misread the statistics too: you could watch unemployment rise above twenty per cent; you could be told that the entire revenue from personal income tax went to pay interest on the national debt; you could look at the emigration figures; but some people lived well in Ireland and maybe the young people we watched that night in Westport were not about to emigrate, but were going to stay to inherit what their parents and grandparents had consolidated. Since the end of the eighteenth century a new Catholic class had emerged in Ireland – people had opened shops, educated their children to enter the professions, slowly increased the size of their farms and gained control over the business life of the towns. This class remained extremely conservative and cautious. They were happier to put money in the bank than take any risks. This was, and is in general, the class from which the Catholic clergy come in Ireland.

It was easy for any external power to control the country once its population was suitably divided between the owners and the dispossessed. And gradually through emigration, and then legislation at the end of the nineteenth century which handed over land to tenant farmers, the threat from the dispossessed decreased and the country became stable but conservative, its population insecure and fearful, desperate to hold on to the small improvements in their lot.

Maybe what we witnessed as we sat on the ground outside Matt Molloy's public house in Westport that night, the music wafting out into the warm summer air, was a new confidence, a new generation wandering around on a Saturday night with no innate fear or insecurity. Or maybe as they grew older they would run their businesses and their lives with the same caution as their parents. For any outsider, it is difficult to judge a small community.

Later that night, we drove out to Murrisk at the foot of Croagh Patrick, and found a pub full of travellers, who sleep in caravans and move around the country, living off the dole and the sale of carpets and furniture. The tens of thousands of pilgrims (somewhere between twenty and sixty thousand) who would climb the reek the next day would each need a roughly-cut wooden staff for support, and there had been a fight outside the pub about who could sell where. The atmosphere in the pub was tense. Drinkers would get up and go outside to see what was going on and come back in to have animated and fierce discussions. Deals were done. A large and muscular traveller man grabbed one of our chairs when it was temporarily vacant. We did not protest.

In the morning there was a dull incessant drizzle which soon became soft rain. We sat having breakfast wondering if we should wait, if the weather would lift. Normally, the landlady told us, you could see Croagh Patrick in the distance from her kitchen window, but now you could see nothing. We drove into Westport and sat in a hotel lounge drinking coffee. I had spare shoes, but no real protection from the rain. My friends were in the same state.

Out at the foot of Croagh Patrick there were lines of cars parked and more making their way to the fields which were being used as car parks for the day. It seemed as though no one else had been worried about the rain. Some people had already been up the mountain and down again. As we bought our sticks for one pound I could see a line of people, like a small coloured stream winding up the mountain and disappearing into the mist.

This was where St Patrick, according to legend, had come and fasted for forty days and forty nights in the fifth century. But it was thought that the tradition of climbing the reek was a much older, pagan ritual which had been incorporated into the Christian calendar. There was also talk that the climbing of the reek had once been accompanied by great festivities, but this had been ended by the clergy, and now the day was dedicated to penance and penance only.

William Makepeace Thackeray was in Westport on the last Sunday in July in 1842 and he ventured out to Murrisk, having heard that 'the priests going up the mountain took care that there should be no sports nor dancing on that day'. He disliked the idea of the pilgrimage: 'it's too hard to think that in our day any priests of any religion should be found superintending such a hideous series of self-sacrifices as are, it appears, performed on this hill.'

We set off in a spirit of self-sacrifice. At first it was easy, like mild hill walking. Some people were barefoot, but most wore shoes. The mist was wet and the ground was uneven and soggy, the staffs becoming more and more necessary as we climbed. Soon, we separated; my two friends went ahead, joining the others who seemed to be vanishing into the sky. The climb became more difficult, and the rain came down harder. I was passed by a travelling woman in bare feet being helped along by her two sons. They did not speak to each other, appearing intent on the climb, a look of furious concentration on their faces. Then the man who had taken our chair in the bar the previous evening passed me, also in bare feet. I had thought that the travellers were only here to make money selling staffs and running stalls, but a good number of them climbed the reek that day, as though it were a crucial part of their fierce Catholicism.

Thackeray did not climb the reek, but received a report from a friend who told him that the ascent 'is a very steep and hard one . . . performed in the company of thousands of people who were making their way barefoot to the several "stations" upon the hill.' One hundred and forty-nine years later the stations are still there, and there are notices instructing pilgrims who arrive at the first station, for example, to walk 'seven times around the mound of stones saying seven Our Fathers, seven Hail Marys and one Creed'.

Beyond the first station there was no visibility. I could see only a few yards ahead as the mountain became steeper. A rescue team climbed past me carrying an empty stretcher; there must have been an accident higher up. A few people were coming down; one man smiled as he passed and said that it would not be long before I reached the top.

Suddenly, there was a shout from behind me. At first I thought that someone had fallen, but when I turned I found that the thick fog had lifted and we could see Clew Bay clearly – all the little islands, grey and silver in the dark water, with the soup of mist hovering over them and then gathering and closing in once more. Everyone had turned to look at it, like a small revelation. Now, we turned and trudged on, the terrain becoming more and more difficult. A few times the mist cleared again, and filtered sunlight shone on the sea so that it seemed like solid metal below us, and then gradually the clouds would block our view once more.

Nothing had prepared me for the last part of the climb. The rise was sheer and there was nothing to hold on to. At every step I sank into a bank of large slippery stones. I moved slowly on my hands and knees in the wind and the driving rain. I stood back to let the stretcher pass, as the injured man was carried down.

Everybody concentrated on each step, and on making

sure not to fall and knock other people over. We clambered forward. It was impossible to see how close the summit was. At times progress seemed impossible; there was no foothold, and if you moved, you displaced rocks and stones, and there was still no foothold. Men and women walked down as best they could, pushing the staff into the ground ahead of them, letting it sink in between the stones, then sliding gingerly down. If they caught your eye, they smiled in encouragement. People kept telling you that you would reach the summit soon.

When I got there I was exhausted and exhilarated. Mass was being said, and everybody, including all the young people, were paying attention. Later, huge numbers went to confession and communion. I felt so well, so happy to have made it that I was half-tempted to tell all my sins to the priest and then receive communion. But I sat back, instead, and watched. People had not climbed the reek simply to keep fit; now, as they reached the top, I could see that they were serious about this pilgrimage, as they all blessed themselves and joined in the prayers, including teenagers and men and women in their twenties. Age did not appear to affect the intensity of devotion.

Why had Catholicism survived like this in Ireland? Why did the Reformation never work? Why does the Catholic faith seem to thrive here among the young as it does not elsewhere? The previous week I had gone to Maynooth, the Catholic seminary and university close to Dublin, founded in 1795, and I had spoken to a lecturer in the Old Irish Department, Muireann Ní Bhrollcháin, about how Christianity had come to Ireland.

We know very little about pre-Christian Ireland, she said. The Celts did not build temples, but tended to honour their gods in open spaces. We know that they believed in another world, but there seems to have been no conflict between them and the first Christians, who came in 431 and 432. There were no martyrs in the early Irish church. The two worlds appear to have worked together. Saint Colmcille, for example, died in 597, and a long poem lamenting his death was apparently written by a pagan poet.

The Roman system did not catch on in Ireland until the mid-twelfth century, she explained, and this is significant. Instead, Christianity was spread by abbots and monks who ran autonomous monasteries. There was no central authority; there were no dioceses until the twelfth century. Thus the monks, instead of going and spreading the word or doing battle against pagan druids, spent time copying out manuscripts, or writing down stories from pagan times, incorporating Christianity with what came before, making gods and goddesses into saints. Some monks went to live in remote places; others founded richly-endowed monasteries where the abbots and monks were like lords and tenants, and power was passed from father to son. Rules and regulations varied from one monastery to another.

Christianity, then, was never imposed on Ireland; Roman structures played no part in introducing the new religion. It grew slowly, and slowly the old set of beliefs faded. Christianity became the faith of the country over five or six centuries using the vernacular; it became a native religion. Having grown so organically, it was more difficult to change or dislodge.

Efforts were made to reform the Church in the ninth century, she said, but they had no effect. However, with the coming of the Vikings there were greater links between the east coast of Ireland and England, which was firmly under Roman control, and the possibility of restructuring the Irish Church increased once the

Vikings in Dublin converted to Christianity. Between 1142 and the end of the century every monastery in Ireland was closed. The religious orders came in from Europe; they did not speak any Irish. It was the first and most significant invasion of Ireland, making the subsequent Norman and English invasions easier. It established structures in the society – parishes, dioceses, religious orders – which any invader would find useful. Ireland, which had been fully Christian, now became part of the Roman Church, but it did so much later than any other country in Europe.

It was still raining on the summit of Croagh Patrick. I assumed that people had also come here on an appointed summer's day in the time before Christianity. And I imagined that the pre-Christian rituals may have continued after its arrival. There seems to have been no battle between the rival religions, no year noted in chronicles when the big day on Croagh Patrick was turned over to the Christians. It is possible that both pagan and Christian rituals were carried on as part of the same thing, and then gradually the pagan disappeared.

I looked around. Another Mass had started and people were kneeling, while others queued for confession. The prayers were said with real seriousness, and when it came to the consecration people bowed their heads, ignoring the rain.

I set off down the mountain. By now the mist had cleared over the summit. Around the islands in the bay cloud was still melting and forming, and there were sudden darts of sunshine, as though the dawn were starting to break over the sea.

The first stretch on the way down was really hard. If anyone pushed against you, you would fall with nothing to hold on to. There had already been several injuries that day. You had to mind every step, use the staff for support and hope for the best. Once I was beyond the stones I knew I was past the worst. It was now the afternoon. The climb had taken about three and a half hours. There were still people coming up, but most were going down.

At the bottom of Croagh Patrick that day the Bishop of Clonfert, Dr Joseph Cassidy, stood dressed in his episcopal robes. He seemed part of what I had been thinking about – the Roman, the man in the official robes, civilised, from the diocese which did not exist until it was imposed from outside in the twelfth century. He was watching the pilgrims descend from their quasi-pagan encounter with rain and a holy mountain. He explained that he couldn't climb Croagh Patrick because of his bad heart. Instead, he waited there, greeting everyone warmly, being greeted in return. He smiled benignly at us all and spoke to anyone who approached him. He seemed pleased that the Church had so many pilgrims ready to climb Croagh Patrick, and happy to preside over the event.

5

Crowds and Power

THE NOISE of cheering in the distance. And then the frantic waving of flags. The noise of cries going up, louder and louder, echoing against the high stone walls of the monastery. There were a million young people down below, all alert now, ready as the Pope arrived. On the top of the monastery walls the clergy stood up to applaud as the Popemobile came into view and slowly made its way through the crowd in the natural amphitheatre below.

It was August 1991 and it would probably be his last visit home. He was becoming old now and frail, and soon these arduous journeys would be too much for him. Earlier that day he had visited his parents' grave and his native town of Wadowice. Now he began moving up the steps to the temporary altar perched on the walls of Jasna Gora, the church of the Black Madonna at Czestochowa, the spiritual capital of Poland.

He was wearing immaculate white; his entourage stayed well behind him and his security men stayed close as he slowly took each step. After the first ten steps there was a platform, and when he reached it he hesitated, as though he could walk no further, and then he turned with that strange melancholy expression, that mixture of bemusement and power, and looked at the crowd. The television lights were on him; his face filled the screens which had been put up all over the field. He stood there, his white vestments clear against the ochre carpet, his face alive to the tricks of light. He eyed the vast crowd below, but he did not wave or make any gesture. It was as though he was oddly surprised by the sight in front of him, and was unsure what to do. And then he turned once more, slowly, as if some terrible weight were still upon him. He did not walk in a straight line, but wandered from side to side in a deep state of reverie and contemplation, and then he turned and waved, taking in the crowd with the side of his eyes. And the spell-binding mixture of strength and weakness, the power of his office and its burden, worked on the crowd, worked on all of us.

I had flown to Warsaw the previous day and, having got my accreditation from the Catholic press office, stood in the railway station waiting for a train to Krakow. Once again, it was a shock being on a European mainland with a huge timetable over the ticket booths listing trains to Leningrad and Paris, Prague and Moscow. It was a glorious afternoon; going south to Krakow along the vast, fertile Polish plain was like watching scenes from pastoral paintings of the nineteenth century. There was hardly any machinery, just a sense that back-breaking toil had been going on since dawn and would continue until darkness fell. How many years more would this last now? The clusters of houses we passed with outhouses for pigs and poultry, with bicycles leaning up against sheds, with summer clothes hanging on a line, seemed caught in a time warp halfway between collectivisation and the regulations of the European Union.

All the journalists were staying in a modern hotel on the edge of Krakow. The bus, for those of us who were following the Pope the next day, would leave at five in the morning. The lobby and the reception rooms were full of fax machines and telex machines and television cameras. Priests moved about like civil servants, busy with fresh press releases and new instructions. I walked into the city, and stood once more in the main square, where the Pope had said Mass earlier in the day. The platform had not been dismantled; the flowers and garlands which had been placed around the altar were still there, but the carpet over the bare wooden steps had been taken away.

It was dark now. Crowds of people climbed the steps to where the Pope had been; people carried their children up to see the altar and the view of the square. They began to take souvenirs, anything they could get their hands on: flowers, plants, banners, pieces of the altar. I sat on the steps watching them haul away whatever they could carry until I was distracted by a jazz band playing against the old market building in the middle of the square. I went over and joined the group standing around listening to them. They played a variety of instruments – drums, a guitar, a saxophone. They all had long hair; they could have been hippies in America or England in the late-1960s. They certainly did not belong to John Paul II's Poland. Even the tunes they played seemed variations on American themes.

I had been watching them only for a few minutes but when I turned there was no one on the platform behind me. Silently, instead, an armed guard had been placed at the bottom of the steps to prevent further souvenir-hunting. The people had been quickly cleared away and order restored. It was as though someone from the army had clicked his fingers and the faithful had scattered. The armed forces had not lost their might.

In the morning we were driven along narrow country

roads from Krakow to Wadowice. We were accompanied by a number of Polish seminarians, who sat away from the press and seemed uncommunicative, gruff. We arrived at a new parish church in Wadowice, an ugly barn-like structure with a large square in front of it. All around the square waiting were dignitaries, bands and choirs, but even so there was a modesty about the scene, a feeling of being on the edge of a small, unimportant place where people did not have much money or influence. Thus the sense that this was an important day seemed to fill the air; there was a brightness in the faces, an air of expectation; people pushed against each other to make sure they would have a good view of the Pope when he arrived.

The people who seemed most excited were, perhaps, the men who conducted the bands and their choirs. This was their day. Just in front of our platform a tall, solemn man with glasses and bushy hair conducted a choir of boys and girls. He looked at them all severely as he began, and then he waved his arms as they sang. It was hard to work out if what he did with his arms had any real effect on the sound they made. It seemed to me that the look in his eye was more powerful, that he would be able to pick out any boy or girl who was not joining in with enough vigour by simply glancing at them. But, none the less, he conducted with great energy, pointing to one group as they became louder and then lowering his hands to indicate to others that they were to keep their voices down. And then letting his two arms gesticulate wildly in the air when his choir were in full flight.

When the Pope arrived they cheered and clapped and waved banners. 'Hail, my native soil, hail my native town on the river Skawa. It was here in this town in an ancient church that I first heard this profession of faith.' As he spoke I could see that mixture of strength and weakness in him which was apparent, too, in the photographs taken in this town in the years before the war when he was in his teens: the stubborn set of the mouth against the softness in his eyes, the expression even and fearless. It is clear that he enjoys the camera, knows how to turn his face to the light. There is always a sense of sadness in his face too, as though he has seen too much and knows too much.

'At twenty,' he said in an interview, 'I had already lost all the people I loved and even the ones that I might have loved, such as the big sister who had died, so I was told, six years before my birth. I was not old enough to make my first communion when I lost my mother.' Women, in his deeply religious household, were absences, figures to be remembered and regretted, rather than flesh and blood. By the time he was twenty his father and his elder brother had died as well.

Unlike earlier Popes, he did not spend his middle age steeped in the day-to-day politics of the Roman Church. In Poland there was no room for internal squabbles or liberal tendencies. It was simple: the Church and the nation were good and the state was evil. Polish Catholicism had no time for the doubting or the faint-hearted. In Krakow in the years before he became Pope, Karol Wojtyla worked hard on his study of human sexuality. 'We need to celebrate human sexuality,' he said in one of his sermons, 'because through it we discover the meaning of life. It is part of our nature to realise that we are "alone" and in constant search for our identity. Because of our loneliness we discover the real meaning of existence when we assume some of the loneliness of our partner in the act of sexual intercourse.'

Sex, for Karol Wojtyla, was not the necessary evil it was for his colleagues. Because he viewed sex as so central and important, he did not favour constant indulgence; on the contrary, sex could be enacted only under certain circumstances. Even within marriage, he was not in favour of frequent sex. Most of the language in which John Paul's view of sex and sexuality is couched is obscure and academic, written to be read by a few specialist Catholic theologians and theology students. His rigid views on whether there will be sex in heaven (there will not) or whether our bodies after the resurrection will keep their sexual characteristics (they will) were formed in a state where there was no dissent or debate about these matters within the Church.

The Pope spoke to his congregation about his youth in Wadowice, how he had friends who were Jewish. He read from a letter he had once received from a Jewish schoolmate. But now, he said, there was not even a synagogue in Wadowice. He knew what war was like, he said, he had a right to speak about war. The war was a part of his life.

In his last prayer he referred to Father Kolbe, the priest who had starved to death in Auschwitz. He began by invoking the Virgin: 'And you, too, be blessed, O Mother, in the mystery of your maidenly sacrifice – you, the patron saint of the old Wadowice parish do transfer your mystery, that maidenly sacrifice of the future Mother of God to this place as well. Fill this new House of God with your motherly presence . . . Teach them Christ – just as you once revealed to me in Christ the full mystery of Man, of his dignity and supreme vocation. Teach them Christ – just the way you did your own knight, Maksymilian Maria, the memory of whose martyrdom in the Auschwitz death bunker renews the Church today. Teach us Christ, O Mother!'

Thus the unsullied woman leads us to God, just

as the martyr in his suffering renews us in our faith. For the congregation in Wadowice that day, this was the essence of their Catholicism: the mystical power of Mary, the purity and innocence of her humanity and the importance of the martyr as saint, the representative of the nation of conscience.

We drove in a bus, along narrow country roads, from Wadowice to Czestochowa. After a while I looked out of the window and saw a signpost for Oswiecim. Here, it seemed like a sign for an ordinary place, another Polish village, but as it appeared a few more times there was something odd and macabre about it, it seemed strange that the communists had never changed its name. No one else on the bus noticed it.

We drove on through the afternoon. The seminarians on the bus kept apart from the journalists, seemed to be avoiding any contact with us, as though this was part of their solemn instructions. When we wondered if there would be any possibility of stopping for food, they pointed out that they had not eaten either. They were a surly bunch. It was now the afternoon and everybody was starving. Approaching Czestochowa we hit bad traffic jams. We could see that the dual carriageway which led into the city was blocked for miles. A priest at the front of the bus got out and spoke to the police. There was very little traffic leaving Czestochowa on the other side of the carriageway. The police directed the driver to cross the margin between the two roads. We now began to drive on the wrong side of the road at full speed, accompanied by a police escort, who made sure that all oncoming cars kept to one lane only. The Church and the state conspired to get the press to Czestochowa.

The press office had no food and no idea where we could spend the night. A million people had descended on this small town, they explained, many had walked for weeks to be here. I found a place selling pizza nearby; I had a pizza and a cup of coffee and then set out to the monastery of Jasna Gora. Crowds were still arriving, the Pope's orderly divisions walking in line carrying back-packs. At the edge of the amphitheatre below the monastery walls there was a thin forest and there were tents pitched everywhere and young people lying around in the sunshine.

The long wait began. The press had access to the monastery, could watch the crowd from above close to where the cardinals and the bishops were slowly gathering. I stood there for a while, realising that I was tired and hungry, then turned back into the monastery and entered the church where a few people were quietly praying. I sat down, enjoying the quietness, the solitude and the dim light when I noticed that along the wall to my left were small, silver objects, like pieces of jewellery. Going over to look, I saw how they were attached to a length of wire mesh which ran right down the wall. At first I could not think what they were. And then I saw that tiny eyes, or legs, or arms were etched into the silver. They were left by people who believed that they had been cured here, through the intercession of the Black Madonna. There were other shapes the size of earrings with the shape of a heart cut into them, or the shape of an infant. Other pieces of silver had nothing at all etched on to them. The walls of the church were festooned with these objects, small symbols of thanksgiving for some recovery, some cure; acts of homage to the power of the Black Madonna.

Outside, everything was now prepared for the Pope's arrival. All the choirs were ready, the church hierarchy was seated, the photographers and reporters were jostling for a good view, and the vast space beneath us between the walls of the monastery and the trees was packed. He was due to arrive at half-past five, but he was late, and the waiting became tense as the crowds below cheered each time a rumour spread that he was on his way. I was carrying a small radio, and was told I could get a simultaneous translation into English of everything that was said if I tuned in to a certain wave-length.

For six hours that night the Pope sat at the altar with television lights beaming on him. He sat for some time on his throne with his head in his hands, as if he was alone in prayer and contemplation. He did not move, he made no sign that he knew we were there, watching him. It was intensely dramatic. Everyone focused on him, fascinated by this display of privacy, the sheer daring of it.

When he spoke first, it was to welcome all the pilgrims, read out a list of all the countries who were represented, giving special mention to Russia's 'passing from slavery'. It was funny; he looked up and smiled when the Spaniards cheered more loudly than all the rest. He could have been a politician in search of votes listing villages and towns to a big patriotic crowd. He went through them all, asking the crowd if they knew where Sierra Leone and Sri Lanka were. When he came to the United States he asked in Polish 'Do you know where that is?' Before they had a chance to reply, the Pope uttered half under his breath 'Perhaps too well.'

The singing began as total darkness fell and the television lights made the colours of the altar solid and rich. The same hymns were repeated over and over so that they came to seem like anthems for the occasion. Some of them were slow and dreamy, one had a particularly beautiful tune and each time it was sung the crowd linked their arms and sang along, swaying back and forth like waves. From the monastery walls, it was an extraordinary sight as a million people moved to this soaring music. Even the bishops in the second row joined hands and sang, but in the front row the prelates sat there stiffly.

There was a break for a while, but there was no food to be had in the monastery and I still had no idea where I could sleep. Somebody said that Lech Walesa's wife, Danuta, who was among the congregation, was going to spend the night with her husband in the monastery and she would be the first woman to sleep in Jasna Gora since it was founded in medieval times. It was getting cold and I wondered what it would be like to lie down on the grass or a park bench without a sleeping-bag or any warm clothes.

When the Pope returned, the tone became more sombre. There were no more jokes, no more opportunities to cheer, no more reading out lists of countries. In the way he walked, in the expression on his face, in how he used his hands, he somehow changed the atmosphere, moved it from a rock concert to the solemn vigil of the fifteenth of August. A large, heavy cross was carried up the steps by a group of young people and placed on the altar. The crowd was now packed in tight; there were screens at the side for those who could not see the altar.

He sat again with his hand over his face as prayers were read by representatives from various countries. He looked up when a group from the Ukraine came up the steps with a present for him as the choirs sang the Ukrainian national anthem. A girl from the Sudan came and read some prayers, referring to the difficulty of Catholics in her country. Suddenly, just before she was due to finish, she turned and sprang, ran up the steps, frantically making her way up to where the Pope sat. Everybody could see her; a gasp came up from the crowd. She made it up two flights before she was held by security men. As they dragged her away, they seemed to twist her arm behind her back, causing her pain, as the Pope sat and watched from his throne, his face now alert, his expression attentive. The crowd began to shout and whistle, calling on the guards to leave the girl alone. She had appeared so innocent and sincere when she spoke. It was clear that she had meant no harm. The Pope stood and gestured towards her. The security men hesitated and then let her go towards the Pope and embrace him. She wrapped her arms around him.

There were more prayers and rituals and hymns. And then the Pope stood up to speak: 'During this night vigil, so full of feelings and enthusiasm, I would wish to bring your attention, my dear young friends, boys and girls, to three terms that are our guides – "I am" – "I remember" – "I watch." ' After exploring the use of the phrase 'I am' in the Scriptures he went on 'You have come, dear friends, to the Holy Shrine of Jasna Gora where since many years is sung the call "I am by you". The world that surrounds you, the modern civilisation, has done a tremendous amount in obliterating from Man's consciousness that "I am" of God. It tries to exist as if God didn't exist . . . You came here, dear friends, to find and confirm, to the very depth, that personal human "I am" in relation to God. Look at the cross in which God's "I am" means "Love". Look at the cross and forget not.'

He then began to preach about 'I remember' and then 'I watch': 'Here in the Shrine of Jasna Gora the words "I watch" are united with the person of the Most Holy Mother of God through her Icon. Her "I watch" embodies the attitude of the mother. Her life, her vocation is expressed by being watchful. It is watching over Man from the first moment of his being . . . The Church took the maternal vigil of Mary with her. Visible signs of this are to be seen in so many sanctuaries all over the world . . . Here on this earth, in this country, where we are, whole generations lived with this consciousness. From here, from the Holy Shrine of Jasna Gora, she watches over the whole nation, over everyone. Especially during difficult moments, at times of trial and danger.

' "Watch furthermore means to notice another person . . . to watch is to love your neighbour – it means fundamental human solidarity." Those words I have spoken before in the Holy Shrine of Jasna Gora on my meeting with the young. It was during a difficult year for Poland, in the year 1983. I am repeating them today: "I am" – "I remember" – "I watch." '

This was a religion I only half recognised, just as the parts of the body etched into silver seemed part of the past but hard to locate. There was something about the singing, the colours and the beauty of the words which reminded me of strange, hard won moments of pure contentment I had experienced in the church as a child.

The Pope had not mentioned sex or sin. He had not hectored us. His words had been suggestive, at times poetic. All around me the journalists and photographers were moved by the crowd below in the night. Now the music grew louder and the hymn I had liked so much was sung again. The Pope stood and gave his blessing in Latin, and then waited, alone and silent. His presence, after the long day, was still mysterious and charismatic. All the humdrum problems of his Church seemed meaningless now, small compared with the size and spirit of this gathering. He watched, his expression sad, otherworldly, bemused, but he appeared, none the less, to maintain all his strength and power.

It was nearly midnight. There would be Mass again

in the morning. I was starving and desperate to get some sleep. Still exhilarated by this brush with crowds and power, I stood at the edge of the monastery walls and looked down: the Pope had disappeared, but the young pilgrims stayed in place, still singing and swaying. I was facing a night in a doorway waiting for the dawn. I walked down to the press bus which would take us to the city centre. A Polish photographer came and sat beside me. He was young, he could have been in his late teens, and friendly. He spoke English with an American accent, and tended to shrug as he spoke, much as Americans do, making clear that he took the world for granted. He had done good work, he said, because some of the western photographers had lent him their lenses, as he had only one basic, cheap lens himself. He smiled. He was relaxed. Where was he staying? I asked him. In a friend's house, he said. He thought there would be no problem if I wanted to stay there too.

We walked through the city that night as a million young people dispersed in groups to find a place to sleep. I told the young photographer about the seminarians on the bus, how distant and unfriendly they had been. I asked him if he knew any seminarians? He did not, he said. They all came from really religious families in small villages. No one from the city became a priest. No one he knew had ever thought of it, even though his family, he said, like all Polish families, was religious.

We caught a tram and alighted in a street full of high, grim, apartment buildings. After a few turns we arrived at a lane which led to a large three-storey nineteenth-century house in its own grounds. The door was answered by a young man who welcomed us in fluent English.

The house was full of young people who had come for the Pope's visit. I was directed to a mattress in a corner of a large room. The photographer was also sleeping there, and he would wake me in the morning so we could get to the press benches early and thus secure a good view.

The dawn had barely broken, I felt that I had not slept at all when he woke me. We would need to get going, he said. It was freezing and there was no hot water in the house. We had breakfast on the way. He loved the Pope, he told me, as we walked along the street. All Polish people loved him.

At nine o'clock the Pope arrived to say Mass. This time, as he ascended the steps he was carrying a crook for support. The morning was bright and warm. As the sun grew stronger, some of the bishops and cardinals had minders who held yellow or white sun umbrellas over them. A priest came to each journalist to explain that there would be an important press conference after the ceremonies and all journalists were expected to attend. A local journalist told me not to bother: the conference would merely explain that Mrs Walesa had not spent the night with her husband in the monastery, that the long tradition of keeping women outside the walls of the monastery at night had been preserved, despite previous reports and rumours.

The sermon once more was philosophical and poetic, at times obscure. At the end of the Gospel the Pope lifted the Testament up in a dramatic gesture. If you knew nothing about this religion, it would seem oddly attractive, wonderfully speculative, the rituals exotic, appearing to place beauty and atmosphere – the colours, the poetry, the music, the setting – above all else. Someone told me that there were groups from the former Soviet Union here who knew nothing about the religion, but had come because of their admiration for the Pope. I wondered would they go away, like the early disciples, wanting to spread the word.

When the Pope came to the consecration there was utter silence down below: no sound from more than a million people as he lifted the Host and then the chalice, for a few moments only stillness and reverence. And then he began the Pater Noster in Latin, the language, he said, which once united Europe. At the end of the Mass he changed once more from the mysterious and powerful overlord to a playful, humorous, fatherly figure. He said farewell in all the languages, expressing his surprise that the Spaniards could recognise the name of their country in Polish, as they cheered below. He had a special blessing for the youth of Cuba. 'I pray for your country every day,' he said. He pointed beyond the trees to the crowds who were watching him on screens as he stood at the edge of the platform. 'Thank God for all these people. Sometimes a lot of evil things are said about the screen. Today we have to thank the screen with all our might.' And then the singing started again, everyone linking arms and swaying. He smiled and waved at the crowd and then turned and walked slowly back into the monastery.

On the way out I stood looking down into one of the cloisters as the twelve cardinals and over two hundred bishops who had attended the ceremonials were disrobed of their splendour by a swarm of nuns. A few others gathered beside me to watch. A prelate, fresh from the altar, would stand with his arms in the air while two nuns removed his richly coloured vestments and carried them to a long clothes-rack to hang them up, leaving the prince of the church with his hair tousled, wearing only black. It was like watching actors backstage after a show, all their magic so perfunctorily removed. The nuns moved briskly, as though making it clear to the elders of the Church that they would take no nonsense.

I walked through the crowded city, there were young people everywhere collecting up their belongings, stretching and yawning in the midday sun. There were crowds in the railway station waiting for the train to Warsaw. Don't bother queuing for a ticket, someone said. You won't need one. Everybody will be travelling back to Warsaw free of charge.

6

The Sweetest Time

ON AN ORDINARY Saturday in March 1992 Stockholm was full of shoppers. People stood in designer shops looking at lamps, sofas, plates, kitchenware and beds, running their expert eyes over fabrics and textures. The coffee shops offered several types of coffee and luxurious chocolate cakes. The second-hand bookshops had shelves full of old art books; all of them with an English language section. I was buying nothing, just observing the casual consumption.

The previous night I had wandered around the city. In the old apartment buildings they did not draw the curtains and as you walked along you could see the rich lamplight, the plants, the well-painted walls, the bookcases, the paintings and framed prints. A settled bourgeois world with all its comforts. Everything seemed more than three times the price it would be in Ireland, even the cinema, but especially the bars. I watched all this with interest, knowing that soon I would be entering a world where electric mixers, microwave ovens and deep freezes were part of people's dreams, where the bourgeois ideal was only in its infancy.

Even on Sunday there were shops open in Stockholm.

In the modern complex around the railway station in the city centre, people were trying on clothes, wandering from boutique to boutique, examining new fashions and different styles. The ferry left from Stockholm at five o'clock that day to go to Tallinn, the capital of Estonia. It sailed down the narrow inlet of the harbour in the encroaching darkness, past tiny islands, with one or two houses with lights on surrounded by bare trees. It would arrive at nine o'clock in the morning.

The cold was new to me, even though I had come from Dublin. It was sharper, fiercer, more exact than the Irish cold. Up on deck it was almost unbearable. Most people stayed indoors. Beside me was a group with American accents. We stood with our elbows on the railings looking out at the small islands. One of them told me that they were Baptists going to Estonia. They were based outside Stockholm, he said, but now that things had opened up in the Baltic states they travelled quite a lot to Tallinn and to other centres in Estonia to set up schools and churches; eventually they hoped to move there.

There were two restaurants on the ferry: one for people with hard currency and the other at the end of a corridor for the rest. The hard currency restaurant had its menu printed in fancy lettering full of French phrases. It offered a five course dinner. The other place had no menu written up and had merely a self-service counter. I ate a sausage, some sauerkraut and a few diced potatoes. This cost less than a dollar but the can of beer I had to wash it down cost two. The atmosphere in the soft currency restaurant was depressing. Even the light bulbs looked cheap.

I was sharing a cabin with a man from Estonia who spoke enough English to tell me that he had been in Stockholm on business. As word spread throughout the boat that the duty free was open, a long queue developed; I watched my cabin mate stand in line examining bottles of spirits. For the new few hours the Estonian passengers and some of the Swedes haunted the duty free. Even when they had already bought things they went in and looked again, studying the objects on sale, picking bottles and cartons up and handling them with a strange intensity.

I went up to the bar where there was a kind of disco and had a few beers. The young man at the bar beside me told me that he was a business student, and had been in Stockholm on a scholarship to look at how things were done in the West. His family had owned a mill before the war and there was now a possibility that they would get it back. His English was good. I asked him if he had found Stockholm expensive. He sighed. He had stayed in an hotel, the bill was paid by a Swedish foundation, but he knew that what it cost per night was more than his family's monthly income, much more. He couldn't get used to the idea. He found it very hard to spend money at the beginning, but soon he started to think in western money and that became OK. He could buy coffees and bus tickets. But the idea of the hotel room was still too much for him.

We arrived in Tallinn in the morning. I intended to change a hundred dollars into roubles, but the bank seemed to think that this was too much. I changed fifty and got quantities of notes. I took a taxi to a modern monstrosity of a hotel near the centre, dumped my bags and began to wander around the city. It was even colder than in Stockholm, a concentrated cold that got into your feet and your hands and the tip of your nose.

Beside a derelict site in the city centre the following sign appeared in four languages: 'Tallinn was bombed by the Soviet Air Forces during the evening and midnight of 9 March 1944, 53 per cent of living space was destroyed, almost 20,000 people lost their houses, 463 people were killed and 659 were wounded.' I stood and watched as three men in coats, who could have been engineers or archaeologists, moved among the ruins. It was clear that there had once been houses here: you could see the basements and the old piping. One of the men had a map which he consulted regularly as he peered into the water-logged holes. Soon, they were joined by a woman in her early forties wearing a black beret.

I approached them and asked if any of them spoke English. Hesitantly, the woman in the beret said that she spoke some. She explained that they were architects working for the city authorities and told me with pride that they had just won a battle to prevent an American trade centre being built on this site. During the years of Soviet rule it had been a park; the bombing of 1944 was never mentioned. Now they wanted to rebuild the façades of the old houses as part of a general plan to restore the old city.

She introduced herself as Mai Lume. She asked me to wait while she spoke to her colleagues, and then took me on a tour of the city, showing me first three of the most beautiful and stately buildings which had been bought by the Swedes, the Finns and the Germans for embassies. At the moment they were just shells, waiting for the builders to finish the structural work. The city centre appeared untouched by Soviet architecture or even by the nineteenth century. The main square was straight out of a Dürer woodcut. There were hardly any cars and no car parks; just a few shoppers wandering around, it was like a vast marketplace. Each building in the square was in a different style. The chemist's shop – Mai Lume called it the 'apotek' – had been there since 1490; it was, she thought, the oldest anywhere in Europe. The shape of the roofs seemed to belong to medieval times; but nothing looked consciously preserved, it was all still used. Now, Mai Lume said, it would be preserved for the future. In the new independent Estonia Tallinn would be the jewel, the showcase.

We met later at about six o'clock. It was an important anniversary, she said, it was the ninth of March. People gathered in the old city, where I had seen the architects at work, they lit candles, which they placed on the ground near where the destroyed houses had been, and they stood in the bitter cold listening to a male choir singing patriotic hymns. Many of them were old enough to remember the bombing, to understand the complex web of motives which led so many Estonians to support the Germans in the Second World War. A single toll of the church bell came at intervals before the choir began to sing 'God Save Estonia'. It was still freezing, people were wearing fur hats. Some old people watched the scene from a window with a single candle lit. This commemoration had been banned under the Soviets, the anniversary had been shrouded in silence, but over the previous three or four years it had taken place not as a mass demonstration but as a quiet event.

Mai Lume invited me to her apartment for dinner. I thought that she did so out of natural politeness and hospitality, but that she also felt a duty to inform a writer from a small country like Ireland who might understand what was happening in Estonia now. The apartment was in a post-war complex within walking distance of my hotel. Outside it looked dingy, like apartment buildings put up in a hurry after the war all over the Eastern bloc. Inside it was warm and comfortable. Mai's husband was there; he was a tall Nordic-looking man. They had two sons in their late teens, both studying music, and a younger daughter. Beside the dining room there was a room full of books, and there was a real sense in this household that education and culture were vital. The children were all studying English and were told to listen carefully as we spoke at the dinner table. Both of their parents could be called, I suppose, Estonian nationalists, although they did not use the term themselves: they were proud of their country, and hugely relieved that it was independent from Russia. Like everyone else I met during this trip to the Baltic, they spoke with intensity, as though no one had ever heard their story before.

When Stalin annexed Estonia the population was 90 per cent Estonian, they said, and 10 per cent Russian and Finn. Every year, they went on (we were in the library, and Mai's husband was doing most of the talking), thousands and thousands of Russians came to Estonia and the country is now more than 40 per cent Russian and the city of Tallinn more than 50 per cent. Because of the number of young Russians in Tallinn, the Russian population is likely to increase over the next few years to maybe 60 per cent.

They believe that they are in Russia, Mai and her husband told me. They can't understand that the situation has changed and they are in Estonia. And parliament has ruled that if you are employed in a shop or an office and somebody comes up to you, you must speak to them in their language. The Russians do not agree with this. And the law doesn't work. And then Mai's husband pointed his finger at me and said: yet. For the previous two years, he said, there has been quite a powerful Russian lobby in Tallinn called A Struggle For Equal Rights. Out of one hundred and five MPs, between twenty and twenty-five belong to the so-called Russian-speaking party.

They don't realise, Mai said, that for five thousand years the Estonian people have been here, that there was a Golden Age of Estonian culture in the sixteenth and seventeenth centuries, that when Estonia was controlled by Sweden, they had the Baltic between themselves and their rulers and thus could flourish as a separate culture. The first secondary school was set up in Tallinn more than four hundred years ago and the university was founded in 1632. But the Russians believed that everybody should be happy to use the Russian language and belong to Russian culture.

The only thing the Russians had which the Estonians needed was oil, her husband told me. Without Russian oil it would be hard but not hopeless. The Scandinavian countries were ready to help. It was clear that Mai and her husband saw Scandinavia as civilised and Russia as dark, foreign and, in certain ways, barbaric. They were indignant at how little Russians knew about the Baltic states, and how they were told in school that they had carried freedom and culture to Estonia, Latvia and Lithuania. In the end, there was no support from Estonians for joining the new commonwealth. Nobody was studying Russian any more, not even in schools, 75 per cent of which were teaching their pupils English.

We have too many Russians, they said, we can't assimilate them. It is a question of culture. They resent Estonia. They live in separate communities. Many of them came to work in the nuclear industry. There were twenty thousand workers, all Russian, building parts of reactors for nuclear plants, but since the Russians will no longer send the raw materials, these people are mostly out of work. The workers blame separation from Russia for being unemployed and feel that if only they could get back to Mother Russia, everything would be all right.

But for Mai and her husband being free of Mother Russia was the priority, restoring Estonia and its culture to pride of place. They could not see how the Russian population could ever become full citizens of the new Estonia, nor dual citizens of Estonia and Russia. They did not know any of the Russians personally – they found the idea absurd – and gave the impression that they shared something with me – an interest in books and culture, the use of English – which they could never share with these outsiders who had come to their country when it was occupied by the Soviets.

I took the train from Tallinn to Vilnius in Lithuania the following morning at seven o'clock. It would take thirteen hours and for the first four or five hours there was no heating. I shared the carriage with a young woman from Vilnius. Every so often we made desperate efforts to communicate with each other: was her book good? was my book good? was she very cold? would I like tea? don't let the Russian woman give you blankets, she only wants dollars, she'll overcharge you. Eventually, we fell silent, slept a bit, were woken by the rattling of the train, read and tried to look out through the filthy windows at the great fertile plain we were crossing. These fields were covered in snow and ice until about midday, when the hot sun rose in the sky. This gave us some heat in the carriage, just as the train's heating system was coming to life.

We passed a large number of isolated holdings, painted wooden houses with galvanised roofs, and small orchards and chicken runs beside them, with trees for shelter. I saw no cars. If someone had assured me that this was the last feudal society in Europe, rather than a place which had been run by the Soviets until recently, I would have almost believed them. There was no sign of any technology or collectivisation. It all seemed traditional and primitive.

My friend from Vilnius did not want me to get a taxi from the station. All day she had been protecting me from people who wanted my dollars. She had hated the tea and the food on the train as much as I did. Now she discovered where I was staying, accompanied me on a tram and then along several streets, and deposited me at the door.

The hotel had been built at the turn of the century and had been slowly deteriorating ever since. The room was either cold or overheated; the restaurant looked more like a discotheque with its tinsel and mirrors. They never had any beer, but sweet champagne and any amount of vodka. The first night, I had my dinner there and went to bed. It was snowing outside. I tried to ring home, but was told that there were no lines available.

In the morning when I wandered out into the city it was like entering a cinema when the movie has already been running for some time. There were crowds in the street, some of them strolling casually along, others moving urgently in the same direction. There was clearly something happening. There were flags everywhere. At the end of a long street which ran from the cathedral to the parliament building I could see that people had climbed trees to witness whatever was going on. The street was still fortified with huge reinforced concrete blocks to prevent Soviet tanks approaching the parliament building, but there were no tanks. Instead, there were constant shouts and cheers. I asked a couple in English what was happening and they explained as best they could that it was the second anniversary of the declaration of independence.

There was a brass band which played in between speeches. Under an archway in a building across the square an army jeep was parked and there were people standing on the bonnet, the mudguards and then the roof to get a better view. Great roars would come up from the crowd – 'Lietuwa!', which I soon discovered meant Lithuania, 'Lietuwa!' Even saying the name appeared to make them all happy, get them excited. I watched a soldier with a video camera taking pictures of the scene. This was, for Lithuanians, a new beginning in their history.

They must have been starved of speeches for so long that right through the freezing afternoon they watched and cheered, staring open-mouthed at the speakers. There were banners in English including one which asked 'Mr Nixon, Save Our Independence' and another which said 'Red Army Go Home'. There were American flags. And all of the time, during the speeches and in between them, they shouted out the name of their country, and everyone became alert, there was a sense of concentration in the air as they roared 'Lietuwa! Lietuwa!'

Then President Landsbergis spoke; when he had finished people raised two fingers of their right hand and cheered and stood erect for the National Anthem. Afterwards, people went to the front of the building to see what was written up on boards and pieces of cardboard. There was a group of women saying the Rosary around a large statue of the Virgin and the Cross, which was surrounded with flowers and votive candles. When the Rosary was finished they started singing hymns. The atmosphere here was completely different from that in Tallinn, where there had been no statues of the Virgin, and where there was a real sense of Protestant aloofness and strictness, even in the way buildings had been preserved, even in the way people sang. It was impossible to imagine Mai Lume's family kneeling in front of a statue.

I had been given the name and address of a newspaper editor, Algis Chekuolis, by a friend in Ireland and I went the next day in search of his offices. It was the early afternoon and his paper *Gimtasis Krastas* had just gone to press. He was in his fifties and spoke good English;

he was friendly and alert and he knew that he had a story to tell and seemed pleased that he had plenty of time to talk. There were things I would understand, he told me, because I was Irish. Ireland and Lithuania had much in common, he said; in fact there were no two countries more similar. Both were roughly eighty-five thousand square kilometres in size; they had more or less the same population. There was nothing in the subsoil of either country, no mineral wealth; both countries grew potatoes and manufactured linen; both had a huge diaspora, which arose from terrible poverty in the nineteenth century; both had big powerful neighbours. And then there was Catholicism: both were Catholic countries, and in both countries Catholicism had come to define the difference between the oppressed nation and the powerful, colonising neighbour.

He talked about the bear and the hedgehog. If a bear swallows a hedgehog, then it is bad for the bear. Thus Russia could never really contain the Baltic states. The Soviets took over Lithuania, which had been independent since 1918, in 1940, but the following year, as the Second World War raged, Lithuania was taken by the Germans. There was considerable anti-Semitic feeling in Lithuania, fuelled by the accusation that some Jews had assisted the Soviet invasion. Ninety-five per cent of the Jews of Lithuania were wiped out during the war years, with the active assistance of the Lithuanians.

In 1944 the Soviets re-took Lithuania, and a guerrilla movement began. Country boys went on the run rather than be drafted into the Russian army; youngsters went into the forest and fought for nine years. But there were no mountains, as in Afghanistan, and most of them had been shot, or captured, or deported by the mid 1950s. In the meantime, a large section of the population, according to Algis, decided to co-operate and a great number of Lithuanians joined the party: there were more than two hundred thousand party members out of a population of three million seven hundred thousand. So in the 1960s and 1970s in Lithuania there was no resistance, no sabotage, just conformity, an entire population keeping its head down.

In June 1988 the real movement for independence began. A committee of thirty-five was set up, sixteen of whom were prominent communists. Later that year the Communist Party in Lithuania split from the Soviet party. There were elections in the spring of 1989 in which all but two deputies were former communists or members of the new movement, an umbrella opposition group. In the 1990 elections 87 per cent of the vote went to the new movement. On 11 March 1990 parliament declared independence. Gorbachev countered with an economic blockade. Algis grew eloquent as he described the Lithuanian response. We made a mockery of it, he said, we told them to stuff their oil where the sun doesn't shine. Lithuania was a big producer and exporter of electricity, we stopped exporting electricity to Byelorussia. We stopped exporting butter and meat, and Moscow television showed not only the defiance but good tables full of food in Vilnius. He was proud that Elena Bonner had said that 11 March 1990, the day Vilnius declared independence, was the last day of the Soviet Union.

In March 1990, then, the hedgehog escaped from the belly of the bear. Eighty per cent of the population was ethnic Lithuanian, 8 per cent Polish, 8 per cent Russian who had settled and integrated, and 4 per cent immigrants who were not happy, who were, in Algis Chekuolis's words, shouting about rights, but who would not get full citizenship until they swore loyalty to Lithuania and spoke three lines in Lithuanian. There could be no double citizenship and non-citizens could not vote or be elected and were restricted in buying property.

He was thinking aloud, his eyes flashing when he recalled the early days of resistance. They used strikes, and organised food lines. They spoke about separation from the Soviet Union on the newly liberalised television station. They were aware that Gorbachev planned to smash independence with military force, but believed they could defeat him with moral force. From spies in the KGB who could monitor and decode intelligence reports, they knew that the building the Soviets wanted was the parliament building, so they put four concentric rings of barricades around it as well as anti-tank trenches and minefields. Since the Soviet tanks were full of high octane gasoline, it made them particularly vulnerable to Molotov cocktails, which, according to Algis, everyone carried.

The Soviets, he said, decided to attack the radio and television building, and there were fourteen killed in the battle, but they were clumsy and arrogant and did not know that there was a second TV station. In a couple of hours the Lithuanians, with the help of the Finns, had found a connection with another satellite and all the world saw the Soviet tanks in Vilnius.

It was dark outside now, and he had been talking for more than two hours. Like Mai Lume and her husband in Tallinn, Algis Chekuolis spoke like someone who had not had a proper chance to tell his story before. I felt that he could happily keep me there all evening as he moved from recent events back to history. Although Lithuania had existed since medieval times, he explained, the idea of a Lithuanian nation did not take root until the mid-nineteenth century, it was only in 1862 that a national consciousness developed. It was just like Ireland he said: songs, the language, newspapers and magazines all gave impetus to the national movement.

What was the role of the Catholic Church in the life of this nation, I asked him, and what was its role in the 1990 declaration of independence? The Poles, he replied, are fanatically Catholic; they personalise Poland and Catholicism, they rally around the Catholic Church, the church as a building and the priests; but in Lithuania things are very different. This was, he said grandly and dramatically, the last tribe in Europe to embrace Christianity only six hundred years ago. And it never totally caught on in Lithuania; pagan beliefs survived; gods were thunder, stone, fire, oak, animals were sacrificed. Later, Christianity took hold as the court became converted; but in villages, paganism and its superstitions continued, Christianity remained skin-deep.

It was relatively easy for the Soviets to suppress Catholicism in Lithuania between 1944 and 1990. Chekuolis estimated that now, in 1992, only 10 per cent of the population were devoted Catholics. It was not like Ireland or Poland; it was easier to undermine the Catholic faith in Lithuania. But Catholicism provided an essential means of resisting the regime. No teacher, for example, could go to church in the Soviet years. So closing the door, shutting the window and praying could be a personal, private resistance.

Algis Chekuolis considered Christmas 1986 a crucial moment in Lithuanian resistance to Soviet rule, and believed that the role of his own newspaper had been vital. Christmas was forbidden during the Soviet years; the authorities would arrange dances in the schools to stop it being celebrated as a family festival. So he decided to run a special issue of the paper dedicated to Christmas, explaining it as a traditional Lithuanian family feast.

He went over to the safe in his office and came back with a precious copy of this edition of his newspaper.

He described how he got it through the official censor. She was Lithuanian, he said, and he told her she had to sign. He used a couple of tricks including the promise of work if she was fired. It was Friday evening. He emphasised to her that there were no state secrets in the newspaper. And she put her stamp of approval on it. It was an important moment, he said, and he covered other aspects of Catholicism in each issue of the paper.

The Catholic Church had stayed in the catacombs during the Soviet years and did not collaborate with the state as much as the Russian Orthodox Church. As a result, only twenty clerical students were accepted every year, and priests were not allowed, for example, into hospitals to attend the dying. The cathedral in Vilnius, like most churches, was closed and used as an art gallery. But in October 1988 it was handed back to the Catholic Church and this was the real public turning point. There was a torchlight procession from the other side of the river to the cathedral. Mass was said on the steps. That period, for Algis, from then until the end of the Soviet blockade was the sweetest time in his life and in everyone's life.

Now, he said, it had all become dull and normal. The circulation of his newspaper had dropped, with no new issues and a great deal of competition. Fifteen per cent of the economy had been privatised. Every Saturday there was an auction when apartments, shops and other property were sold to the highest bidder. Each citizen had state bonds; a husband and wife could club together and bid for an apartment, or they could join a larger conglomerate and bid for a shop or a business. It was a far cry from building barricades and carrying Molotov cocktails. He went over to the safe and put back the precious Christmas 1986 edition of his newspaper.

Vilnius was a Lithuanian city now, the capital of an independent country. But it had a shadow named Wilno, the Polish name for Vilnius, where the poet Czeslaw Milocz grew up speaking Polish in the years before the Second World War when the city was a Polish and Jewish enclave in Lithuania. His friend the poet Tomas Venclova grew up after the war in the same city, but now it had different street-names, its Jewish population was decimated and it had a new language. 'None the less,' Milocz wrote, 'it is the same city, its architecture, the landscape of the surrounding region, and its sky, shaped us both.'

Czeslaw Milocz's Wilno had disappeared. I could not find the 'German Street' he described in his memoir *Beginning With My Streets*: 'It seemed that on German Street every house concealed an infinite number of inhabitants who engaged in every possible trade. Beneath enormous painted signs, shop after shop fronted on the street, but the faces of lions, the pictures of stockings of monstrous proportions, of gloves and corsets, also advertised shops inside the courtyards, while the signs inside the gates gave information about dentists, seamstresses, hosiers, pleaters, shoemakers, and so forth.' It was not there. The city he remembered no longer existed.

In my notes I have written down: this is the dullest city I have ever been to. There were theatres and concerts and cinemas, but the streets themselves and the atmosphere seemed oddly shadowy as though we were caught in what Milocz had called in one poem the 'City without a Name', in which the bars closed early and no one went out at night. It was as though the old streets which Milocz remembered in his city of Wilno had still not given up the ghost, and the new city had not yet fully come into being.

This Vilnius, the Lithuanian city, however, had once

been a dream too. For Lithuanian nationalists, it is, Tomas Venclova wrote, 'a symbol of continuity and historical identity like Jerusalem. In the nineteenth and twentieth centuries, the myth of royal, holy Vilnius, torn away by force, shaped the Lithuanian imagination to a significant degree . . . Vilnius is very different from Riga or Tallinn, because it was not a Hanseatic Centre but was a capital city, a sacral city . . . Lithuania without Vilnius is an ephemeral state, but with Vilnius it regains all its past and all its historic obligations.'

It was the dream-city the Lithuanians wanted back from the Poles, and the Poles, having lost it, dreamed about it too and still called it Wilno. Once darkness fell it was empty and strange.

One day, one of the women in the press office of the parliament made an appointment for me with Monsignor Vasiliauskas, the priest who ran the cathedral, and came along to interpret. She used the word 'parishoner' for him, but it was obvious that he was not a parish priest. He was in his late fifties, a mild-looking man with glasses. We met in the large, old-fashioned vestry.

He remembered how he was raised to the priesthood in this very cathedral in 1946. Even at that time quite a number of priests had been arrested, although the real persecution began in 1948. The churches were being closed, and by 1949 it was forbidden to say Mass. The last class of priests was ordained in 1947. The cathedral was finally closed in 1950, to be used first as a grain store, then left empty, and in 1956 to become an art museum. In 1949 he himself was arrested and sent to Siberia, where he spent ten years working as a coal miner. About 25 per cent of the priests were arrested, he said, and four out of five of the bishops.

In Lithuania almost everyone was forbidden to go to church, particularly professional people and students. Only the old continued to practise religion. In Monsignor Vasiliauskas's camp in Siberia there were eight hundred Lithuanians among the four thousand prisoners. There were ten Catholic priests who said Mass every day, celebrated Christmas and Easter and heard confessions. He showed me a photograph of a group of miners taken in the camp in the 1950s. Which of them is you? I asked him. The youngest and the most handsome, he said and laughed.

In the camps, he said, the Lithuanians were always the bravest. He remembered an old man dying, he was an old believer, a member of the Russian Orthodox Church, the priests from his Church were afraid to give him the last rites. But the Lithuanian Catholic priests were not afraid. After the death of Stalin things became easier, they were allowed to organise games and sport, and eventually he was released and exiled to Latvia for ten years, working for five years in a collective farm as a bookkeeper, forbidden all the time to say Mass in public. His papers had the words 'Especially Dangerous' written on them. Later, he was allowed to live thirty kilometres from the Lithuanian border, and in 1969 he returned home.

Lithuanians had not kept the faith like the Poles, he said. This was the reality. There was no education. There were no rights for the Church in schools or hospitals or prisons. The figures for Mass attendance on Sunday even now were not high. In Poland, all the time, he said, they had priests and religious literature. Now, in Lithuania, there were hardly any priests, and many were old, and the only religious books they had were from the beginning of the century. There was also an atheistic spirit which had crept into society: 50 per cent of all pregnancies ended in abortion. I had heard similar figures from other people and I asked the Monsignor if the Church had plans to ban abortion. He was careful: the Church, he said, had always had a negative attitude to abortion, and the Church will fight this because it is a problem.

In October 1988 when it was decided to hand the cathedral back to the Catholic Church, he set to work calling bishops all over Lithuania, telling them to come, and finding people to sing for the first Mass, which was shown on television. The former director of the art gallery welcomed them whole-heartedly. In three months the cathedral was redecorated.

There was one outstanding matter which the Monsignor felt was important and wished to explain: previously, the Bishopric of Vilnius had belonged to Poland; making, theologically, Lithuania a part of Poland, but a month before we spoke the Vatican had recognised Vilnius as Lithuanian. For this, he said, Lithuanians were very grateful to the Pope.

Although everybody I spoke to agreed that religious practice had genuinely died out even within Catholic families, and many people under the age of fifty knew nothing about the Church, except as a symbol of resistance, and did not avail themselves of the new freedom to worship and take the sacraments, the churches were packed on the only Sunday I spent in Vilnius. The cathedral was full of very young children and their parents, the Jesuit church also; and there was a strange shrine to the Virgin at the top of a long flight of stairs in another church beyond the Jesuit one, which had remained open during all the years of religious persecution. It was where the old people went, someone told me. Now, on Sunday morning people knelt in front of the shrine and prayed.

There was silence in what was a narrow corridor with flowers and candles surrounding a small shrine, a silence broken only by the shuffling of people standing up and the whispering of prayers. There was a large number of old people; but even the young looked like figures from the 1950s, unlike, say, the young women who worked in the press office who dressed smartly and could have been Americans. The shrine and its pilgrims seemed locked in the days when it was the only Catholic haven in the city, visited only by those who had nothing to lose under the Soviet regime.

The hotel where I was staying had been bought by a Scandinavian consortium, someone told me, and would soon be closed for renovations. I wondered what would happen to the receptionist who refused to make international telephone connections for me, insisting always that she could not get a line, until one day I went down to the desk and told her I must make a call to Dublin now and was prepared to wait at the desk until I got through. She put me through immediately. Towards the end of my stay I watched a Scandinavian man who had checked out trying to carry his suitcases to a waiting taxi and hold the door open at the same time. Two uniformed hotel waiters watched him nonchalantly: it simply did not occur to them that they should help him. He pointed at his cases and said something to them, but they still stood there looking at him. Eventually, he shouted at them in his native tongue. But they had no idea why he was angry.

It still snowed a few times a day, and once darkness fell there was a forlorn atmosphere in the city. I kept looking at a map of the former Soviet Union wondering where I should go now. One day I went to the Aeroflot office to see if they had cheap flights, and I bought a one-way ticket to Kiev, the capital of the Ukraine. I had no plans, no reason to stay or go, but there was one more person in Vilnius I wanted to see: his name was Alfonsas Svarinskas and he was the Catholic priest who had become a member of parliament. Again the press office made contact with him for me and agreed to interpret. We arranged to meet at the priest/politician's home one evening, just before I left.

Father Svarinskas was a large, brusque, strong-looking man. He tended to fidget and look around as he spoke. Whereas Monsignor Vasiliauskas in the cathedral had listened carefully to the questions and made sure I understood the interpreter, this man was less accommodating. He went into the seminary in 1942, he said. Under the Germans conditions were good, even though the number of seminarians was restricted. The problem began with the Soviets. He was arrested in 1946 and sentenced to ten years in Siberia. He was secretly ordained in the camp by a bishop in 1954.

I tried to ask him about his years in various gulags. (He was not finally released until 1988.) But his answers were vague. He told me how the guards were detailed to watch him on Sunday in case he said Mass, but he, like the other Catholics, learned to pray wherever he could. It was pressure, he said, from Reagan and Dan Quayle which had him released, particularly Dan Quayle. He believed that there should now be a monument built to Reagan in front of the Kremlin; it was he who had called the Soviet Union 'the evil empire'. He had met the president in Washington after his release and was full of admiration for him.

After his release he spent forty days in Lithuania and forty days in Frankfurt and then travelled around the world for two years. He returned to Vilnius in 1990 and the following year he was elected to parliament. He wanted a free, democratic, independent Lithuania. What role did he see for the Catholic Church? Lithuania was now almost all Catholic, he said. The Catholic Church was a leader throughout the years. He started to list: one bishop shot, two bishops exiled, the cardinal exiled . . .

It would be easy, he said, to re-build the material church after fifty years, but not souls. He was concerned about the increase in drinking and crime, and about the number of communists still in public life. They were collaborators, he said, quislings – we'll get rid of them. Before there had been only 4 per cent of Russians in Lithuania, now there were 9 per cent. It would be difficult to do anything about abortion, he continued, until the parliament was cleared of communists. He told me that before the war it was usual for priests to be in parliament. In the 1920s one priest was Minister for Agriculture and made great reforms, giving every person eighty acres of land, which ensured that there was no support for communism in Lithuania. In Slovakia, during the war years, he said, Father Tiso had been the president.

In the 1930s all the commerce in Lithuania was in the hands of the Jews. They were not popular. There were rich Jews and poor Jews. The poor Jews, he said – and this is a common view in Lithuania – helped the Soviets in 1941. If it had not been for their behaviour more of them would have been saved from the Germans in 1944, he asserted. In the end they were wiped out. There were maybe a few hundred left in Lithuania; many survivors went to Israel, he said. He did not seem to know – he spoke fast and I could not see his eyes clearly behind his strong glasses – how the Holocaust is viewed now in the West, as an enormous crime, an unspeakable tragedy. He had spent most of his life in work camps, and I knew that I could not expect him to have picked up the language of western liberalism when he did not share its politics. I asked him, finally, what the immediate priorities were for Lithuania.

First of all, he said, agriculture had to be developed. Lithuanians had never starved and living conditions had, compared with other places in the world, always been good. There was a shortage of technology and that needed to be rectified. Second, he said, this year Lithuania needed to get rid of the eighty thousand Soviet soldiers on its soil. These were the real priorities.

The following day I flew to Kiev and got a taxi from the airport to a hotel in the centre. Maybe there is no reason why people who work in hotels should be polite and should smile at you. I don't know why I minded so much when a woman at reception refused to deal with me while she wrote in a ledger, and then was hostile when she discovered that I had no reservation. I would have to pay in cash, she said, in advance. I told her that was OK. Passport? she snapped. I gave her my passport.

The hotel was undergoing reconstruction, so the residents' bar was a tiny former bedroom at the end of a corridor. My room was small. But the dining room was splendid, high and bright, one wall was window from floor to ceiling. The tables were set in the elaborate old-fashioned way which had not died out under the Soviets, the waiters were formally dressed.

The streets were busy and the shops were all full. It would not take long for capitalism to catch on here. I could easily imagine Benetton, Habitat and Marks and Spencer in the city centre. I passed a bookshop which was selling Russian art books for next to nothing. When I went in and asked if anyone spoke English or French, the assistant smiled at me and produced a book of reproductions of wall paintings and mosaics; the colours were so delicate I felt I would damage them if I touched them with my hand, all chalky golds and yellows. I bought a few books and carried them back to the hotel. Soon, I thought, the Russians would not have the money to print these books anymore.

As I walked back, I knew that I was going to the Aeroflot office to see if they had any cheap tickets. This time I wanted to go west, to Poland if I could, and then home, as soon as possible. I did not admit this to myself as I walked along, I allowed myself delusions that I would go into the Aeroflot office only if I passed it, and even then I might buy a ticket for next week.

I found the office easily, and I bought a cheap one-way ticket to Warsaw for two days later. On the way into the office I had noticed a man in his twenties or early thirties wearing a woollen cap that covered his ears. He asked me in a foreign accent if I spoke English. I thought he wanted to change money and I passed by. Now, on the way out, my ticket to Warsaw firmly in my pocket, I noticed him again. This time he asked me in English if I wanted an interpreter. I said no, that I was all right and began to walk back towards the hotel.

Once I had walked one block I realised that I was not all right, that an interpreter, even one wearing a woollen cap that covered his ears, was precisely what I needed. I doubled back. He was still there. I told him I needed an interpreter, explained that I was in Kiev for another day and a half, that I was interested in looking at churches and maybe meeting a Catholic priest or a bishop.

His name, I discovered as we walked together, was Andrew Katrus. He was married and had one son, aged twelve. He spoke good English, but what he did best, he said, was play tennis. He could play equally well with his left hand or his right hand. He did not want to talk about money: I could pay him whatever I thought he had earned. I realised that whatever I paid him would probably make his standing outside the Aeroflot foreign ticket office more worthwhile than holding down a standard soft currency job.

He took me to a Ukrainian Orthodox church, which was full of icons and candles, shadowy spaces and old-fashioned smells. It was crowded on this ordinary afternoon with people moving from altar to altar, lighting candles and praying. The atmosphere was much more intimate than the atmosphere in a Catholic church, as though this interior wanted to be amenable to the individual as well as the community. Maybe it was because it was dark and low-ceilinged, which made it easier for people to stand in states of reverie without any self-consciousness at all.

Andrew told me that he belonged to no religion; it was all strange to him, he said. In school and at home, he heard nothing about religion. He loathed the communist system because of Chernobyl. He had learned most of his English from the BBC World Service, and he heard about the explosion in the hours before dawn on the radio. His wife was away. He knew what to do. He spoke about it with great emotion: he was going to make sure that his son survived. He knew about taping the windows and taking iodine. And he telephoned all his friends, imploring them to stay indoors and do as he was doing. He listened to the radio all of the time, waiting for the World Service and the Voice of America, realising the extent of the accident. He had trouble convincing people, because in the days after the accident at Chernobyl there were no official warnings from the state, no announcements, merely rumours, and large numbers were placed in danger as a result. He could not believe that the authorities could do this to the people of Kiev and the Ukraine. He could never forgive them for this.

He took me to look at some more Orthodox churches. The most spectacular one was closed because there was a conflict between the Russian Orthodox Church and the Ukrainian Orthodox Church about who owned it and controlled it. Huge posters had been stuck up on the gates by Ukrainian nationalists, some of whom stood around in the freezing late afternoon. We went to a Catholic church but it was closed – it seemed grey and unattractive compared to all this Orthodox gold – and there was no answer when we rang the bell in what looked like the presbytery. Andrew said that he would try tonight and the next morning to find me a priest to interview.

He came to the hotel at around eleven in the morning. He was still wearing his woollen cap. He had found a priest, he said, and if we went to the cathedral now we could speak to him for as long as we wished. The cathedral looked normal outside, but entering it we could see how it had been made into a three or four storey building using cheap wood and cheap plasterwork. There was an altar, but the lofty impact that cathedrals are meant to have was missing. I thought of the English poet Philip Larkin wondering 'When churches fall completely out of use/ What we shall turn them into, if we shall keep/ A few cathedrals chronically on show/ Their parchment, plate and pyx in locked cases,/ And let the rest rent-free to rain and sheep./ Shall we avoid them as unlucky places?'

We were walking down the stairs from the first floor looking for the priest when we met the Bishop. He was dressed in full regalia, and he had that wonderful well-fed, lived-in look that reminded me of several Irish bishops. I expected him to greet me in a warm Irish accent. He smiled and shook our hands, and when Andrew told him what I was doing he agreed to talk to us now if we accompanied him to the top floor office.

While he was immaculately robed, all around there was chaos. He found us chairs, apologising for the state of things, appearing to be half amused at how bad it was. His name was Jan Purwinski and he was the Bishop of Zhytomir, which consisted of the north and the east of the Ukraine. He had been back in Kiev for one year now, he said, having previously lived in Riga and the western Ukraine. There were no big problems, he said, and laughed. This cathedral was built in 1842 and it had been used by the Catholic Church until 1937. It was used thereafter (*pace* Larkin) as a dormitory for workers, a planetarium, a club of atheism, and then a place 'for dubious video films'. He now had thirty priests in his diocese, seventeen of them Polish, the rest Ukrainian.

The building had been given back to the Church, he said, but it was now devastated. There was a need for money to restore it. The Church had also owned three other buildings, houses for the bishop and the priests and a monastery, but these had not been handed back. Thus the Bishop and three priests were living up here in what used to be the choir and the organ loft – he pointed at a room beside the one we were sitting in, which, he said, was his bedroom. When the cathedral was reconstructed they would have to find places to live.

How many Catholics were there now in Kiev? I asked him. He smiled and shook his head: I didn't understand, he said. He had no idea. There were no registers; nobody had any religion. He raised his two arms and shrugged. It had all been destroyed. The first service since 1937 was held in the cathedral on 15 January 1991 and was attended by between five hundred and seven hundred people. Different numbers attended Mass on Sunday. There was no Catholic community; there had been so much displacement in the Ukraine since 1937 that nothing had survived. There was also competition from the two main religions – the Russian and Ukrainian Orthodox churches.

He was the first Catholic clergyman I had met who had no power. I wondered if that was why he smiled so much, or seemed so bemused and easy-going. His Church had depended for almost two thousand years on continuity, on the faith being passed from generation to generation. He was sitting now among the ruins of that. He had twenty-five churches to be restored. He lacked the most basic things such as chalices, monstrances, Bibles, religious books. There was a need now, he said, for at least half a million dollars. As he showed us down the stairs, he pointed to the damage which had been done to the interior of his building, and laughed half in despair, half in wonder at the task which was facing him.

The following morning I flew to Warsaw. It was like entering a whole new universe. The woman at the Polish airline counter smiled at me as I approached. She had a computer to check flights to London. She spoke English, and explained, smiling all the while, that I would have to go to the other airport to catch my flight later that afternoon. She sold me a ticket.

This did not look like Eastern Europe. They were building a huge new airport, the taxi was a fancy car. I dropped my bags at the left luggage and went into the city. The open spaces which for me previously had been full of absences now made the city look habitable and comfortable. I asked the taxi driver to drop me at the Hotel Europecski, where I had stayed before. After

Tallinn and Vilnius and Kiev the downstairs bar seemed graceful, the staff warm and friendly. I wondered if I was changing or if Warsaw was changing.

When I went outside I discovered that it was Warsaw which was changing. The Hotel Bristol, which had been under construction the August before, was nearly finished. The old façade had been left intact and cleaned up. Towards the old city on a corner was a brand new bar: an Irish bar, with decorations for St Patrick's Day, which falls on 17 March. One of the staff was Irish and he told me that it stayed open until eleven thirty at night. I had a coffee; it didn't look much like an Irish bar, more an imitation of one, with sepia posters and imitation old wood, but since there had been no bars at all in Warsaw the year before, this was a great step forward. There were big plate-glass windows which meant you could look out on to the street.

Nearby was a shop where I had bought CDs at very low prices in 1991. They had even more stock now, but prices were edging up. Outside, in the old city, the sun had come out. It was almost a warm spring day. I had escaped once more into a familiar world. I felt lighter, almost at home, as I caught a taxi to the airport for my flight to London.

7

The Old World Order

THE SINGLE-DECKER BUSES moved stealthily, like great silent cats, through the old streets. They didn't make a sound. One day I watched an old woman crossing the street and I realised that she did not know there was a bus coming directly towards her. I waited for someone to shout at her, or the bus to swerve or blow its horn, but the bus simply came noiselessly to a stop in front of her, and waited for her to get out of its path, without blowing the horn, and slid by, full of civility, as though nothing had happened.

I had flown to Munich and taken a train to Regensburg in Bavaria on the Danube, the city where Mephistopheles flew with Dr Faustus. If you come from Ireland, an island which the Romans never bothered with, nor Napoleon, nor the Nazis, there is something overwhelming and daunting about cities on the Danube which were conquered by the Romans, and grew under the Holy Roman Empire, and were visited by Napoleon and saw the rise and fall of Hitler. It was a dream-world I had known only from books. Thus the real thing – the old bridge over the Danube, or the house where Kepler was born in 1571 and died in 1630, still preserved in his memory, or the plaque commemorating Napoleon's visit, or what John Banville in his novel *Kepler* called 'the sullen surge' of the Danube itself – was to me impressive beyond belief.

The tourist office was in the main square; they found me a cheap hotel in an old building down a narrow side street, as I asked them. There were tickets on sale for concerts and outings. A poster announced a recital of Bach's St John's Passion on Good Friday in a nearby church. This was the music I often listened to on Sunday mornings in Dublin. I could not believe my luck. I bought a ticket, even though it was in a Protestant church.

I had arranged to telephone a theologian, Professor Norbert Brox, as soon as I arrived. He agreed to come to the hotel that afternoon. He was in his fifties, keen-eyed, intelligent, concerned that his English did not allow him to say precisely what he wished, but polite enough to try hard all of the time to make himself clear. I was still star-struck at the idea of being here, at the way in which the unbombed city appeared perfectly preserved without seeming to be dead or in aspic, and Professor Brox's courteous style of talking and explaining things added to my delight.

This was Easter 1992. As we walked through the city towards the river I asked him if the revolutions in Eastern Europe had had any effect on Regensburg. When the border opened, he said, the Czechs came in buses to look at the city; it was a strange, unexpected sort of mass tourism as they wandered around the big shops making small purchases and then went back across the border. Now, he said, workers came across every day, they started at five in the morning and got home at ten o'clock at night. They slept in their own country, but worked in Bavaria. Even though they were badly paid, the money was more than they could ever earn at home.

We went into a restaurant and ordered coffee. Once

more, everything was perfect: the linen tablecloths, the unvarnished floorboards, the old-fashioned double-glazing. Professor Brox told me that I was in the right place if I wanted to write about Catholic Europe. Bavaria was 60 to 70 per cent Catholic; Cardinal Ratzinger, the Pope's right-hand prelate, was born here; his brother, indeed, was master of the choir in the cathedral.

Most of the priests, he said, came from villages and farms, where life was more conventional than in the city. Numbers were down to about fifteen a year. How had the Pope and his teaching affected the way theology was taught? I asked. For conservative clergy, he said, it had been important, it had made their ideas seem legitimate. But for simple people it was clear that the Church was a disaster.

I thought that he was talking about *Humanae Vitae* and the Church's teaching on contraception. He smiled when he realised this, and said, yes, that as I was Irish, obviously the Church's teaching on sexual matters would come to my mind, since the emphasis in Ireland was on these things. But contraception was not really the issue for him, he was more concerned with matters of faith and dogma. He thought that there was too much emphasis now on the Virgin Mary in the Church; it was important to teach how devotion to her began, to place it all in its historical context.

The increasing significance of Mary in Catholicism he ascribed to John Paul II, and to the legacy of the worship of Mary in Poland. As a child, he said, the Pope had learned about Mary as a divine figure and never questioned it. Polish Catholicism was very special. There had been no Reformation in Poland and no Enlightenment, and the Polish brand of Catholicism had become inextricably linked with Polish nationalism. It was, to his German mind, a matter of wonder and sadness that someone coming from this tradition now controlled the Catholic Church.

Professor Brox's English was good, but he was still unhappy communicating in a language he did not speak fluently. Jesus Christ, he said, for him, was especially a human being. God perhaps, but God was not a simple name for a being. Jesus had ideas, he had lived a life in such a way that he was a good example to many people. For us now it was more interesting that he was human – his divinity could be symbolic.

Could be symbolic? Professor Brox taught in a Catholic seminary; he was a calm, rational man who had put a great deal of thought into this. I had never heard anybody from within the Church saying this before; Professor Brox did not think that there had been too much discussion of this in Ireland. Did he believe in statues? He thought that statues in churches should be good pieces of sculpture, he said. He did not believe in miracles and had no interest in them. Transubstantiation? No, he said, he did not believe that the bread and wine was literally changed into the body and blood of Jesus. In the philosophical and metaphysical sense, yes, but in the literal sense, no.

Life after death? He would like to think that there was, but he did not know. Hell? Hell, he said, was a special problem. If there was a hell in eternity, then there was a God who enjoyed to see . . . He stopped, and shook his head. Such a God could not be the God of his belief, he said. He preferred, he said, not to believe in hell. It was an idea that could not be thought out to the end. What was the difference between his religion and the Protestant religions in Germany? For him the Lutheran liturgy was too abstract, too rational. Only the word, not the symbol. He loved, he said, the richness of Catholicism.

He left me thinking about all of this – he was as

puzzled by my naivety as I was by his theology – and said he would come and collect me on Easter Sunday morning and take me to his house for breakfast. I sat there wondering if I was not a Catholic too: if you could doubt the divinity of Jesus and the efficacy of miracles and life after death and still be a member of the Church, then maybe we should all join, or re-join. It struck me that these new ideas were being fostered once more in the fertility of the German mind, and were so far from what is dreamed of in John Paul II's philosophy that he probably would not know how to counteract them.

That night the narrow medieval streets of the city were full of fashionable venues, bars and coffee shops which could have been constructed to keep poor old Faust happy when darkness fell. The trendiest places had plate-glass windows as though they were emporia for selling clothes, and inside carefully designed people stood around wearing expensive and carefully-chosen styles in suede, leather and wool. The atmosphere was one of mild, studied animation. Nobody laughed too much, or talked too loud. Nobody was too old, or had taken one of their parents along. They gave the impression of being ex-art students who worked in advertising, people who made money out of their creative selves. I couldn't stop looking at them.

The newest bar, Kaminski's, was perhaps the most cool, the most studied, the most ironic. I stood on my own looking around; the staff were wearing uniforms, and the place had the feeling of being crowded, without, in fact, being so. It was about ten-thirty at night. I made my way towards the bar, but I was intercepted by a woman in her late twenties who was wearing an expensive black tailored suit and designer glasses. She asked me in excessively polite English if I wanted a drink. I slowly realised that she worked here. I asked her for a beer; she went to the bar and fetched it for me and then merged once more into the crowd, chatting to people, constantly looking around her, full of discretion and charm. Every so often she smiled at me. I was, after all, a customer. Everything in Regensburg was so comfortable, so thoughtfully planned.

On Good Friday I arrived at the church where St John's Passion was to be performed just as the doors opened and thus secured an aisle seat at the front. The programme gave all the words in German and a note at the bottom said *Bitte kein Applaus*. This was not to be a performance for our entertainment then, we could not applaud the singers and the orchestra, it had to be a form of worship on a Good Friday. The radiators were under the seats; the church was cosy and warm, unlike the vast Catholic cathedral. It filled up quickly. The audience, even the young, were serious-looking, modestly dressed people. I would have known that they were Protestants a mile away, I thought to myself.

The opening words of the first chorus were even more arresting in that small church now that the occasion was sacred, the context restored, the language full of resonance and meaning, than they were on a CD-player in a small house in Dublin on a Sunday morning. The choir sang with immense commitment, letting the slow unfolding of the drama work like magic on the audience.

This was more beautiful than the Mass in B-minor or the St Matthew Passion because the choruses had, in their overwhelming harmonies, huge healing qualities, enormous power that seemed to soar beyond the story that was being told. Sometimes, the Evangelist whispered a phrase for extra effect, and when it came to the solo parts for instruments the players stood up to perform as the singers did. I was spellbound. Every time the chorus stood I knew that once more the sound would be uplifting, that they would combine the notions of sin and of redemption, that they would capture the sense of man as fallen and as saved. They were the raw crowd in the street as much as the disciples.

There was a genuine excitement in the voices in the scene where Peter betrayed Jesus. And the Evangelist's words '*und weinete bitterlich* (and wept bitterly) were profoundly moving. It was as though the audience had never heard the story before, were waiting for it to be told.

When it came to the part after the scourging at the pillar, the violinist and the viola player stood up to play; the atmosphere grew more tense as the bass began *Betrachte, meine Seel, mit ängstlichem Vergnügen* (Bethink thee, o my soul, in agony and rapture), which sounded like a melancholy German song about love and death. The next piece for the tenor started with the word *Erwage* (Imagine) repeated. Both were sung with feeling as though the bass and tenor wanted to rouse us, spark something off in us.

From these moments of rapture we went back to the narrative, the simple music of the Evangelist telling us *Also ging Jesus heraus* (Then Jesus came forth) to a silence in the church, followed by Pilate singing his *Sehet, welch ein Mensch* (Behold the man) with enormous solemnity. Some of the choruses were sung softly; others were more declamatory. I was waiting for the contralto's 'All is fulfilled'. I knew the aria in English sung by Kathleen Ferrier. The tempo suddenly changes halfway through as she sings 'The lion of Judah fought the fight'. Now it was in German: *Es ist vollbracht*, and the 'cellist had moved out to the front. I wanted this moment to last as the contralto began to sing. I was worried in case

I was not concentrating enough. And then it came: the sudden change to signify that one world had ended and another had come into place. When the Evangelist sang now about the veil of the temple being rent in twain and the earth quaking there was dark drama in his voice.

The Passion came to an end with two choruses, the second more subtle in its harmonies, the rhymes in the German original more absolute than before, each couplet complete, like something being accomplished, reaching its inevitable end, hearing its own echo soaring beyond it. The choir stood still and let their voices resonate around this small Protestant church. There was no applause. No one moved. The conductor did not move. There was a sort of stunned silence, but it was deliberate. It lasted one minute maybe, perhaps more. And then there was a shuffling of paper, but no coughs or whispers. The performers remained still. No one spoke. People began quietly to move from their seats.

'Protestants one, Catholics nil,' I said to myself as I went to midnight Mass the following evening in the Catholic cathedral in Regensburg. But then I thought about it: they won on music and sheer, solemn style, and their churches were charming and pretty and neat. But their churches were small. Our Catholic cathedral in Regensburg, on the other hand, was a big soaring, shadowy gothic structure, by far the most imposing building in the city. They had Bach; we had buttressing.

I had been to the cathedral two or three times over the previous few days, but the ceremonies were dull, and the singing insipid. All my hopes were on this midnight Mass, even though it was being held at nine o'clock, which was not promising. In Enniscorthy the Holy Saturday Mass had been changed from twelve o'clock to nine as well, because, it was said, there were always drunks at the back shouting up slogans and causing havoc when the Mass was at midnight. There was an old story, in fact, about a midnight Mass in Enniscorthy years ago when a man got very enthusiastic as the priest was inviting people to renew their baptismal vows. 'Do you renounce Satan and all his works and pomps?' the priest asked the congregation. 'I do, the fucker,' the man shouted. I had a feeling as I took my seat among the congregation in Regensburg Cathedral that such an outrage had not occurred here; there was a sense of an ancient and august order which had been in place for a very long time, passed on from one Bavarian generation to the next. One man behind me was even in traditional Bavarian costume; he looked like someone who had walked out of a postcard.

This was a drama of darkness and light, as all the electric lights in the vast cold cathedral were turned off and everyone lit a candle, the flame being passed from the huge Paschal candle on the high altar. 'Lumens Christi,' the priest intoned and we replied, 'Deo gratias'. Then there was a procession of church dignitaries – Cardinal, bishops, priests and altar boys carrying a covered crucifix towards the baroque high altar. There was a wonderful smell of incense. (Did Protestants use incense? I wondered.) After the readings, two electric lights were turned on near the altar and the singing, a sort of plainchant, started. Then the lights were turned off again and more readings were done by candlelight. The singing grew more complex and the parts more elaborate. Then the Cardinal began: 'Gloria in excelsis Deo' and all the light came on, the organ blared and the bells started to ring and our candles were lit with tapers carried by the altar boys. There was more incense and more singing and an interminable period where we all stood up as it grew colder and colder. My feet were freezing. I knew when the priest was asking us to renew our baptismal vows. The smell of candle grease and the darkness took me back years, but the service was mechanical as though everyone was going through a tired ritual. It was livened up a little by the arrival of a baby to be baptised, with video cameras to record the occasion and an extended family to witness it. When this was over, a bishop moved down the centre aisle with a small brush and a container of holy water, blessing everyone, and bowls for money were passed around. The singing continued, but I think I had been spoiled by the singing of the night before.

The following morning at nine o'clock Professor Brox arrived at the hotel to take me to his house for breakfast. He and his wife lived in a large comfortable house about two miles outside the town across the Danube. He had invited several of his students for breakfast too, but none of them was a seminarian, they were all lay students studying theology. They were all polite and formal. There was coffee and local traditional Easter eggs, but there was also brandy and champagne. After breakfast, we sat in the living room having more drinks. I had viewed Professor Brox as an austere man, the idea that he would drink on Easter Sunday morning had not occurred to me. He did not drink as much as I did, or his students, but he continued to pour brandy and champagne to celebrate Easter.

That afternoon when I had recovered from breakfast I went to look at various museums in the city, including the Old Town Hall, which had a magnificent main reception hall and a very dark and frightening dungeon, complete with torture chamber, and the City Museum, which had artefacts from the Roman city and a room full of cannons. I was amazed by the cannons, the size of the carriages and the cannon balls. I realised that I had never seen cannons like this before, except in films and drawings in history books. Once more, I understood that I was in the real Europe, the place which had been fought over, the vast fertile plain over which these massive machines could be pulled. There was a stately, grim beauty about many of the buildings in Regensburg, including the flat medieval bridge over the Danube, but it was these cannons in the museum that afternoon that held my attention most. They belonged to a world that I did not inhabit; for natives of Regensburg, I supposed, they would be another ordinary relic of the wars that had engulfed the region since Roman times.

The weather was warm and later that afternoon I tried to go for a walk along the banks of the Danube, but I ended up at a disused factory and had to make my way back. Near the Town Hall I had noticed a large and stodgy looking restaurant-cum-beer hall. It looked like a place for tourists, but on my way back I stopped off there. Now it was crowded with men, women and children. The noise was astonishing. The men and women looked like country people; their clothes were plain and sensible and the women wore no make-up and did not have their hair styled. They talked and chatted to each other, and to families at other tables, with immense animation and good cheer. Barmen came by with trays full of glass tankards of beer and plates of food. The place was enormous, and every table I inspected was the same: a family group talking and laughing and drinking beer.

I had one drink and then went back to the hotel. I had been reading Pete Dexter's novel *Paris Trout* without paying too much attention to it, but the previous night, after the so-called midnight Mass, I had become gripped by the book. I was still another hundred and fifty pages from the end. I thought that I would go back to the beer hall and finish it there, in the company of all the Bavarian drinkers. I had expected Bavarian beer halls to be full of loud, overweight men swilling beer and shouting. The men here were quiet types. They drank solidly. But the women drank just as much, and did most of the talking, the men smiling and laughing at their remarks, the children listening as well, or quietly wandering about.

I found an empty table and ordered a beer. I was given a plate of ham and tomatoes and bread with the compliments of the house. Every drink I had was noted down on a beer mat. As soon as I had half finished one beer another one was put in front of me. A family joined me at the table, having politely ascertained that they would not be disturbing me. After a while, they asked to see the title of the book I was reading, and they made various comments about it in German.

I spent the evening between my book, which was utterly absorbing and seemed easier to read the more I drank, and the beer hall, which remained completely full, the noise levels rising and rising, the Bavarians drinking beer after beer. The beer, I should say, was deliciously fresh-tasting and sweet without being sugary and the food was solid, sensible soakage for the beer. Everything remained orderly, nobody sang, people just talked and laughed. At one stage I laughed out loud at a scene I was reading, and this amused the people at my table no end.

I stayed there until near midnight when the beer hall closed. Towards the end of the evening a few people who spoke English came to my table, and since I had finished the book, which was just as well since I was clearly drunk, we talked for a while. I cannot remember, or indeed imagine, what we talked about. The bill was staggering. I staggered back to the hotel.

It was a new sort of hangover. I did not have a headache, or an urge to get sick. I felt, instead, that I had been run over by a train. Every single part of me ached. Sleep did not help. I lay there, motionless, until I realised that it was time to check out of the hotel. I moved towards one of the coffee shops and ordered lots of coffee and mineral water. Even the shadowy light of the side street offended my eyes. I did not know what to do. I thought of checking back into the hotel and staying in bed for the rest of the day, but instead I collected my bag and walked up towards the railway station. I did not want to go back to Munich; I wanted somewhere small, with another old-fashioned hotel and a comfortable bed. One of Professor Brox's students had told me that I should go to Passau, south of Regensburg on the Danube, and since there was a train going there that afternoon, I bought a ticket for it. I had no idea what it would be like.

I went to the main door of the station and looked back at the city. It was bank holiday Monday, crowds were strolling in the streets. Two or three skinhead youths came towards the station, two of them carrying folded banners; they had obviously been to a demonstration. I didn't like the look of them. I knew that they personified Germany now, the Germany of neo-Nazis, racism, xenophobia. I, instead, had been looking at an abiding Germany of choirs, theologians, beer halls. In the Bavaria of Franz Josef Strauss, I had done nothing except enjoy myself. In *Danube*, Claudio Magris had written of Strauss: 'his physiognomy gives him all the right qualifications to emerge with his vigorous, superabundant blend of sweatiness, outstanding flair for politics . . . vulgarity, energy and demagogy of a plebeian and reactionary nature.' The people in the beer hall, at the recital and at the midnight Mass must have voted for him and his Christlich-Sozial Union. I had spent some days in the world which they sought to preserve.

I remember sitting in a square somewhere near the railway station at Passau having an ice-cream. There was pale sunshine and there were families walking lazily along. My hangover had become a gnawing pain behind the eyes. The city seemed desolate and I thought of going somewhere else until I found myself at the riverfront looking at the fortress on the hill across the river and the range of boats that lay moored there. I found an hotel which looked on to the river and took a room for one night, then went out to one of the offices along the quay front and booked a seat for the next morning on the boat to travel from Passau to Linz along the Danube.

Passau had that same feeling of planned cleanliness and civic order as Regensburg, but it had none of Regensburg's splendour and wealth of architecture. Near the river, away from the hotel, there was an exhibition of work by Egon Schiele. I went hoping that this would give me something to focus on, keep my mind off the excesses of the night before. It was an exhibition of paintings, drawings and posters with some photographs of Schiele and his circle, all beautifully presented in small rooms which overlooked the river. Schiele was so brave in the way he let colour decorate his paintings, in the way he would allow pure moments of delight to happen, revelling in the richness of the materials at his disposal so that his sense of mingled disgust and desire at the nature of the body is always mysterious and oddly comic.

In the morning we sailed down a dream-Danube, with hills on both sides, crowned with forests and turreted castles and thin-spired churches. The sky was completely blue and there was a frosty edge to the wind. Birds of prey moved stealthily over a nearby hill. We passed old farm houses and an old stone storehouse that could have come from a woodcut; there were small, fertile meadows between the river and the hills; old flat barges passed us, one of them carrying stacks of logs. It was still cold and most of the other passengers stayed down below drinking coffee and beer, but I braved the open top deck, looking out at the swans, the distant trees winter-purple and the green water of the river.

Once we passed a hydro-electric dam the land around grew flatter and plainer; there were bicycle paths on each side of the river, and a few cyclists with bright, plastic back-packs. We passed another story-book castle on a hill, with a black-spired church beside it. Soon, the river turned and the black spire of Linz Cathedral came into view. We were in Austria now.

Hitler was born near here, and this was the city he thought of retiring to when his life's work was done. He must have dreamed about strolling in the vast main square where all the buildings were painted a different colour, looking at the hills in the distance and the boats arriving on the Danube. The tourist office found me a hotel with a room overlooking the square. The hotel had the same atmosphere as the city itself – it was like being in Eastern Europe: the shopfronts were old-fashioned, the trams and the tramlines looked as though they had not changed since the nineteenth century. The hotel was big, but it had no computer, instead there was an enormous ledger for bookings with a pencil and a large rubber, which surely dated from the time of the Kaiser. Elsewhere, paperwork and the art of rubbing out had disappeared. Here, they were thriving and taken very seriously. The furniture in my bedroom was more than a hundred years old.

On the way to the city's art gallery I stopped for cake; since I was in Austria I felt that I was entitled to drool over varieties of chocolate torte and apple strudel. The gallery had a superb collection of paintings from between the wars, including portraits by Kokoschka, Corinth and Schiele. In Kokoschka's 1929 portrait of Mercel von Nemes, the sitter was painted as both icon and actual flesh and blood, the painting fluid and the work full of self-conscious delight in its own making. As with Schiele or Otto Dix there was no naturalistic detail in the brushwork on the face and yet something real shone through, some absolute and sensual individuality, an uneasy, half-guilty bourgeois self, as though the spirit of Marx and Freud hovered there with Faust. This spirit was made into paint, into glistening colours and it was everywhere in the work by these painters.

But, for the most part, it had gone and would not come back. There was a small Karl Appel show in Linz and the following day in Munich I also saw an exhibition by Georg Baselitz. There was no individuality in their figures; they painted icons, they were concerned with brushwork and colour and how the space of the canvas would be filled. This was the work being made now that would be shown in museums in the future. It was brilliant, but I could have done instead with one Otto Dix portrait of a German man, puzzled by the world, isolated, almost ugly, except for the light in his eyes and the sense of appetite in his face, standing not just for the painter as himself, but standing, like the figures in Joyce and Kafka, for his time and his circumstance as well. I had never realised before that this sort of art is mostly over. For a reason I do not know, the face or the head of a man or a woman has ceased very much to be a true subject for a painter. I spent a good hour of that day in Linz taking in what I could of the great German painters of the century, before beginning a tour of the beer halls of the city.

8

The Sign of the Cross

MAYBE THERE ARE things I should explain. In the early 1980s I edited an Irish current affairs magazine called *Magill*, and that is how I met June Levine. I remember reading the first draft of a long article I had commissioned from her – she is a well-known Irish writer and feminist – about the life of Lyn Madden who had worked for years as a prostitute in Dublin.

I went to her home to talk to her about the article. She asked me to stay for dinner. I cannot remember if I knew or not that she lived with the psychiatrist Ivor Browne – I had seen him many times on television – but he arrived just before dinner. I noticed that they watched me and listened to me in a way that was new to me. Ivor asked what sort of music I liked and I said that I liked traditional Irish singing and chamber music. He seemed excited by this, and played me pieces which he liked; he seemed disturbed that I did not like jazz.

June's article grew longer; we were going to run it as a cover story. A few evenings a week I travelled out to her house to see how the work was going – it was the era before the fax machine. Usually, I had dinner with June and Ivor; often Lyn Madden, who had moved in with them, joined us. There were policemen outside to guard Lyn as she had agreed to give evidence against her former lover who was charged with murdering a friend of hers.

Ivor had evolved a radical system for dealing with trauma and blocked experience and had been treating Lyn. She had discovered in one of the sessions that she was raped as a child, a totally blocked experience, something she had never remembered before. This was all new to me; I did not know that such things were possible. A few times we talked about it late into the night, Ivor explaining how patients experienced their birth as though for the first time, or grief, or a trauma from childhood. And over these weeks the idea came up that I should do a few sessions with Ivor. I'm sure I laughed and tried to change the subject. I might have said that I was afraid.

In the years that followed I often had dinner in the house that Ivor and June bought in Ranelagh, near the centre of Dublin. I don't know what year it was, but it was towards the end of the 1980s, and there was a crowded table and a lot of talking, when Ivor, who has no small talk, was sitting beside me and asked me if my parents were still alive. I was surprised at the question: I thought he knew that my father was dead. I told him that my father had died when I was twelve.

I can see him watching me, holding my gaze, as he asked if this had affected me very deeply. I must have shrugged as I tried to explain that my father was a secondary teacher, and he died just before I was due to go to his secondary school, and I dreaded him teaching me, so in a way, when he died I was relieved. Did you know him well? Ivor asked me. No, I said, no, there were four other children, three older than me, and he was very sick for the last four years of his life. But did you ever have a relationship with him? Ivor continued. Oh yes, I said, when I was younger before he became sick, I used to go down to the museum he had founded in the town every day with him after school, and when I was even younger I used to go and sit at the back of his class, or write on the blackboard. Suddenly, as I spoke, as Ivor still watched me – his look was always even and open – my eyes filled up with tears. Do you realise, he asked me, that you have blocked the experience of his death, all your grief, and you're going to have to do something about it?

Over the next couple of years June and Ivor came back to the subject: I really ought to go to one of Ivor's workshops. He held these sessions in the disused Protestant church in the grounds of Grangegorman Mental Hospital where Ivor was chief psychiatrist. He had formulated a way of treating blocked experience, and he was especially interested in working with groups of artists. I said that I would love to come some time; but I always managed to be away when a workshop was happening.

In May 1992 June telephoned me. She herself wanted to do one of the sessions and she needed someone to come with her, as you had to work in pairs. She needed someone that she could trust, she said. I knew that she had had her own troubles, and she probably needed to do the session. I said I would do it. I made it clear that I was terrified. So was she, she said.

It would take from Friday morning to Sunday afternoon and there was accommodation in the hospital for those attending. Some of them were Ivor's patients, people who had been disabled by traumas which they had not fully experienced; others were merely people interested in the workshop, or whose reasons for being there were not entirely obvious. I put myself in the last category as I drove into the hospital early on that Friday morning. I was wearing loose clothes and I had not eaten anything heavy, as instructed.

At first it was like group therapy from a movie or a manual. There were a few therapists, Ivor and a nurse. We all drank tea and talked nervously and then sat around in a ring and introduced ourselves. Nothing much happened that morning. A Jungian therapist asked us to write out an account of our lives now and our problems, and then when this was written, he asked us to put it behind us, or put it away. He warned us that we should not predict or expect some particular experience to come up in the later sessions; often, he said, what we least expected was what surfaced. He asked us to close our eyes and conjure up a symbol, an object, an image, something that appeared. He made us take our time, go slowly. I closed my eyes and tried to leave my mind blank. At first, I think, I was trying too hard to see something, so I made an effort to relax. It is hard to pin-point colours, but if the background was black, then what appeared was yellow, or just bright, and it seemed to come of its own accord, floating in: it was a cross, large, made of gold, or painted gold, and soon it faded and I saw a comb, or something shaped like a comb, but I had no idea what these things meant and I wondered if they were not random images which came from nowhere. I suppose I was sceptical about this part of the session, but I tried to suppress this, because I felt that there was no point in my being here if I could not take what was going on seriously. Ivor Browne was there all the time, in the background, watching everything. I trusted him, and I believed that whatever was happening had a reason.

We had lunch. June and I sat on the grass afterwards. It was a warm day, the sky completely blue. In the afternoon we were given paint and paper and told to paint anything we liked. Once more, I had to allow this to happen, had to keep to myself my natural aversion to being in a group of people all painting as a form of therapy, and slowly try and rid myself of it. I became absorbed in the painting. I daubed the paint any way I could. At the beginning I was not sure if it was taking on a shape, and sometimes I didn't bother to look.

I have that painting I did here now as I write this. It was done in red and black with a grey shape in the middle like a whirlpool. There are some red bars and spikes at the sides. It looks untidy. June worked beside me as I painted; she painted a delicate flower. It had never occurred to me to do anything like that. There were discussion groups then, where we showed one another our paintings and tried to make sense of why we had painted them. I didn't know what mine was about; it seemed very dark.

We were ready after that for the real session. We had to split into pairs. June and I had arranged that I would go first; she would have her session on Saturday morning and Sunday morning; I would have mine now and on Saturday afternoon. She had done it before. We fetched mattresses and I was advised to put mine into a corner. I remembered June saying once that these sessions could be very violent. There was talk of a drug called ketamine, but I did not know what it was.

I took off my shoes and loosened my clothes and lay down on the mattress. June sat on a beanbag beside me. Twenty other pairs, maybe more, settled down as well. I closed my eyes as this soft voice, which I recognised as belonging to one of Ivor's colleagues, started to speak through a sound system. He asked us first to relax and then to breathe softly. There was soothing music in the background, and perhaps a drum sound. He spoke slowly and told us to breathe as though our breath was liquid. I did what he said. He then told us to begin to breathe faster as though our life depended on it. The music changed and the drum sound became louder. I'm not sure at what moment it happened but I had suddenly moved into a different state of consciousness. I don't know if some of the crying and moaning sounds came from the PA system or from the people around me, but I think from both.

I was in terrible distress. I knew that June was there beside me. I could ask her for Kleenex if I needed it, or to hold my hand, or to stay close. I knew that I could stand up and go out to the toilet if I needed to. But I had entered another world which was more urgent and real than the one I had left. I had to breathe hard, breathe like hell, to stay there. It was all dark in the church, but sometimes lights came on; there were always heavy drum sounds and wild music and cries, babies crying, someone moaning in pain.

And I was moaning too and screaming. I was in my parents' bedroom on the morning that my father died. My mother was downstairs. It is difficult to know how time passed, or how long things went on for. I know that I screamed 'I cannot deal with this' over and over. I know that I screamed at the top of my voice. I know that June grew worried about me and Ivor came over to look at me. I know that I would ask for Kleenex and blow my nose and then go back into myself almost whispering to myself and then start screaming and thrashing around on the mattress. I was not afraid. June's being close was important, but she was outside of what was happening to me. What was happening was real, and the distress was absolute. I started to shout, 'Will you put your arms around me?' I had to gesture to June that I did not mean her, that I was all right. I was a twelve-year-old boy in the front upstairs bedroom of a small house, with neighbours and friends visiting downstairs, expressing their condolences in quiet voices, with my aunt having told me that my father had died during the night in a hospital not far from the town. I was crying all of the time now and shouting out to my father and my mother 'Will you put your arms around me?' 'Will you please?' 'Please?' June and I had agreed to give each other space and never to interfere and touch only when invited. Sometimes, the crying sounded terrible, like howling, but I couldn't stop, or at least I did not know whether I could or not because I did not try: I seemed to want this to happen.

It was a summer's morning in 1967. I was in one bed and my older brother in another bed across the room. I pretended to be asleep when my aunt came into the room and whispered something to him. He said nothing, but quietly got up and put on his clothes and left the room. My father was in hospital, and we knew that he was bad. He had had a stroke, and maybe a heart attack, I'm not sure. But I did not believe that he was going to die. I lay in bed listening for some sign. Eventually, I got out of bed and went into my parents' bedroom. My mother had been in the hospital all night; my aunt had stayed to mind myself and my two sisters and two brothers. I watched from the window as one neighbour crossed the street to talk to another. They looked up at our house; and I knew by the way they were talking that one was telling the other that my father was dead. I knew that my mother was downstairs, and I dreaded the idea that she would have to tell me the news. I wanted to hide. I remember that I was turning to go back to my bedroom when my aunt appeared and she told me that my father had died in the hospital during the night, her voice catching and breaking as she explained that if my father had lived he would have been incapacitated, and he would not have wanted that. He had gone to heaven, she said, and my mother, who had shared her life with him, was going to need us all now. I turned away from her, crying, but she told me I wasn't to cry. I went into my room and got dressed.

I was back there now in that bedroom, on that summer morning. An hour, two hours must have gone by. I kept blowing my nose and calming down and then starting off again. I felt the shock and the powerlessness and the grief; fierce, absolute things; the realisation that he was dead would cause me to seize up on the mattress and start to scream and cry out. Ivor came over at one stage and I thought he was going to take me out of this ordeal – sometimes I wanted desperately to stop – but he made me turn on all fours and he held my stomach. 'Get it all up now,' he said as he pushed in my stomach muscles. He had brought a metal bowl with him and I screamed so hard I started to vomit mucus into the bowl, and when I lay down he told me to breathe heavily again. The whole terrible pain came back; like before, I began to sob and then cry and then call out and then scream, but it was worse now, this sense of pure loss, of being abandoned, of someone being torn away forever, of being utterly forlorn, but more than anything of not being able to deal with it.

I do not know how much longer it went on. It could have been half an hour or more. The music changed all of the time, but there were always drums, and sounds of voices, with other music in the background – African or South American music. Eventually, Ivor came and said I could rest now. June held my hand and I lay there. I felt that I had got something over with, but I was confused.

Ivor asked me if I wanted to try the drug he had mentioned: ketamine. The effect would be different, he said. I thought he meant that it would take me further towards the distress, and felt that I should try it, since I had gone so far I should go further, see it through in some way. So I said that I wanted the drug. I expected a tablet, but soon a nurse came with a needle and asked me to drop my trousers. The injection hurt me, the needle seemed to go right into muscles and then further again, it was a thin, hard pain. When she finished I pulled up my trousers and lay back. I was waiting for worse things to happen. I closed my eyes.

Nothing did happen for a while. But then I began to laugh. I made a sound like 'Hey!' and grinned. I could not stop smiling. Slowly, I was inundated with these beautiful colours: a dark orange colour which glistened at the edges, and then a luscious light blue which floated in front of me the way you see clouds from an aeroplane window. Then the colours became formal arrangements, like big Willem de Kooning paintings, a huge swathe of orange or white and then different shapes of blue or pink. The colours had an extraordinary life in them: parts seemed wet at the edges as though recently painted, in others you could see the texture of the paint, how it had been applied. At one stage I shouted out, 'Hello Jackson Pollock!'

I had been looking at these paintings for years, taking great delight in them, reading about the New York School and the rise of Abstract Expressionism. But nothing dark came, nothing from Mark Rothko, for example. Only the light beauty, the unembarrassed use of pink and lemon in big ambitious paintings. I saw things that were even more beautiful and more formally pure than anything by de Kooning or Sam Francis. I knew they were passing in front of me, floating dreams that made me smile, but they were so real, the view I had of them was so pure that I did not believe they would fade. I watched them intensely and shouted out in delight. I looked at June and smiled at her. She smiled back.

Later, some poetry came, and bits of songs: lines by Louis MacNeice ('World is crazier and more of it than we think,/ Incorrigibly plural. I feel and portion/ A tangerine and spit the pips and feel/ The drunkenness of things being various.') and a whole verse of 'What A Wonderful World'.

Slowly, the visions became weaker and the real world around me more noticeable and present. The lights were coming up and the music changing. The same voice that had initiated the session now brought it to an end. I sat up. I did not know how I felt. Ivor put on jazz.

Saturday was another beautiful day as we all settled in the dark church for two more sessions. I had gone home and slept well in my own bed. This time it was my turn to mind June. I just had to sit with her and wait until she asked me to do something. Thus I had a good chance to look around. Once the fast breathing started, it was like a vision of hell, everyone on the mattresses was involved in a private nightmare, as though there was a story being told to them which made them scream and cry out and then lie quietly for a while. I knew that some of the women had been raped and sexually abused and I knew they were trying to work this out.

The ketamine affected people in different ways: one woman just cried; another man wanted to hit everyone he looked at, and had to be sat upon. All the time I was aware that I would be facing this again at six o'clock. I did not expect to return to my father's death. I was surprised by what had happened to me the previous evening, but I did not think it would come back.

In the afternoon we started painting again. The first paintings I did were very dark. I looked at the painting from the day before and it seemed to me to be about death – the sense of the body entering the dark. I worked on a few more paintings that afternoon: one is almost comically black, but I let myself do whatever it was came into my mind. I was now much more willing to concentrate on painting than I had been the previous day. I had to do something, and this, if I used it properly, might help to interpret and deal with what had happened to me the previous night.

I wondered if I could paint the ketamine: the glorious, glistening colours, the happiness. I mixed white and red and then every bright colour I had, daubing white into the mixture all the time, and then putting it down on the surface of the paper, in any shape it came, moving it around the way you play with mud when you're a child. It was thick and bright. I sat and watched it dry. I had let myself register what happened when I took the drug.

There was plenty of time left, and everyone else was busy. I thought that I had finished painting. But I got another sheet of paper and painted a black square on it. I still don't know whether the impulse to paint one thing rather than another has any meaning or not. I did the painting of the square slowly, as though it was important that each stroke of the brush was right. I did not know what else I was going to do, but I think that I intended to leave it like that. I sat on the ground looking at it, and wondering what to do. Gradually, I thought of surrounding it with bright colours, like I had in the painting of the drug. It began as an idea which I resisted. I felt that doing this would be giving into something: some clichéd version of the previous night's experience which mixed darkness and light. But the idea stayed in my mind; I found that I wanted to do it. Soon, I was busy surrounding the black paint with bright pink and orange.

It was almost time for the next session. I still expected this to be about something else. I thought that I could not delve any further into the experience of my father's death. I thought that something new would arise, as we fetched the mattresses and rolled them out. I lay down just as I had done the previous evening. And it began again.

I would blow my nose and start to breathe heavily and then the crying would begin and become uncontrollable and I couldn't stop myself shouting and screaming. The music was always there, constantly changing, throwing out violent and disturbing sounds against snatches of opera and classical music, but I was only barely aware of it. I held June's hand, and shouted out 'Will you let me go?' and started to cry as though no answer was coming or would ever come, as though I would be held all of my life by something which had happened all that time ago.

It began to change. The change was gradual and soft. But I started shouting, 'I will let you go.' I lay on my back and made gestures as though releasing air from my mouth, and then whispering 'I will let you go' and repeating it again and again in whispers. I don't know whether I did let him go or not, but I felt happy as I lay there, saying something that I had never dared to think.

Once more, it is hard to judge how much time passed, but the change from shouting out 'Will you let me go?' to 'I will let you go' seemed to happen fast, in maybe twenty minutes or half an hour. I still lay there making gestures with my hands as though releasing something from my mouth.

I thought that I had come to the end, I could see no other way in which this could develop. I signalled to June that I'd had enough, and she got Ivor. I was content, thinking that I had gone through enough. But Ivor said I should go on, I should start the fast breathing again. There was more, he said.

So I lay on the mattress and took deep breaths and began to listen to the sounds all around me. I went straight back into my private, hidden world. Now I felt warmly towards my father rather than frightened by his death. I became overwhelmed by a compulsion to thank my father for life, but I was embarrassed by it. It sounded like the sort of thing you hear at a bad funeral service. But I needed to do it. I lay there feeling it, trying to let myself do it, say the words, thank my father for life. I held back: I had to let myself use language that I would not normally use. I had to say: 'Thank you for giving me life' and I had to say it over and over until I was sure that I meant it and was no longer embarrassed by it.

In the end I wanted to bless him. It was the first time in my life I had ever thought of anything like this. I wanted to make the sign of the cross over him. It was not just an idea that came into my head for a moment. It was a compelling need, something I had to do. But I did not want to be seen doing it; I did not want to see myself doing it. I was shamed by this need to bless my dead father, to make the sign of the cross over him. I tried to hold back. I couldn't do this. I was, for the first time, embarrassed that June was beside me. I would find this hard to explain.

And then I did it. I made the sign of the cross in the air, over and over. I had no choice. I knew afterwards that I could go no further. Ivor told me to rest.

Before it all ended we sat around in a ring as we had at the beginning and talked. We were warned not to go to pubs or mix with large groups of strangers over the next few days. We were all too open, too raw. We talked about the symbols we had conjured up the first day. Mine was a cross. I saw it now as the cross which the altar boy had carried in front of my father's coffin as it was wheeled down the centre aisle of Enniscorthy Cathedral, but I was not sure. I had an explanation for the comb, but I am certain now it was too far-fetched, too neat. I did not know if I would be different and changed. And I still do not know.

It was late afternoon, Sunday. The sky was still blue and the sunlight warm and hard on our eyes after we had been indoors all day. I sat on the grass with June and Ivor for a while before collecting my paintings, which I put in the boot of the car, where they remained until recently. Ivor told me that I had taken on a lot in three days, but I should work on it more, I should visit my father's grave, and I should come back for another weekend. He was sure there were more things I needed to explore. And I should try listening to jazz, he laughed. Honestly, he said, it would do you good.

9

A Walk to the End of the Earth

TWO MONTHS LATER, on a Sunday in July, I set out to walk from Leon in the north of Spain to Santiago de Compostela. I did not check the distance because I knew, from the very beginning, that I was going to cheat. In fact, starting at Leon was, in itself, a kind of cheating since serious pilgrims should begin in Paris or from one of three other designated points in France, or at least at the Spanish border. Every time I saw serious pilgrims they put fear into my heart: they were wearing thick shorts and good walking boots and carrying staves and good maps. They knew where they were going: where the refuges for pilgrims were and where to get your cards stamped so you could prove you had really walked and get a certificate from the authorities on arrival in Santiago.

I had nothing. I had an old rucksack with some clothes and a few books, a pair of running shoes and a pair of sandals. I woke up late that Sunday morning in Leon, and I did not want to walk anywhere. It was hot. I went to see the Romanesque frescoes in the Panteon de los Reyes in the church of San Isidoro El Real. There was a beautiful, vivid centrepiece of the Christ figure, with a rich dark blue background, two long, slender fingers on his raised right hand, and a swirling gold border on his tunic. Around him were Matthew,

Mark, Luke and John; two of them had animal heads, one the head of a bird, and one a human head. They had books in their hands and marvellous brown and white wings. Some of the colours had faded, but most of the figures were perfect, and the details, such as the food on the table for the Last Supper, were startling. It was a two-dimensional world, where the faces had no expressions, and the animals, plants and patterns were painted with the same care and exactness as the humans.

I had left my rucksack at the hotel, and every time I felt ready to go back and get it and set out on my walk I was distracted by another wonderful building, or a café which looked promising, or a seat where I could sit and watch everybody. The pilgrims' route to Santiago, on which I was so unwilling to embark, is one of the great mysterious European journeys. Charlemagne's journey there was recounted in the eleventh-century *Song of Roland*, even though he did not travel as far as Galicia. And the remains of Saint James were said to have been taken to Santiago by boat, though they were not discovered until the ninth century.

The journey and its origins, then, were surrounded by rumour and vagueness and superstition. By the twelfth century, rogues as well as religious made the pilgrimage. It was an adventure and people came from all over Europe, often travelling in large groups to avoid bandits; they visited shrines where the relics of various saints were on display; they opened trade routes. They, too, would have looked at the frescoes in the Panteon de los Reyes in the church of San Isidoro El Real, and for them, perhaps, the mixing of pastoral scenes, calendars and moments from the New Testament would not have seemed so strange. And perhaps the most important thing about their journey was that they moved westwards every day, towards the setting sun, toward the shrine of Saint James at Santiago.

The route remained popular even after the discovery of America, dying out only for a while in the nineteenth century. But now, since Spain is in the European Union, there are constant improvements in signposting and hospitality and new grant-aided hostels and refuges for pilgrims. Galicia is known to be unspoiled, full of green fields and small villages. (It is also a traditional, tightly-knit world where smuggling and petty corruption thrive.) The route is suitable for modern pilgrims as well as those in search of a healthy holiday and what Michael Jacobs in *The Road to Santiago de Compostela* called 'slightly bogus medieval nostalgia', which Bunuel satirised in his film *The Milky Way*.

I collected my rucksack, put on a hat to protect my head from the sun and set off. The first temptation came very soon; came, in fact, before I had even left the town. It was called the Hostal de San Marcos, a sixteenth century monastery, solidly square and imposing, with ornate details on the façade, which had been made into a luxury hotel, part of the state-owned Parador chain. It suddenly struck me that I would benefit greatly from spending a night here. I went into the cool hallway and established that there were rooms free and then turned and sat on a stone bench in the cloisters. I closed my eyes and listened to the birdsong and opened them again and looked all around at the arches, the cut stone, the decorations. The beds would have clean, white sheets. I thought about it for a while. There had been a monastery and hospital on this site since the twelfth century; pilgrims had slept here then. I realised that if I gave in to this first temptation I would be full of guilt for the rest of the journey. I picked up my rucksack and walked.

I walked through the interminable suburbs of Leon,

past factories and garages and warehouses, along dull streets, and then more factories and garages and warehouses. I expected all the time to find a sign to tell me that there would soon be a path, or a lane, or a special walkway for pilgrims, but instead there was a busy road. My hat was blown off by a lorry's slipstream, and every time I saw a lorry coming thereafter I had to put my hand on my hat to save it. It became very hot and there was a rumble of thunder in the distant hills and ripples of lightning in the western sky, and as the afternoon wore on a faint drizzle began, but there was still no path, even though there were signs explaining that this was part of the route to Santiago. Lorries, cars and motorbikes sped by, there was no sign or sight of the medieval world, instead there was a fly-over and later a dirt-track running beside the road. The landscape was flat and unpromising. But I knew I was on the right road when I met a German pilgrim who had a good map. He was miserable as well and suggested we walk together for a while, but I said I was going to stop in the next village which was only a few kilometres away.

It was bearable when I kept distances out of my mind, when I just walked and did not think about the time or the number of kilometres still to go. I had no idea what my destination was – I had now been walking for about four hours – but I counted every step of the last two kilometres to a place called Hospital de Orbigo, becoming tired and impatient as the drizzle grew worse and the journey more miserable. I sat in a bar in the main street of the one-horse town, where men were playing cards, and had a few shandies and then a coffee. I had three or four hours of daylight still, and there was nothing to do but walk on. After a while the weather cleared, and gradually it became a warm summer's evening, with a blue sky and a few languorous clouds on the horizon. I didn't know where I was going, but I wanted a town with a few bars and a restaurant and a decent square, and as I tramped on I realised that there was nothing like that within walking distance.

At about eight o'clock in the evening, having walked for miles along a soft dirt-track beside the road, I came to a modern road-house, which had a restaurant and rooms. It was in the middle of nowhere and it looked dull. I could picture myself finishing my dinner at ten, having a few drinks and then making my way upstairs to bed. It was not, I thought, what the medieval pilgrims came along this route for. Just before the road-house there was a long straight road, with a signpost to a train station. I stopped when I saw a man sitting beside his car listening to a transistor and asked him if there was a train due soon. He looked at his watch and gave one of those doubtful, more or less expressions at which Spaniards of all types excel. I decided to walk down the road anyway, even though I could see no sign of a railway station or a railway track anywhere. Several times I was going to turn back and content myself with the road-house, but I kept on. I asked a woman who was working in her garden if the train had gone; she said she wasn't sure. The railway station building looked as though it had not been used for years. I found a timetable, however, and discovered that the last train to Astorga, the next city to the west, had been due fifteen minutes earlier, and there were no other trains. I stood and looked at all the names cut into the plasterwork, and then went out and inspected the platforms.

As I turned to go I noticed something moving in the far distance. I knew what it was: I had seen it in movies. It was the swimming headlights of a train refracted in the warm air and smoke, and it was slowly approaching. I had no ticket and there was no one else in the station, so I put out my hand to stop it, and slowly it came into the station and drew to a halt. I was so happy I did not even realise that this was cheating. I smiled at the people in the carriage and sat down. It would take us about half an hour to get to Astorga; it would have taken me a day to walk it. I had placed myself in the company of the rogue pilgrims of medieval times who surely must have cheated too, and it felt good as I sat back and began to appreciate the subtle colours of the landscape in the evening light.

Astorga offered a grand hotel in the centre, Hotel Gaudí, with windows overlooking a broad square. I sat in the bar and had a few drinks and then had dinner beside an open window in the dining room. In the morning I went to look at the bishop's palace, now a museum, one of the few commissions which Gaudí undertook outside Catalonia. It had all his references to medieval architecture, with columns and vaultings and narrow windows, spires and buttresses and turrets, and a vague sense of menace. It is closest, perhaps, to his Palau Güell in Barcelona. And it seems reasonable that both the Palau Güell and the bishop's palace in Astorga were built to be lived in but are now museums: no one could live in them. Gaudí loved the idea of rooms flowing into each other, of nothing being a uniform shape; thus there are no doors in the bishop's palace, and there are constant vantage points to see from one floor what is going on on the floor below. Gaudí designed a palace of intrigue, a paradise for spies and eavesdroppers. There was no place for the bishop to be alone, no place where he could be comfortable. Gaudí had little interest in comfort himself, and he certainly saw no reason why bishops should be comfortable, which is, I presumed that day, why the bishop lives elsewhere.

I set out walking again, cutting across the open countryside to avoid the busy road, but obviously not paying enough attention to the signposts. I had walked for about two hours before I approached a new luxury hotel. I asked the porter if this was the route to Santiago and he informed me I was going in the wrong direction. I would have to walk back to Astorga, he said. I felt like a fool. I had lunch in the hotel and ordered a taxi to take me to the bus station in Astorga where I bought a ticket to Ponferrada and from there to Villafranca, two of the main villages along the route. It would have taken me two or three days to walk this stretch. As the bus began to nose out of the station on to the street I caught sight of the German, whom I had met on the road just twenty-four hours earlier. He was still walking. I turned my face away so that he would not see me, so that he would not know how much I was cheating.

They showed us a movie on the bus, as though we were on a transatlantic flight. It was full of lurid scenes of screaming and torture. I realised halfway through that it was *The Silence of the Lambs*. The whole bus was looking at it in a state of terror and wonder. I tried to go to sleep but I was woken up by the screaming.

In Villafranca I walked up to the top of the town and sat on the steps of the Church of Santiago, a plain, small Romanesque building. There seemed to be a refuge or a hostel beside it. I went and inspected this: it was full of young people who were busy cooking their evening meal. A few of them had guitars. I did not want to stay and witness a sing-song. I turned and went to the northern doorway of the church, which is known as the Portal del Perdon: in medieval times, pilgrims who could go no further, who would not make it to Santiago, stopped here and asked for forgiveness, ran their hands along the worn stone, looked at the stone carvings, and received the same absolution as they would have received had they gone the whole way. I did not know if pilgrims who cheated could come here too, but I sat on the steps for a while, none the less, looking over the rooftops of the town, asking the old stone to give me lanes, country pathways and bucolic beauty for the rest of my journey.

I checked the next stage of the route and it, too, was along a busy road. The last bus had gone so I went to the main road and began to hitchhike. This, I thought, was the last straw; it was public, bare-faced cheating. I got a lift with a guy who was going to the coast to join his family; he would take me all the way, if I wanted, he said. I told him that I was doing the pilgrimage to Santiago. Pilgrims are meant to walk, he said. He laughed.

He dropped me just after the sign which announced that the province of Leon had come to an end and we were now in Galicia. Thus anyone who had walked from France would here be encountering their fourth language: French, Basque, Spanish and Gallego. And entering a new world, much greener and more rained upon, poorer and less technologically advanced than Leon and Castile, with a tradition, like Ireland, of emigration, Gallegos having populated many of the countries of South America.

The evening was mild and calm; it was perfect for walking. I now had a better map and believed that a turn to the left, down a river valley, would take me to an official refuge. I still had not registered as an official pilgrim. I had no little book, or stamps, or signatures, and this, I thought as I walked along, was my opportunity to join.

Once more, however, I had taken a wrong turn, and as I doubled back I realised that it was getting dark, that

I had at most only another hour of daylight left. I made a vow to concentrate on directions in future and stop fooling around and I walked as fast as I could. In the village of Pedrafita a man told me that the pilgrims' refuge was about half an hour's walk up a hill so I decided to go there.

It always happened like this: once I started to count the time or the kilometres the journey seemed never to come to an end. Darkness fell and a mist came down and the mist grew heavier until it was rain. And I walked; at every turn I expected to find the lights of the refuge; all I found were signs leading me towards it. The rain came at me in slanting gusts. There seemed no end to this. I tried not to think about it, concentrated instead on other things as the road twisted and turned. But this brought the refuge no nearer. I had been walking now for more than an hour. I wondered if the man who directed me here meant that it took half an hour in a car; no one could walk it in half an hour. I trudged on imagining a small cell with a clean bed and a hot shower, and a dining room full of other pilgrims, with hot soup on offer and local wine. I hoped my clothes were dry in the rucksack. I was desperate to arrive.

Eventually, I turned a corner in the driving rain and the sanctuary was ahead of me. I could see the lights and as I grew closer a number of buses. There were tents pitched in the grounds. I expected sympathy for having walked so long in the rain. I expected care and solicitude. I walked into a packed dining room, and when I approached the waiter, he made me stand aside, and then went back to the kitchen ignoring me. There was a bottle of wine on every table, and plates of hot soup, and steak and chips. I was starving and anxious to have a shower and put on some clean clothes. The waiter came back, and when I got his attention he told me brusquely that the place was full, not just the restaurant but the refuge itself. As soon as he said this he walked into the kitchen, disappeared.

Another older man came out of the kitchen but he was equally brusque: full, the place was full. He went to a nearby table and began to take orders. I waylayed him as he left. What can I do? I asked. He shrugged his shoulders. I could ring for a taxi, he told me, and walked back into the kitchen. I followed him and used the phone; the taxi driver agreed to come and collect me. The man in the kitchen told me that the call would cost twenty-five pesetas and it would be better if I waited out in the hall.

I was still soaking wet. I sat in the hall with my rucksack beside me, and everyone who came in and out of the dining room examined me as though I was on exhibition. Eventually, the taxi came and the driver told me that he owned a hotel and restaurant in Pedrafita as well and I was welcome to stay there. It was bad luck walking all the way up in the rain to find that the place was full, he said. I wondered if he was being sarcastic.

The next morning was dull and cloudy. There was a market open beside the hotel. I bought a pair of runners to replace my old ones, which were still wet. A red-haired man was cooking huge squid in barrels. The water had turned pink and was bubbling over, like some strange, unnatural brew. At intervals, the man stirred the squid around with an oar. Later, when it was cooked and cut into segments, it would be delicious, but just now it looked like something that should not be eaten, or even examined too carefully, with all its little rubbery pustules, protuberances and knobs.

I walked up the mountain again, as the day began to clear. This time, since I knew how far it was to the refuge, I expected nothing. I did not count my steps or count the time. I stood and looked at the gorse in full bloom and the view across the hills to the mountains in the distance. I stopped a few times and sat down. I knew that there was a village called Triacastela that I could probably reach in one day, but the route was mainly along lanes, so there could be no catching trains or buses or hitchhiking.

But there always seemed to be temptations. As I came to the refuge from which I had been turned away the previous evening, I wondered if I should not have an early lunch. And as soon as the thought came into my head, it would not go away. I almost walked by it, but I knew that I was going to turn in, and at the crucial moment of decision, I did.

Lunch had begun; a few of the tables were occupied. I waited until my friend, the waiter from the previous evening, came out of the kitchen and told him I wanted a table for one for lunch. He looked around the dining room and then replied in the same brusque tone as the night before: We don't have any tables for one. I pointed to a long table at which five or six people were sitting, but where there was room for five or six others. Can I not sit at the end of that table? I asked. He shrugged and said if I wanted to I could, but he did not encourage me. I sat down.

As I looked at the menu I realised that the other people at the table were of the English persuasion and did not look like pilgrims. Nor did they look like a family on holiday; most of them were in their thirties and it was hard to work out the relationship between them. I looked at one of them and was sure I knew him from somewhere; he was careful to look away. I asked them a question about the pilgrimage and found out quickly that they were a television crew from the BBC making a film about the route to Santiago. I told them I was writing a book about it, and wondered out loud if everyone else in the dining room was engaged in similar activities. They were all jolly and friendly in a very English way, a great relief from the gruff Galicians I had been dealing with.

I looked at the man who had looked away earlier: he had glasses and straight hair, he was in his late forties. Suddenly, I realised who he was.

'What did Chad's family make their fortune from in Henry James' "The Ambassadors"?' I asked him.

'No one knows,' he replied. He did not seem surprised by the question.

'But there's a solution in your first novel,' I said.

'In my second novel,' he corrected me.

'You're David Lodge,' I said, and he agreed that he was. He was the presenter of the BBC film.

We had lunch then. The crew was full of jokes and nicknames for each other, completely bonded as a group. They even called David Lodge 'Lodgie'. He seemed disturbed that I had not got an official book of the route which should be stamped regularly. I knew he was trying to be helpful but brief exchanges between Irish people and English people can often be difficult, and I thought for a moment that he felt he was hectoring me, and he soon stopped and smiled and I smiled back.

He and his crew had a minibus. I really wanted to go with them and abandon my own solitary manoeuvrings. I sat for ages over my coffee talking to them, but I knew that it could not last and I stood up to go. It was now the early afternoon and I expected little from the rest of the day as I began to walk westwards in the direction of Triacastela. The sky was blue with white, puffed-up clouds banked on the horizon; the road was narrow and there was hardly any traffic. In the distance over a ridge to the north I could see a falcon immobile in the sky, like something held by a taut string from the ground, but steadier, and then swooping slowly not to capture any prey but to draw nearer to a companion hovering closer to the ground.

The road led along a ridge between two valleys: the ditches were feasts of weeds – ragwort, thistles, daisies, clover, ferns, nettles, blackberry bushes – and each field was a different size and shape, with a different colour and texture. I passed through a small village and on to a path beside the road; the two valleys kept appearing and reappearing as I moved along. The sky was different from the sky in southern Spain or in Catalonia; the clouds changed all the time, they covered the sun, and then dispersed in the breeze. I passed a sign in Spanish which had been crossed out and replaced by Gallego. I was now walking along a lane, with a full view of the hillside of brilliant gorse across the valley. The only sounds were constant birdsong, the tinny sound of the bells which hung around cows' necks, and tractor and farm machines in the distance. For miles I met nobody.

When two lanes diverged there was a piece of yellow plastic tied to a bush to tell pilgrims which lane to take. The lanes still followed the ridge, and the view remained delightful: small hills of soft greens and yellows and far-away ranges of mountains. I occasionally passed small houses and there were always people, usually old people, working in the fields, bent over weeding, or digging in the hot afternoon. The young people, someone told me later, had all left the land, observed the usual Gallego custom of moving away, travelling. Most of the time there were birds of prey – dark, solitary specks in the sky – hovering over the hills. When they came closer I could sit and watch them, huge, merciless creatures, motionless, ready to swoop like an arrow.

Along this world of tiny narrow lanes and dry stone

walls and pieces of yellow plastic to direct pilgrims there were a few small villages. Some of them had retained the old-style round thatched houses but had built modern houses alongside. I was told that there was still a good length to go before Triacastela, but if I kept on, they said, I would make it before dark. They spoke in Spanish, but it sounded like Gallego, with 'o' sounds at the end of words coming out like 'u', with 's' sounds coming out like 'sh'. It mattered that I was walking westwards, towards the Atlantic ocean and the setting sun; it made the walking easier, even though my feet and back were sore. Once more, I began to dream of a clean bed and a good dinner with lots of wine.

I started to walk down a hill of purple heather. The sun was straight ahead of me. Soon it would be getting dark, the sun would sink into the Atlantic. The colours of the vast panorama before me were sumptuous. The people were still working in the fields and I asked everyone if it was far to Triacastela. Four kilometres downhill, they said. The smell of grass and clover was sweet and powerful, and it was a great happiness, for once, not to have cheated. But it was more than four kilometres and it was not all downhill. It's not far, they told me, when I asked again. Obviously, they were used to this. They told the same story to all pilgrims. The last half an hour's walking was pure agony, but the pain was nothing to the pleasure and the expectation as the rooftops of Triacastela gradually came into view. Just outside the village there was a huge sign announcing the imminent construction of a new hotel for pilgrims as part of the development, with EC aid, of the route to Santiago.

Triacastela had been a pilgrims' stop, according to my guide-book, for more than a thousand years. An old man told me that there were two hotels and pointed out what he believed to be the better one. This hotel offered me a small room with a bare wooden floor and a narrow iron bed. It was like a convent and it was cheap. I had a shower and changed my clothes and had a dinner of soup and trout and white wine. The only other person in the little dining room was a Frenchman. He had been walking for twenty-one days, he said. He would start again at eight o'clock in the morning. What time did I intend to start at? he asked. Eleven, I said, eleven. You're lazy, he remarked and shook his head. Lazy? I said. You don't know the half of it.

The following morning I sat in the café on the ground floor of the hotel, drinking coffee and eating croissants. I could have stayed in bed all day, and got up only because the landlady came knocking on my door. She told me that Samos, where there was another refuge, was two hours' walk away. I set out with the idea in my head that I would walk for two hours and then rest. My feet were sore and I felt exhausted. I could not stop timing myself, translating kilometres into miles by dividing by eight and then multiplying by five. It was a warm day; there were no lanes and the road's surface was hard. After a while I tried lying in a field, but I could not relax. I would just have to walk on, put up with the pain. I was passed by several large groups on bicycles as I made my way, slowly and painfully, towards Samos. My guide-book promised a medieval monastery and a cool, clean river. I wondered if there was a bar and a restaurant.

There was, but the bicycle people had got there first, and there was a long wait for service. After lunch I crossed the bridge and walked across a field and lay down by the river. The water was cold, but after all the walking it was a great relief to strip off and wallow in the river and lie on the grass drying out afterwards and think about plans.

I loved being in Spain: the heat, the food, the wine, the way people looked and spoke. I lay there and thought about it. I remembered when I was about seventeen getting a summer job working in the bar of a big hotel in the south east of Ireland. I brought a few books with me, and one day, when I had the afternoon off, I went down to the beach and I read Hemingway's *The Sun Also Rises*, which was in a book called *The Essential Hemingway*. I had never been out of Ireland and I had never read prose like that before. There was a real delight in every aspect of Spain: the way a waiter watched you, the way a tablecloth was folded, the way crowds gathered.

A friend, the Irish novelist Joseph O'Connor, was due to arrive in Vigo, to the south of Galicia the following morning. I took a taxi to the nearest bus station and caught the last bus to Vigo. The bus had seen better days and drove fast along the rocky road south. Every house and holding had an *horreo* – I later learned the word – in front; this was a little house on stilts with a roof and usually a cross on top. It could have been for dead ancestors, if this was another society. Some of them seemed to be as big as the houses themselves; they were barns for storing straw and perishables. For the first half of the journey, before I asked a fellow traveller what they were, I stared at them and guessed at various possible uses for them.

It was dark when the bus arrived in Vigo, and the taxi driver at the head of the queue was grumpy. There was no centre, he said, when I asked him to take me to the centre. Was there not a part of the city with shops and bars and old-fashioned hotels? I asked him. He'd drop me near the port, he said, and sighed as though passengers caused him infinite pain and sorrow.

He drove me down a narrow, steep hill which appeared to lead to the waterfront. He left me at an old-fashioned hotel whose bar and front windows gave on to the port. I filled in the form at reception and realised as I climbed up the stairs that my legs were still stiff and painful. It was even worse later as I tried to walk up the badly-lit street in search of a restaurant. Maybe I was lucky that I could not go far, because just around the corner there was a long street of restaurants. I found a table outside one of them and sat back as the waiter came to change the tablecloth.

There were stalls in front of the outdoor tables which sold only oysters; the women at the stalls seemed to be allowed to sell their oysters to clients of the restaurant. They now descended on me, and I took half a dozen oysters from them, and ordered prawns and white wine from the waiter. My stiff legs and sore feet were a great excuse not to do any more walking, I thought. Maybe I would be better just to eat and drink and lie in bed.

The following morning I met Joseph O'Connor at the airport, having booked him a room at the hotel, and we stayed two days in Vigo, not moving far from the hotel, eating crabs and prawns and oysters and drinking wine and beer. The crabs were called 'buey', the word for ox, and they were huge, with thick brown meat inside. Eating them, eeking out the meat from the claws, must have been a sort of art because various waiters complained that we had not mastered this. The white wine in Galicia, Ribeiro, was light enough for us to drink several bottles of it at each meal.

The big day for all pilgrims to arrive in Santiago de Compostela is the 24 July. On the eve, Joe and I set out too from Vigo by train. My legs had recovered, and I suffered merely from a small regret that I had not walked the final stretch and seen the towers of Santiago after a long day's walk rather than from the railway station.

We found a cheap place to stay in the centre and started to wander around the intimate, small scale streets of the city, which is full of houses with big bay windows like porches on the upper storeys, and old fashioned shops on the ground floors. There were pilgrims everywhere, weather-beaten men and women wearing hats and shorts, with the scallop shell which is the symbol of the route around their necks, staves in their hands and big back-packs. They looked healthy and serious minded, but business in the city carried on despite them and as the evening began whole families from the suburbs and the towns around Santiago arrived in the centre and took over restaurants and bars and walked up and down looking at everyone who passed them as though they were searching for lost loved ones.

The city is built on a hill. The old streets and squares seem like mere arteries and veins leading to the heart of the city: the cathedral. It combines several styles and can be approached and entered in many different ways. In the city's main square, Plaza del Obradoiro, it is a massive baroque structure with a double ramp staircase, which stands alone and dominates the square. But the Portico de la Gloria, which you approach intimately from a side street a good distance away, seems part of another church altogether; it is a delicate Romanesque doorway with elaborate and beautiful stone carvings of saints, figures from the Bible and representations of heaven and hell.

'Up to as late as the sixteenth century,' Michael Jacobs wrote in *The Road to Santiago de Compostela*, 'Santiago Cathedral remained open throughout the day and night

. . . Scandalous activity resulting from pilgrims sleeping in the cathedral led to the portal being enclosed by outer doors.' It is easy to imagine a city which camped around the mass and power of the cathedral, where the cathedral was the principal dormitory and refectory for a wandering population of pilgrims, tradesmen and adventurers.

That evening, 23 July 1992, the eve of the feast of Saint James, it would not have made much difference to the frenzied atmosphere inside the cathedral if there had been people lying on the ground asleep. There was Mass being said at the high altar with a huge congregation answering the prayers. There were tourists everywhere, including pilgrims, still carrying their staves and rucksacks, wandering around the cathedral as though it were a marketplace. As I looked around at the soaring interior I noticed a woman going to confession, kneeling in an old confessional right beside where I stood. I felt that if I moved closer I could hear what she was saying, but I moved away and looked instead at the priest's calm face as he heard her telling her sins. People stood in line waiting for her to finish so that they could go to confession before the feast day.

You can buy tickets to visit the vaults and cloisters and the exhibitions of sacred objects, but the main interest of this magnificent building is open to every eye: the strange, forceful power and beauty of the interior, the splendid spaces, the long elegant vistas, the sense of the Catholic Church at the height of its wealth and ambition.

Pilgrims who arrive in the city with their certificates proving that they walked the route have a right to a drink in the Pilgrims' Hospital in the Plaza del Obradoiro, which is another link in the chain of Paradors. This year the staff were on strike, and maintained a steely picket at the front door preventing pilgrims, both real and phoney, from getting their free drink. We went and had dinner in an old restaurant, squeezing our way between well-fed families, and tables laden with empty wine bottles and empty shells of prawn, mussel, crab and various other shellfish we could not identify. We were told to be back in the Plaza del Obradoiro by eleven o'clock or eleven thirty. Even as we began to eat, the families were leaving to secure good places in the square for the traditional fireworks.

The square was packed when we arrived. We stood at the edge for a while and then tried to push our way in towards the centre. Soon, we could go no further as everybody waited. The fireworks were attached to all the old buildings in the square. We watched the first ones sweeping up into the sky and exploding into colour; we cheered and held our breath with the rest of the crowd. You could never tell from where the next fireworks would be released; suddenly, they would come from a building behind you, and break up into coloured stars in the sky. This went on for more than half an hour. They left the best and most spectacular ones for last.

Santiago that night after the fireworks was one vast bar. I seem to remember having my last drink at about six o'clock in the morning. All that day I had noticed posters advertising a meeting of the youth branch of the Falange, the old Spanish fascist movement, in a square in the old city at lunchtime the next day. There was a bar in the square, and we made our way there for a cure and to see how many people would turn up for the fascist meeting.

Galicia has its own autonomous parliament now, and its own government known as the Xunta. It is run by one of the most fascinating survivors in modern Spanish history, Manuel Fraga. (In Barcelona in 1976, when Fraga who had served under Franco was one of the chief hate figures, we used to shout: '*Fraga, fraga, la gente no te traga*' – 'Fraga, Fraga, the people won't swallow you.') Fraga had founded Alianza Popular, a right-wing party which would slowly become the main opposition in Spain to the socialists. Fraga himself, once he resigned as leader of his party, had been swallowed with great relish by his native Galicia and he gave the impression of being a strong man, a populist leader who enjoyed democracy, now that he had discovered he could hold power under its systems as well. He was famous for the grand gesture: in the 1960s when someone claimed that a stretch of the Spanish coast was polluted, Fraga, one of the architects of modern Spanish tourism, gathered the press and went swimming in the water himself.

Over the next few days, as we wallowed on a beach near Santiago, Fraga entertained Fidel Castro, who was visiting Spain, took him to his ancestral home and seemed to enjoy being photographed with him. Both men were strong Gallegos – like Franco himself – who had survived, Castro with his charisma intact, Fraga with his beefy confidence. There was a sense of happy defiance in Fraga's expression when he appeared with Castro on television in the beach bar: ideology doesn't matter, he seemed to say, it's being in power that counts.

I wondered when I saw the posters for the Falange meeting how successful Fraga had been in soaking up all the right-wing energy and rage for public order in Galicia. I expected a small crowd. Instead, there was nobody, except a few youths in military garb and a megaphone. It was a feast day, people sauntered by, examining the youths as a mild curiosity, but not stopping. Nobody stopped. The young fascists might as well have been talking to the wall.

The coast of Galicia is full of small inlets, tiny

resorts and fishing villages. We got a bus to a beach called San Francisco, rented an apartment and lay on the beach for a few days. But there was something else I had on my mind. In medieval times, the route did not end in Santiago. People wanted to see the end of the world, and that meant travelling further to the west. There was no America then, no Cuba, the world could have been flat with steep edges; it was all mystery, waiting there to be discovered. If you walked westwards you could come to the end of Europe, to the place called Finis Terrae in Latin, Finisterre in Spanish and Fisterre in Gallego.

We caught a bus to Fisterre which left us in the old village with more than a mile's walk uphill to see the end of the world. There were pilgrims, with rucksacks and staves and scallop shells around their necks, just as tanned and pleased with themselves as the pilgrims I had seen in Leon when I started my journey. The hills on the promontory which overlooked the end of the world were wild with gorse and heather; as we walked up we could see small fishing craft like silver specks in the bay below. This must be a smugglers' paradise.

At the top of the hill there were two makeshift bars selling cold drinks, an old house in ruins, and beyond that a magnificent lighthouse in perfect order, the stone and the paintwork glistening. And behind the lighthouse there was rock and scrub and a path leading down to the sea. I stood and watched as the waves hit the point – the first and the last piece of land in the world – and crashed back leaving a creamy foam in their wake.

In the years before 1492 you could have stood here contemplating the deep blue sea and the flat earth and the hot sun in the brilliant sky, knowing that you had come to the end of things, speculating what was beyond: great wealth and unimagined possibilities or nothing, the abyss that these same waves had touched or come close to. And then the turning back: the walk homewards, away from the setting sun, in the direction of the dull east, and all the places to revisit, and all the time in the world.

10

The Language of The Tribe

I WENT TO SCOTLAND in February 1993 expecting a shadowy version of Northern Ireland. I arrived armed with certain information: it was a deeply sectarian and divided society; there was discrimination against Catholics; the Scottish Labour Party was mainly Catholic while the Scottish National Party was mainly Protestant; the football matches between Rangers and Celtic were examples of pure, naked hatred between Protestants and Catholics.

There were things I needed to know. Why, for example, had the violent conflict between Catholics and Protestants in Northern Ireland not flared up in Scotland? Could it do so in the future? How exactly were Catholics discriminated against? What exactly was the atmosphere like in these famous Rangers–Celtic encounters?

In 1986 I had gone to Belfast to report for a Dublin radio programme on the difference between a night's drinking on the Protestant Shankill and on the Catholic Falls. I had no trouble making contact with the Catholics, and I had no fears for my safety. It took some time, however, to get in touch with people from the Shankill who could take me drinking and guarantee my safety. It was the summer after the Anglo–Irish Agreement, and sectarian assassinations had resumed in Belfast; there was considerable ill-feeling against the Republic and its citizens among Protestants in the Shankill.

Friday night was to be the Protestant night; I met my minders in the Crown Bar in the neutral territory of the centre of Belfast. I did not expect my Catholic minders to be there as well; I was surprised to see them. But it is a popular bar. I could not introduce my two sets of minders to each other. My Catholic friends did not think I should go up the Shankill; they would never do so. They viewed my Protestant minders suspiciously and suggested that I stay in the Crown Bar. I told them I'd see them the following night. I knew that they were worried.

My Protestant friends took me in a taxi to a place called the Malvern Bar. They asked if the name meant anything to me. I replied that it was where a Catholic barman had been murdered in the 1960s. They thought this was a huge black joke, taking me to this bar, the site of such a famous sectarian murder. There was very little malice in their laughter; it was more a sort of banter which is common in Belfast. They were amused at my being an outsider.

I survived the Malvern, several other bars, a great deal of drink and a lot of grim laughter. I was not introduced to many people. (My name is clearly Catholic.) After the bars shut we went to a drinking club which looked more like a sports hall full of tables and loud talk. After a few drinks, I noticed that my minders were missing. One of them, after a while, walked over casually, sat down opposite me and said, 'Our instructions are: "Get your Fenian friend out of here now." So turn around this second and walk out, don't look at anyone, and get on to the main road as quickly as you can.'

I did what he said.

The next night, I went to a Republican drinking

club with my Catholic minders. There was a sign on the wall saying that any band who played too loudly would not be allowed to play again. One of my companions, making sure he had the attention of the entire company, asked me if I knew what this meant. I replied that I did not. 'It means they'll be shot,' he said. 'Any band who plays too loud will be shot.' They all laughed. Their Fenian friend had no trouble getting into other Catholic drinking clubs in the city, and felt much more relaxed that evening with his own tribe than he did with the Shankill Protestants.

A month after this, I set off walking along the Irish border, and I wrote a book, called *Bad Blood*, about my experiences. Every step of the way I was aware of the Protestant/Catholic divide. Sometimes it took the form of hatred or deep hurt, but often it was simply there: it lay under everything, and it explained most things. When I went to Glasgow in 1993 I carried with me all this baggage about conflict between Catholics and Protestants; my view of the place was profoundly affected by my experiences in Northern Ireland. It is possible that I asked all the wrong questions.

It was easy at first. I arrived in the city a few days before a Rangers and Celtic match, and I moved among journalists and academics asking about the background to the famous rivalry between the two football teams. Here are some of the things I heard:

'Protestants are richer. The poorer classes, the Catholics, who came here first from Ireland after the potato famine, vote Labour. But it is not discussed: people here are too afraid to bring religion into it.'

'There are a lot of Masons in the police, but also some Catholics. Rather than religion, it would be social standing, but that would favour Protestants.'

'Eighty-five per cent of the prison population is Catholic.'

[When I contacted The Scottish Office to check this, I received the following information:

Below are the percentage figures for 1993 of receptions within Scottish prisons broken down by religion.

Church of Scotland	57·7*
Roman Catholic	33·7
Church of England	1.1
Other Religion	0.6
No Religion	6.8
	—
	100

*Components may not add to total due to rounding.

These figures should be treated with some degree of caution as the information is collected by asking the prisoner when he is first received into the establishment. Please also note that we do not know whether the prisoner is a practising or non-practising churchgoer.]

'Sixty-five per cent of the population is Protestant; thirty per cent is Catholic.'

[According to The Scottish Office, this is not a question asked on the census form.]

'Protestant kids still have better schools, but there was a bigger gap in the 1950s than there is today.'

'There is tremendous sympathy among Catholics here towards Catholics in Northern Ireland. There was bitterness during the hunger strikes. When Bobby Sands died open conflict would have been easy if a leader had emerged. It would have just taken one man.'

'People here are afraid to talk too much about the Protestant/Catholic/Irish subject. It's taboo. People here will say a Dundee bastard, but not a Protestant bastard or a Catholic bastard. People don't want a Northern Ireland situation.'

'On The Scotsman [newspaper] in Edinburgh I could have told you who was Protestant and who was Catholic the minute I went there.'

'In Glasgow the Rangers and Celtic matches channel away energies and bigotry. If they didn't have great intensity, things might spill over into violence.'

'Celtic [the Catholic team] dominated Scottish football in the mid-1960s. In 1967 it was the first British team to win the European Cup. It won the Scottish League nine years in a row. Now it has gone right into reverse. Poor old Celtic! It is run by two old families who are suspicious of change. The club is going backwards, while Rangers is buying up all the best players.'

'I always said that I wouldn't attend the game. The atmosphere is evil. For ninety minutes normal rational, good-living people . . . [pauses] . . . you can feel the hatred in the air. Don't go.'

'Rangers were incensed when Celtic won nine in a row. They went around Scotland and bought everyone's best players.'

'Evil? You could go tomorrow and it could be a quiet game. The popular theory is that it is a cathartic exercise for both sides.'

'Until 1912 you could still find Catholic players playing for Rangers. Round about 1910/1912 Harland & Woolf [the Belfast shipbuilding company] came over to Clyde and brought a large section of Protestant foremen from Belfast. Rangers was going through a bad patch and somebody saw that you could ally a club to a side. Things stayed like that from 1912; Rangers never knowingly fielded a Catholic. Celtic maintained an open recruiting policy.'

'There are reasons why you didn't have Northern Ireland here. Municipal housing was never allocated on the basis of religion. There was no discrimination and Catholics had allied themselves with the Labour Party in Scotland. The discrimination against Catholics was in banking and insurance. Politically, Catholics had power at local level and at party level.'

'More than half the population of Glasgow has Irish connections.'

'Most of the police are Protestants. Most people in jail are Catholics.'

'The match is a tribal ritual. Celtic has had two very bad seasons, but the fans turn out. It has nothing to do with Scotland. It is an Irish situation imported into Scotland. The Catholic population in Glasgow is Irish.'

'The fans are turning against the management of Celtic.'

'There were no Catholic broadcasters on BBC radio in the 1950s. Things changed when commercial TV came in.'

'The two sides have a different way of looking at the world. The Church of Scotland has great virtues – thrift, an ability to work hard. Calvinist theology is a better training for accountants than Catholic theology. Catholicism is romantic and fanciful. I'm not sure that you want romantic and fanciful accountants.'

'The signing up of Maurice Johnson [a Catholic, to Rangers, in 1987] was a stroke of pure genius. At a stroke it removed an area in which Rangers were vulnerable. He was extremely courageous and a good player.'

'The Rangers/Celtic divide is the focus for a sectarianism in Glasgow which doesn't exist. Ninety per cent of the Irish came from Donegal, they were labourers and second class citizens. Celtic became their focus, a way of celebrating their identity. You couldn't work in a bank; you couldn't be a lawyer, or a journalist – in those years The Glasgow Herald wouldn't employ a Catholic – you could be a publican or a bookie – dear God the property they own in Glasgow now!'

'You would die of dullness in Scotland if it wasn't for the Irish element.'

'In 1890 Glasgow was the richest city in the world per capita.'

'The Celtic style of playing is full of panache; the Rangers style is dull and boring.'

'The virtues here are wit, intelligence, enthusiasm and irony.'

'Scottish people are more concerned about the nature of the union with England than with the Protestant/Catholic divide.'

'The Pope's visit was important. There was great pride that he had come. It was beautiful sunny weather. It was felt to be a Scottish occasion. It was a distinct watershed in the history of the nation. The Catholic community changed because of it.'

In one of my early encounters in Glasgow I asked an innocent question. There is a new movement in Scottish writing, full of social engagement and formal energy. I could list ten or twelve Scottish writers, most of them uncompromising figures, distant from southern English gentility. I casually asked a journalist in Glasgow who among the writers was Catholic and who was not. I presumed that maybe half the writers were Catholics. He stopped and thought for a while. He shook his head.

He said it was funny that he had never been asked the question before, or thought about it. There must be one, he replied, but he couldn't think of a name.

Unless I wanted to include Muriel Spark. She was a convert, I said, that was different. Do you mean, I asked him, that all of the writers, with their street credibility and their working-class heroes, are Protestants? Yes, he said. And do you mean, I went on, that no one has ever raised this matter? Correct, he said. And do you mean that most people do not think it is a significant fact? Correct, once more.

Irish nationalism was constructed by writers as much as by politicians or revolutionaries; some of these – Yeats, for example, or Lady Gregory, or Synge – were Protestants but they had offered their power and support to a Catholic nation. In Northern Ireland writers like Brian Friel or Seamus Heaney, both Catholics, were essential aspects of the nationalist community's sense of itself, even when they did not write about politics. In the Republic, writers like Patrick Kavanagh and John McGahern had named our world for us. Maybe it was my problem: but I could not imagine coming from a nation, or a community or a place which did not have writers.

And surely, I thought, there were stories to be told: the arrival of unskilled and unlettered men and women from Donegal in Ireland into this strange world of factory-work and mines and labour politics; the slow melting into Glasgow of these outsiders; the adherence to Celtic football club; the pub life of the city; the idea for the generation which benefited from free education that they belonged in the city and were outsiders at the same time. I could not understand why there were no Catholic writers in Scotland.

Late one night during the Edinburgh Festival in 1993

I raised the matter with a distinguished Scottish poet. He couldn't think of a Catholic writer either, and, as the night wore on, I mentioned the discrimination against Catholics in banking and insurance in Scotland, the Masonic influence in the police. And the no writers. I happened to state that this sounded to me, an outsider, like Alabama in, say, 1954. Scotland was now the only place in the world where to be a Catholic was to be at a distinct disadvantage. Northern Ireland was just as bad, but there was a general recognition of the problem and numerous committees and bodies to deal with it. No one in Scotland even admitted it was happening.

My friend, the poet, told me I was completely wrong. It just wasn't like that. I came from Ireland where Catholics and Protestants openly opposed each other. It wasn't like that in Scotland, he repeated. I was asking the wrong questions, he said. I asked him how he would reply if there were no women writers in Scotland, or, in another society where blacks represented 30 per cent of the population (as Catholics do in Scotland), no black writers?

On the Thursday before the Celtic versus Rangers match I telephoned a journalist in London, whom I knew to be a Glasgow Catholic, and asked him if he knew of any Catholic writers in Scotland. I was in luck. He did not hesitate. He gave me a name – Thomas Healy – and a telephone number. I went to a bookshop and bought the two books by Healy which were on sale. They were both published by Polygon, the first, *It Might Have Been Jerusalem* in 1991, the second, *Rolling*, in 1992. I began to read *Rolling*.

It was a novel about manic drinking and pure loneliness and the desperate search for redemption. There was a knotted, tortured edge to the prose, and there was no effort to make things easy for the reader. I presumed – maybe I had no right to presume this – that the novel came directly from personal experience. There was a sense that nothing in it had been made up, and that it had taken real honesty and effort to write down and shape what had happened. It had that same sharpness as a great deal of the best modern Scottish writing.

I telephoned Thomas Healy and we arranged to meet that evening. He nominated a modern, well-lit pub in the suburbs. I ordered a pint and sat there waiting for him. He was a tall, thin man in his forties, nervous and polite. He explained that he was not drinking himself, but made clear that he did not mind if I had another pint. He had gone up to the priest, he said, and taken the pledge. I knew about the pledge. It was something that people in Ireland had done up to the 1950s, and maybe later. If you were a heavy drinker and you wanted to stop, you went to see a priest and made a pledge never to drink again, or not to drink for a certain period. But it was, at least in my experience in Ireland, a thing of the past. But not here.

Things were bad at home, he said. His mother had been in hospital but he did not think she was happy there and he had taken her home. He had to look after her: it was important that she was well looked after.

He'd had a difficult time, he told me, with London agents and publishers. At one point, he said, he was in such a rage that he threw the only copy of a typescript into the fire, as did the protagonist of *Rolling*. He had made very little money from his two books. We talked then about money and publishing.

I mentioned that there seemed to be a great camaraderie among Scottish writers. I mentioned James Kelman, Alisdair Gray and Jeff Torrington. He nodded, but said that he did not know any of them. I asked him if he was the only Catholic writer in Scotland, or if he could think of any others. He thought for a while and then laughed. No one, he said, had ever raised the subject before. He had never thought about it; but it was true. Maybe there were one or two others, but he couldn't think of them. He shook his head and looked into his drink. It was odd, he said, that no one had ever raised the matter before.

He was quiet-spoken and, of course, sober. His eyes grew bright when he talked about books and writing. Sometimes he mentioned a detail about his own life that tallied with the narrative in *Rolling*: stories about cycling or boxing or time spent in Germany. I hadn't finished the book yet, but that night after I left Thomas Healy I read it to the end, to the raw, brutal honesty of the last pages, so full of ambiguity and unresolved pain that it did not matter whether he was Protestant, Catholic or Hindu. Nevertheless, it remained true that he was the only Catholic writer in Scotland that anyone could think of.

On my first day in Glasgow I met Dr Andrew Noble from the English Department of Strathclyde University and asked him if there was anyone I should see over the next few days. He suggested an ex-student, one of the most brilliant he had come across, who now taught English. He gave me his name, Jim McCormack and his number. We arranged to meet at my hotel.

I was surprised to find a man in his fifties, more or less the same age as Andrew Noble. Once more, this was something which would not happen in Ireland. People go to university after school, in general, or not at all. There is no state grant system in the Republic of Ireland for adults. Jim McCormack's name is Irish, and there was a sort of soft, immediate friendliness about him which reminded me of home. I asked him about his Irish forebears.

His father came from Ireland in 1934 to work in the pits, joining his uncle and cousins; his mother was born in Scotland, but her parents were from Newry in Ireland. Her father had been in the British Army; he had served in Ireland. The owner of the mine where his father worked also owned the village, but he invested no money in the mines, which became death traps. Jim McCormack remembered talk about priests having to go down and minister to those who were dying or dead in the pits, phrases like 'they brought him up in a bag' being used in stories told about accidents, women in black shawls living in dread of rock falls or explosions.

His father was deeply Catholic, not pious, but devoted, he barely drank at all and was fiercely respectable. You were never far from Ireland. If you listened to Mass on the radio and the priest had an English accent, someone would say 'put that off, it's not our kind of Mass.' During the war, his father had a plot of land. He would hold up a piece of clay and say: 'That could be your grandfather's place in Lisnaskea [in Northern Ireland], clay is the same all over the world.'

St Patrick's Day was the big day for Catholics in Scotland; Lent was suspended for the celebration. They knew all the hymns as their hymns: 'Hail glorious St Patrick, dear saint of our isle.' When the King and Queen came to Scotland after the war, his mother and father would not go to see them.

A real battle was fought in Scotland, he said, between the Church and the political left. The priests were demented about it. It was a sin to read the *Daily Worker*. He met men on the plots who had fought in Spain against Franco, lay scholars, men who had educated themselves on Voltaire, Shaw, O'Casey, Hugh

MacDiarmid and Dominic Behan. It was common in Catholic families for the father to be a communist and the mother a devout Catholic who never missed Mass.

There were Protestants down the mines too, but they could also get jobs in the steelworks. There was a joke about people with Catholic names: 'He needn't apply for a job in the Bank of Scotland.' In Glasgow, Catholics who did law tended to become criminal lawyers because they couldn't get jobs as business lawyers.

His father told him that he would break his back before he would allow him to become a miner. He won a place in a secondary school and began to read. The cult of Fatima was huge at the time and the discussion over how long you could kiss a girl before committing a sin was current. He read Jacques Maritain, Bloy and Peguy and Waugh. But he loved and respected the older men who had tried to run a revolution in Scotland, men who had spoken to Lenin. There was a spirit in Scotland which could have done well, he said.

That radical spirit in Glasgow survived, he believed, and emerged again in the arts, in the theatre with groups such as 7:84 and the Citizens' Theatre. The place was alive with singers, poets, writers, drama groups, and that to him was the flowering of the old socialist/communist world.

He himself came to work in the city as a clerk in a shipping office. He discovered jazz and began to write poetry. Over the years he published a good deal of poetry in magazines and periodicals. He continued to read. In 1959 he got married and started to work as a bus conductor. In 1964 he went to university to study English and got a good first. He became head of the English Department in a Catholic school. Nowadays, he said, things were becoming more strictly Catholic in such schools; for certain promotions you needed to get a certificate from the local parish priest, which you never needed before. They would not bother the older teachers but they were tightening up. The state schools in Glasgow were essentially Protestant schools; he taught in a Catholic school by choice. He understood the jokes, he said drily.

The Thatcher thing had had a dreadful effect on Glasgow, he said; the kids all wanted to be accountants and lawyers whereas before they wanted to be writers. In the late 1960s the students would read you their poems over the phone. Now you didn't have poets coming out of schools any more. At the same time there was huge unemployment and the place was jumping with drugs.

He mentioned reading James Baldwin and realising that the Irish working class in Scotland tended to despise themselves. For him, then, the idea of communism gave you a sort of dignity as an Irish Catholic in Glasgow. I asked him about Catholic writers, told him how no one seemed to have thought of this before I had come along with my Irish sectarian attitudes. He hadn't thought of it before either. He supposed Protestants had a sense of belonging that Catholics did not have. As a writer, he had been invited by Philip Hobsbawm, who had helped writers both in Northern Ireland and Scotland, to come to his workshop, but he had never gone along.

'I'm not sure,' he said, 'that it's easy to be creative in a culture in which you're not at home. The Protestants feel at home in their province, shout how they may about independence.'

To be a Catholic in Scotland, he said, is to be fundamentally different. The same Unionist mind-set exists in Scotland as in Northern Ireland; the feeling that this country belongs to them rather than to Catholics. Catholics are not really trusted. And it should be remembered, he added, that when people came over from Ireland they took any job, and they undercut local workers, and this caused bitterness.

The writers, he said, came from foremen's homes and felt a terrible anger at petit-bourgeois values. They belonged, he said. I could see he was thinking about this as he spoke; he was unsure if he could put his finger on what it was that caused him never to strike out as a writer, never to feel confident enough to make it his life. It still seemed to me astonishing that no one of his class or generation had become a writer, and only Thomas Healy represented the next generation.

I asked him why there had never been a civil rights movement in Scotland or a spill-over of the violence from Northern Ireland? Catholics in Scotland simply did not know enough about Northern Ireland, he said; their enemy was not Britain, but the Rangers' symbol. The conflict was about wages and conditions, and there was no discrimination in the allocation of state housing. The Catholics accepted that it was not their country. They gloried in that fact. And there was a romantic element in the Irish connection rather than anything real.

The Catholic zeal of his youth was something that still amazed him, the amount of energy the Church invested in keeping Scottish Catholics safe from communism. They had staged plays about Our Lady of Fatima, the apparitions at Knock, the history of St Dominic; bishops came to see the performances. We had been drinking and talking for some time now and I could sense that what he had told me had stirred things in him, old ideas and memories. I don't remember if I said that there were at least two or three novels in what he had told me, and more, perhaps, in what he had left out, and that his country, despite itself, needs Catholic novelists, especially lapsed ones.

The following night, the eve of the match, I went to Hereghty's pub, one of the famous bastions for Celtic supporters in the city, and joined in the festivities. They were drinking with speed and ferocity. The group of young men to my right ordered treble whiskys and gulped them back in one go, shaking their heads and gasping when they had finished. One of them looked as if he was going to be sick. I was introduced as a journalist from Ireland, and people bought me pint after pint until I had three of them lined up in front of me. I was with my tribe.

There was only one woman in the bar; she was sitting near the door. When I remarked on this, I was informed that she might feel isolated, but what about the Rangers supporter? I didn't believe that there was a Rangers supporter in the bar, but they pointed to him and one of the company took me over and introduced me. Was he sure he was in the right bar? I asked him. He laughed. This wasn't Belfast, he said. He was a regular here, and he was always made welcome. Once, he said, when Celtic had lost really badly he had come into the bar as usual, and the fans had thanked him for coming that night, as though his presence cheered them up.

It would not be as easy, he said, for a Celtic fan to drink in a Rangers pub on the night before a match, although no harm would probably come to him. He didn't know why, he said, but the atmosphere would be more tense.

The atmosphere grew tense in Hereghty's during the last ten minutes of drinking time. People swallowed pints in two gulps and reached for another one or a double whisky. When they talked about Celtic, they moaned about the management. Rangers had a better ground, they had more money and could buy in top-class players.

Celtic was now a poor relation and the fans hated the idea because Celtic had once been their main source of pride.

The next day, half an hour before the match, a group of Celtic fans stood close to where the Rangers supporters entered the stands and shouted, 'Oou, aah, up the 'RA! Oou, aah, up the 'RA!' The 'RA was the IRA. They waved an Irish tricolour. Some police came by on horseback and others in a car. The fans continued to shout, 'Oou, aah, up the 'RA!' until one of them was snatched and put in the back of a police car. 'Scum,' one of his friends shouted at the police on horseback. And then there was more trouble as the police tried to detain this fan as well.

All this was noteworthy because it was isolated. The two groups of supporters were not involved in any scuffles or fights with each other. They took different routes to the ground. There was no real sense of aggression or violence. Everything was carefully monitored by the police. It could have been an ordinary match between two competing sides in any English city.

In my search for a ticket I had mentioned that I didn't care whether I sat with the Rangers fans or the Celtic supporters. Everyone thought that I was mad. As a Southern Irish Catholic I had no place on the Rangers side, I was assured. I was, by definition, a Celtic supporter.

When the match started I did not feel like a Celtic supporter. Celtic waved the Irish tricolour; Rangers waved Union Jacks. Celtic sang the Irish national anthem, 'The Soldiers' Song'; Rangers sang 'Rule Britannia'. There was a peculiar unreality about it, since this was Glasgow, and it was unlikely that either side had spent much time in England or in Ireland, places to which they now swore such fierce loyalty. All this emotion seemed wasted on these clapped-out images and clapped-out songs. This was parody without any humour, without the slightest hint of irony. It was intense, misplaced fanaticism. The Rangers crowd now sang 'The Sash', a Unionist anthem from Northern Ireland. A big group of Celtic supporters massed together in what is known as The Jungle chanted, 'Oou, aah, up the 'RA!'

At the beginning the Celtic fans excelled at exuding a feeling of grievance. If there was the least foul which escaped the referee's notice, they all booed and whistled and pointed their fingers. And then at dull moments in the game they chanted their sectarian slogans. But the rest of the time they forgot themselves, they simply wanted their team to win, and they went crazy if there was the remotest possibility of Celtic scoring a goal. They went wild when there was a near miss; they howled with despair and disappointment at bad play. And in the thirty-seventh minute when Celtic scored a goal, they danced with joy and screamed with delight. The Jungle, thick with green and white scarves and Irish flags, was transformed into a soup of smiling, yelping fans. I suddenly discovered that I was a Celtic fan too, that I was shouting and jumping as well. I wanted Celtic to win.

Then the Celtic fans had some great fun taunting the Rangers supporters. 'Can you hear Rangers sing? No, no, no', and 'What's It Like To Follow Shite?' and 'It's So Fucking Easy'. The goal had made all the difference. The match was now exciting. I watched every move, wanting our side to score again, wanting another goal to come and transform us all.

In the second half Rangers sang 'We are the Billy Boys', a reference to King William of Orange and the Battle of the Boyne, in which the Protestant side defeated the Catholics in 1690, and our side came back with 'Roddy McCorley', a rousing if melancholy ballad about an Irish Catholic hero on his way to be hanged. In the eighth minute we scored a goal. The Rangers fans did not move. There was not a sound from them, and thus it was easy to point over and shout 'Can you hear Rangers sing? No, no, no' once more.

It was not long before Rangers scored. It shouldn't have happened and our goalie, Packie Bonner from Donegal, hit the ground with his fist in rage and frustration. But we were still winning, even though Rangers were way ahead in the League, still in line for the European Cup and were now singing about being a Euro-army.

After the game most of the supporters stayed behind for a while to roar and cheer and wave their flags and shout abuse. As they left there were police everywhere to make sure that each group stuck to its own patch and went back to its watering hole in an orderly fashion. I stood in the car park and watched the Rangers fans leaving the stadium. A few Celtic fans stood on the other side of the wire and jeered them, making very rude signs. And a few of the Rangers fans made rude signs in return, but soon they grew bored and went off.

They were only half in earnest, just as the sectarian confrontation at the match seemed only half serious, a game full of empty slogans which meant nothing to the participants, left-over parts of what had been imported from Ireland. These slogans meant nothing much in Scotland, where there was no IRA and where the followers of William of Orange did not control political parties.

Back in the hotel later, Irish supporters of Celtic, who had come all the way from Dublin, and others who had come from England, were too drunk to talk. They moved unsteadily around the bar, muttering things I could only half understand. One of them had fallen asleep on a bench and his friends were trying to wake him up so they could go out on the town and celebrate some more. They were having a great time: their team had won, they were with their tribe, and there was hope still.

II

Croatia at Prayer

OPPOSITE THE HOTEL entrance, across the tiny canal, there was a two-storey building for sale. It was built of brick, and the pale pink plasterwork was faded and some of it had fallen off. I began to dream, to let my mind wander. What would it be like to live here, to know these streets as home? To go to the market and the shops? To curse the noisy barges moving down the canal with blocks and cement rather than watch them fascinated? To keep away from the railway station and Piazza San Marco where the tourists are? Venice as much as Paris was a city I knew through the lives of writers who had lived here. I wondered that day where Ezra Pound lived with Olga Rudge, and a snatch from the Cantos about St Mark's Church came into my mind: 'the gold gathers the light against it'. I promised myself that when I went home to Dublin I would look up where Pound lived in Venice and the other lines he wrote about the gold mosaic-work on the front of the church.

'The gold gathers the light against it'. I wasn't sure as I walked around Venice and went to a concert in Vivaldi's church on the waterfront that I wasn't misquoting the lines, but they stayed in my head. I don't know why. It was years since I had read them.

It was years, too, since I had read Henry James's *The Wings of the Dove*, but the name Merton Densher was in my mind as well, the name of the man who had come to Venice to court the heiress Milly Theale, who was dying. He was a journalist too, and penniless (we had that much in common), and he managed to find his apartment in Venice by noticing a piece of white cloth tied to a balcony. They still do that in Barcelona, but less and less, and I presumed that the property business in Venice had also become more sophisticated.

As I walked the streets of Venice and found a bar and had a few beers looking out on to the water ('the gold gathers the light against it') I began to think again about *The Wings of the Dove*. Phrases from the book came into my mind: the doctor's advice to Milly Theale – 'live all you can, it would be a mistake not to', or the news of Milly's discovery of Merton Densher's supposed treachery – 'she has turned her face to the wall'. Or Densher's sudden sighting of his arch-enemy Lord Mark in Venice, like the scenes in *Don't Look Now* where Donald Sutherland and Julie Christie keep believing that they see their dead child flitting through the streets.

I tried to recall the title of the Henry James short story, in which an old woman remembers as she travels with a companion along the Grand Canal that an ardent admirer once gave her a palace there, and in the story the two old ladies go and visit it. It was years since I had read that story and I wondered that night as I walked back to the hotel through the empty streets if I would not be better at home in Dublin reading, turning a page just now in a lamp-lit room, rather than hanging around a strange city with my mind full of half-baked quotations.

In the morning I walked towards the Frari, knowing that a map in Venice is no use as there are too many unmarked side streets, and you miss too much if you are concentrating on the map. The only thing to do is to walk in the general direction of your destination and hope to reach it by a route you had never come before. There were two bars I liked just across from the Frari, one for coffee and the other for *prosecco*, Italian champagne, which they served by the glass. But it was hard to idle in bars here. Nobody did. You spent your day on the streets, or in your hotel. In Venice, space was money, and you were expected to drink your coffee and leave within a reasonable time.

It was Holy Week now and I counted back sixteen years to when I had casually wandered into the Frari for the first time to peruse another churchload of paintings and seen Titian's *Assumption* above the high altar. I was amazed then by the soaring colours, the sense of drama, the world above us ready to receive the Virgin assumed body and soul into heaven while the world below held arms outstretched as she flew into the sky. I loved the size and scope of the painting and I had gone back again and again to look at it, and bought reproductions of it.

In Venice it was difficult to focus on paintings, the streets were so rich with beautiful faces and colours. It was hard to know sometimes why you were in a gallery standing staring at a painting when you could be outside in the world.

I settled on one painting, and in the years when I managed to go to Venice I went back to look at it. Maybe because they charged a small entrance fee the Frari was usually peaceful; a few people sat quietly taking in the painting. I stayed there for a while that day looking at the richness of the folds in the Virgin's dress, the flesh tone of the arms, and the light in the eyes of the mere mortals at witnessing a miracle.

I tried to look at it without thinking, just taking it in, but my mind wandered all the time. I knew that I would be back here in two weeks, and that I would come and sit here again, and I hoped that I would be safe where I was going. I promised that I would take no risks, until I reminded myself of the hero in Hemingway's *The Sun Also Rises* who went into the church on the day of the fiesta to pray that the fiesta would be good and the bulls would be brave. He, too, was a journalist. I remembered as I stood up to go that the fiesta for him was a bit of a disaster.

I had a train to catch. The previous day when I arrived I had bought my ticket for Zagreb in the railway station in Venice. I remembered that in Italy sometimes you have to go to another window to reserve your seat but when I asked the ticket-seller, he looked up at me and shook his head. No, he said, he didn't think I would need to do that, there would not be many people on the train. And when he said it I realised it was probably true. The war in the former Yugoslavia was still raging. Not many people would be travelling from Venice to Zagreb that Easter.

After Trieste the train was empty and there were several long stops and visits by passport control and customs control and security control. From Venice at first we had gone along by the sea, past beautiful villas in the hills. Now we were going south-west into the heart of Croatia, but there was no sign anywhere of the war, just half-shabby, old-fashioned stations and a landscape of tree-lined hills and slow rivers. Darkness fell. I read Mark Thompson's book *A Paper House: The Fall of Yugoslavia.* He lived in Zagreb and I would see him the next day, if he was free. An Englishman who had lived here for some years, he had written his book as the catastrophe of Yugoslavia was about to take place.

It was clear that he loved the country, its variety, its mixtures. Now that very variety and mixture had caused the war, and the news was full of the Vance-Owen plan, a complex and elaborate division of Bosnia into ethnic regions where there would be no variety. But this plan offered compromise, and at this time, Easter 1993, there were too many forces who had nothing to gain from compromise.

It was late when the train arrived in Zagreb and as far as I could make out only two other passengers got off at this, the final station. I walked to the Esplanade Hotel next door where I had a reservation. It was almost midnight.

The hotel was large, expensive and elaborately decorated. The rooms, however, were small and functional; the bathroom was like a bathroom on a train. I had a shower and changed my clothes and went downstairs to investigate what was what going on in the Esplanade Hotel. The nightclub was open, I was told at the desk, and the casino would be open until four.

As I walked to the nightclub I saw a big poster on a board. It was in English. RIJEKA AUGUST 1–21, it said in big letters: SUMMER SCHOOL WAR MEDICINE CROATIAN EXPERIENCE. And below it read: 'In the name of truth and science we feel obligated to offer the world our experiences, hoping that you will never use them in your practice. If you decide to come to Summer School War Medicine Croatian Experience you'll get a unique and high quality science concept, carefully prepared social programme and a lot of fun. Looking forward to seeing you this summer in beautiful Rijeka.' I couldn't wait.

The club was all mirrors and hidden lights. There was a Japanese man sitting alone, a group of young women at the bar, and a few Germans at another table.

The rest of the tables were empty, but when I tried to sit at a table beside the wall, one of the women came and told me that it was reserved. So I sat at a table in the middle, ordered a beer and remained there in the semi-darkness with loud disco music playing all around me until a show started. This involved a few girls going up on the stage and dancing to the music. They had clearly put some work into this, as their steps were in harmony, and they were lithe, well-built, good-looking, thus holding the attention of most of the nightclub. I had a second beer during the break in the music. Some men came and stood in the doorway as the girls came back, this time wearing nothing on top, and danced some more for us to the sound of loud American music. Silver globes hung from the ceiling, carrying the light with them, as the girls smiled at us as though we were a large and receptive audience.

There was a small bar outside the casino and four American men were having supper and drinking beers. One was much younger and went in, at regular intervals, to play at the casino, sometimes winning and sometimes losing, but always confident, bright-eyed, almost swaggering as he came back to his colleagues and his drink. A few times he talked about hookers until one of the older men remarked that he sounded pretty keen on them. It was interesting to see how he was going to deal with this.

'I just like talking about it,' he said confidently.

They talked, the three older ones, about their days at military academy. One of them told the story of finishing at Westpoint some time in the 1950s – he gave the date, but I was not taking notes, just sitting sipping a beer a good distance away, pretending I did not understand English – still in uniform, he said, he had turned up in Las Vegas with a friend and they were entertained there for free, just because they were two boys in uniform; put up free, free meals, free tickets to shows, because they were military boys, young American heroes. It was different then, he said, if you appeared anywhere in uniform you could have a ball. The others listened carefully, but said nothing. The younger man disappeared again and the three others talked then about places in what had been Yugoslavia with a sort of casual knowledge, just as they talked about superior officers and colleagues. They seemed at home here, at ease, as though nothing would surprise them.

In the morning I telephoned Mark Thompson and arranged to meet him at his apartment later in the day. I paid my hotel bill, and walked to the bus station. I knew that at some stage every day there was a bus to Medjugorje, in western Hercegovina. It was now Holy Thursday. The previous Easter Medjugorje had been closed to pilgrims because of the war, but now it was open to pilgrims again. In this remote place in the summer of 1981 the Virgin was reported to have appeared to four young people, three girls and a boy, known as the visionaries, and the apparitions, it was said, had continued ever since. Some pilgrims could see the sun spinning in the sky. In Ireland it had become, like Lourdes and Fatima and the shrine of Padre Pio, a place where pilgrims went in the summer, and many people had great devotion to it.

The bus station was a new glass and steel building; the woman in information directed me to the booth where they were selling tickets to Medjugorje. The bus left at seven in the evening. They did not know how long it would take, they told me, and they seemed to enjoy shrugging, making clear that any journey south from here would take God knows how long. Here, as in the railway station and the hotel, there was no sense of a war going on just twenty miles south. I don't know what I expected: stretchers everywhere, or men on crutches with bandaged heads. And I did not know if the quietness, the feeling of things absent, had been there before the war or not.

I caught a taxi up to the old city of Zagreb, to the Jesuit church behind which was an exhibition space showing the glories of the Jesuit legacy in Croatia, full of old paintings and religious objects. Outside, it was a warm spring day, with soft white clouds in the sky. The church itself looked like one of those dark, eighteenth-century constructs but it was different and surprising when I went inside. The plasterwork on the walls and ceiling was pure pink and white, which made the interior seem light-hearted, luminous, sweet, as though a new religion had been invented, one that treasured laughter and smiling, small acts of kindness and a light step above all other things. The pink would certainly never be allowed in Ireland.

I walked down through the city to the main square, where the cafés, bars and restaurants had put chairs and tables out and people were sitting enjoying the spring. A few times men in green camouflage uniforms went by – big, determined, rough-looking fellows – but mostly the atmosphere in the square was polite and pleasant. The cafés had a peculiar opulence which was mirrored in the shops and the goods for sale in the market. There was still no sign of war, only of plenty, of an Eastern European city used to a market economy, of a city where certain luxuries were taken for granted.

In the way the city centre was built, in the way people sold flowers and fruit at the stalls in the market, there was an airy light-heartedness, as in the decoration of the Jesuit church. The cathedral was a huge, high gothic structure, with soaring stone pillars. It could have been in Spain or France, except that the sombre style and shadowy grandeur of the interior was mellowed by the ceiling, which was painted blue with gold stars.

One might have imagined Croatian Catholicism as a lighter version of the religion, except that the evidence for this was vested merely in the interior decor of churches and was deceptive. The Serbs had another version of Croatian Catholicism, as an aspect of Croatian nationalism, which had come into its own when Croatia had autonomy under Hitler in the years between 1941 and 1946, and had involved the mass murder of Serbs and the forced conversion of Serbs to Catholicism. And this, in turn, in the years after the war, had become part of the state-sponsored history of Yugoslavia so that it was easy now to stir up emotions in Serbia and Bosnia and even in the areas of Croatia inhabited by Serbs, especially since the new Croatian government refused to distance itself from the crimes committed during the war, and insisted on using all the old symbols of the Croatian nation.

It was lunchtime on Holy Thursday. In Zagreb Cathedral there was a queue ten or twelve people long for confession. Most of those standing waiting were young. A few whispered to each other, but mostly they waited in silence. I went across the road and had my lunch, which was served with old-fashioned ceremony. There was a big table in the middle of the restaurant occupied by a single family, and there was a great deal of talk and laughter. Most of the other tables were occupied. The idea that there was a war on, that I was sitting in Zagreb during the height of the war in former Yugoslavia seemed a bizarre notion, something I had to keep reminding myself about. I kept searching for signs and clues but could find none.

Afterwards I walked along one of the main shopping streets, buying a CD of Bach harpsichord music at a fraction of the price I would have paid at home. It was wrapped up for me in brown paper in that meticulous style which reminded me of old shops in my home town where the assistants were expert at handling twine and making packages. At a junction there were flower sellers and there was a taxi rank. The shops were all busy and well-stocked. I collected my bag from the hotel and took a taxi to Mark Thompson's apartment in the suburbs.

The apartment was in a new block; the kitchen we sat in was bright. Mark's Croatian wife was heavily pregnant. He had a sauce for the spaghetti on the cooker as he tried to explain the deeply complex and fascinating nature of the society I had just stepped into. Every so often he had to turn and stir it as he tried to explain the background to what was happening in Croatia and then he would forget about the sauce and have to rush over and stir it once more. I sat and watched him, aware that I should probably stay here for days, taking notes and listening. He spoke about the legacy of 1941–46 and the failure of the Croatian leadership to come to terms with this period. They looked back on it as a period of independence, freedom and self-determination. For the Serbs it was a time of terror when the Croatians were prepared to expel them, convert them or exterminate them.

I asked Mark about Medjugorje. He had been there once, he said, and had seen all the objects – statues, holy pictures, rosary beads for sale. He didn't like the place and hadn't stayed long. I could sense his hostility to this sort of religion, but it didn't last because he knew so much about the roots of the war and the nature of the regions, and there was so little time to explain that he had to talk fast, while making sure that the sauce didn't burn.

Medjugorje was in western Hercegovina, he said, which believed itself to be Croatian. The Virgin, who had been appearing there, spoke pure Croatian. It was a strange, barren part of the world, clannish, with fierce loyalty to the mystical and abstract idea of Croatia. Within the new administration in Zagreb, there was an identifiable Hercegovinian lobby which operated as a sort of mafia.

When we had finished eating Mark drove me to the bus station. The bus was due to leave at seven o'clock but would not arrive until after midday the next day, we were told. Before the war, he said, you could get a train to Mostar, the nearest large town to Medjugorje, at night and arrive in Zagreb in the morning, two separate, rich cultures within the same country, but not now. Now even the land route was disputed and impassable. I could sense from him the real pain he felt at what was happening to the former Yugoslavia.

I did not wear a watch, but had a small traveller's clock in my pocket, which I decided not to consult during the journey. It would only make me miserable counting all the hours ahead, knowing how long this was going to take. There were a few people standing, and I wondered if they were going the whole way, or what they were going to do when darkness fell. A few men in camouflage uniforms were among the passengers, but as far as I could make out they were not armed. The seats were too small and the man beside me was already taking up too much space. I consoled myself with the thought that I had tried to get a flight to Dubrovnik but they were all booked up: this was the only way to get to Medjugorje.

It was going to be long, uncomfortable and boring, but it would have to be done. At the same time I felt a strange contentment. I was not going to a war, but to a shrine, and I was excited by this travelling and glad that there was nothing to be afraid of.

After a few hours we reached the coast. I could see the almost full moon reflected in the blackness of the sea. We stopped at a bar on the side of the road. The driver and his companion seemed to know people there; they sat together and after a while some food was put in front of them. The rest of us crowded around the bar. I had a beer, and stood outside in the stillness looking at the clear night sky and the moon.

The narrow road followed the coastline. There was no light in the bus, which felt overcrowded and claustrophobic. The man beside me fell asleep with loud snores and regularly lurched against me as though I were a pillow, or a soft object for making him comfortable. I pushed him back over to his own side with my elbow but it was not long before he had collapsed on top of me again. Once he woke and looked at me, but I stared out of the window, and he fell quietly asleep like most of the passengers.

When the bus came to a complete stop behind a line of lorries most people woke up, moving in their seats wondering what this delay was for, as the driver's companion, who had been up at the front of the bus, got out and walked in the darkness to the lorries. People whispered softly; a baby woke and whimpered and went back to sleep; there was no other sound. Half an hour went by; then another half an hour. I did not know whether this delay was included on the schedule or whether it meant that we would arrive an hour late in Medjugorje. This was something that would preoccupy me for much of the night, as we waited in long queues of lorries, vans and cars.

Suddenly, the driver's companion came running back, clearly telling the driver to start up now. Everyone on the bus came to life again as the engine revved and we began to drive on the opposite side of the road for maybe two or three miles, passing out lines of lorries. Then we were stopped and made to wait again, many of the passengers getting out to stretch their legs, and the driver's companion going up and standing with the officials, trying to negotiate a way for us to pass.

At times that night the scene was like something out of a dream. The sky was clear and the moon could be seen reflected in the sea below us. The road still twisted along the coast. And the few times I could see for miles ahead, I could make out the shape of queues of lorries in the moonlight. The intention was clear that, despite the war, trade would go on, goods would be moved up and down the country, there would be shortages only in the places under siege. Again and again we were given priority, the driver's companion was a skilled diplomat. But progress was slow; we were stopped all the time and then let drive ahead a bit and then stopped again until it became boring when all I wanted to do was sleep.

Well into the night we were stopped once more, and made to drive at speed on the other side of the road until we saw the ferry and the long island in the distance. I had seen it on the map, a small section of the coast that was held by the Serbs. No one was sure if it could be passed. It was obvious now that our only option was to go out on to the islands and make our way down using ferries. This explained the delays. We waited in the queue for the ferries, leaving twenty or thirty miles of queuing vehicles behind us. People stood up excitedly to watch and comment as the driver's companion, our hero, convinced the authorities to let us go ahead. We cheered him when he came back to the bus.

We made slow progress through the night until it was dawn. The bus was quiet, most people were asleep. The man beside me leaned his head on the back of his seat rather than on me, but he was restless, and I found it impossible to sleep.

We stopped for half an hour at Split. The man beside me took his bag and got off. A few people got on. I guessed it was about eight o'clock in the morning. There was still no sign of the war here; people seemed to be going to work and shops were opening. It was a clear day, and there were hints of a mild spring heat. As we drove south we passed through small villages, where the shops were open and where people wandered in the streets. The countryside grew wilder, with rocky, scrub-filled fields with wooded hills in the distance and snow-capped mountains beyond.

Once we passed through a village which had been destroyed. Every building was in ruins, the stone-work remaining but the roofs all caved in; there were indications that some houses had been burned down. No one on the bus paid much attention to it. It could have been a Muslim village destroyed by the Croatians, or a mixed village, but it had to be the Croatians who destroyed it since they controlled everything around here. By this time we had probably crossed from Croatia into Hercegovina, which was, as Mark Thompson had explained, even more fiercely Croatian.

I wrote the word Medjugorje on a piece of paper and handed it to a man sitting across from me. It was now close to midday. He nodded in recognition and pointed up ahead, signalling that it was not the next stop but the one following.

When I got off the bus I walked along a street of new buildings. Some had notices up saying there were rooms free. I went into a large building marked Hotel, but it was full. When I said I was Irish, the people at the desk smiled. A lot of Irish people came here, they said. They phoned another hotel nearby which had rooms free, and directed me there.

It was hard to work out, once I began wandering around the village, what buildings had been here before the apparition in 1981. The church, certainly, and the church buildings, but very little else. It seemed to me that the church had previously been some distance away from an old village, but now in front of it were brand new tea-shops and souvenir shops and shops which sold religious objects and postcards. There was a taxi rank, even, with a line of brand new BMWs. I sat down outside a tea-shop and listened to American voices at the table beside me talking about Sister Shirley who had just left for Vienna, how she was promised three days of darkness on the mountain. The woman talking was wearing a T-shirt with five words printed on it in big type: Prayer, Penance, Faith, Fasting, Conversion.

There were pilgrims waiting at the door of the priests' house. A young Australian priest told me they were all busy now, but Father Philip Pavich would presently be conducting the Good Friday ceremonies in English in the church and he would speak to me afterwards.

I had not thought about Christ's Passion for a long time. What I had experienced in Poland and Seville and Bavaria over the previous three Easters served to distract from the Crucifixion rather than draw attention to it. The reading on Good Friday in Medjugorje was from St John: 'After this, Jesus knew that everything had now been completed, and to fulfil the scripture perfectly he said: "I am thirsty." A jar of vinegar stood there, so putting a sponge soaked in the vinegar on a hyssop stick they held it up to his mouth. After Jesus had taken the vinegar he said, "It is accomplished": and bowing his head he gave up his spirit.'

I found myself listening carefully, like I would to any other story I had heard in childhood. This held my interest, caught me unawares. Suddenly, I found the story moving, and was now absorbed in the ceremonies, like everyone else in the packed church. Most of us were pilgrims. I could have been six or seven years old, at home, watching the ritual for the first time.

And then Father Pavich began to preach. He held up the cross and spoke in an American accent. He wanted to present to us 'an image of Jesus as a bloody victim on the cross'. The Church, he said, 'has always had the crucifix as a visible symbol. Let us ask today as we remember the crucifixion that the Lord would in his mercy show us the crucifix, that it would not disappear from our churches.'

He went on to speak about a movement gaining 'great momentum' to remove the crucifix from churches, to offer to us an image of the liturgy as merely a meal, 'completely devoid of its full meaning'. We must take, he said, 'this crucified body, sacrificed in this bloody fashion'. He was still bearing the cross aloft with his two hands. 'Jesus defeated Satan on the cross,' he said. 'It was for this that I came into the world.' He stopped and looked around the church. He held our gaze. And then he shouted at the top of his voice: 'Look at the cross!' There was silence and we all sat there in the church staring up at the ornate, silver cross in his hands and listening to the echo of his voice.

'The cross,' he said, 'will always be the central sign in our worship.' And he held it up again in silence. The congregation began to sing, 'Were you there when they crucified the Lord?' The second verse began, 'Were you there when they nailed him to the cross?' and the third, 'Were you there when they pierced him in the side?'

We had not prayed for peace. Instead, the images presented were of sacrifice and blood and violence. Just over the hill, maybe twenty miles away, there was a war going on, and the war would come closer during the months that followed. The Croatians would lay siege to the Muslims in Mostar, the nearest town, and the people of Medjugorje would block the convoys of aid and food on its way there, they would sit down and block the road. The ceremony I attended on Good Friday seemed more like a part of the war itself than something to heal the hatred that had caused the war.

Father Pavich, an American of Croatian descent, had a small office in a tiny house near the church. He is, like all the priests at Medjugorje, a Franciscan. He agreed to see me. He first visited Medjugorje, he said, in 1985, and came to stay two years later. Last Easter, he said, Medjugorje had been closed because the shrine was in danger of being bombed from the air. The bombing had gone on from April to June 1992. He had shut the church then and taken the Blessed Sacrament into the basement. But on 24 June 1992, the eleventh anniversary of the apparition, when it was clear that the bombing had been stopped and the shrine was safe, several thousands came and the church had been open since then. 'The Serbs set out to destroy us,' he said. 'They boasted that they were going to eliminate us.' But there was no physical damage done to the shrine.

'The Irish always knew who the English were,' he went on, 'and we always knew who the Serbs were. We couldn't trust anyone to protect us. We had no organised army. The local men mobilised themselves and effectively defended this area from Serbian aggression.'

'This country,' he said, 'between 1945 and 1990

was basically a disguise for a greater Serbia. It should have been called Serboslavia. After the war the Serbs got everything.' I asked him if the Serbs were all Orthodox. 'The Serbian Orthodox Church . . .' he began and as he spoke now he grew agitated, as though angry. 'This really is a fiction, a nominal thing. It is a store-front religion, a Hollywood set. Croatia, on the other hand, has been Catholic for thirteen hundred years.'

I asked him about the war years. 'There were attacks against the Serbs in Croatia between 1941 and 1945,' he said. 'There were some killings and unjust elimination of Serbs. Now they remind the world of this and they don't just want an eye for an eye, they want our head and legs and everything else. They razed the Croatian villages and there was no outcry, no reaction.'

I wondered if he felt as suspicious of his Muslim neighbours as he did of the Serbs. 'The Muslims will betray us', he said, 'if we don't defend ourselves.' He spoke about the downtrodden nature of Croatian Catholicism and managed a smile as he said: 'Only Croatian Catholics would live on this rockpile.'

There was an Irish pilgrim waiting for Father Pavich who wanted medals blessed. They went into the other room together as the man whispered the names of neighbours who also wanted to be prayed for at Medjugorje. Father Pavich was gentle now, pastor rather than political preacher. All his fanaticism had gone as he carefully noted each intention and request, promising that he would do precisely as the man asked. The man left to go back to the church and pray. He thanked the priest and smiled at me as he left. He seemed content. I asked Father Pavich as I was leaving why he had not prayed for peace. He presumed, he said, that most people would do that themselves privately; and he wanted to speak to the congregation about the importance of the crucifix as it was becoming an issue in the United States.

Outside the door to the church gallery a small crowd had gathered, hoping to be let in to pray before a framed painting of the Virgin. It was likely that Ivan, one of the visionaries, would come here to pray too – he usually did – and there was excitement about the possibility of his arrival. One Irishwoman was telling another how she had been to Fatima the previous year, but it was not the same, you don't have the same urge to go back, she said. 'This is living,' she said to her friend. It was true: the shrine was still small, and this year, because of the war, there were no big crowds, and all the visionaries were in their twenties. And as they lived here, they could be seen and visited.

The women told me that there was a special pilgrimage to the top of the hill beyond the church where the huge cross had been put up in 1933. The Virgin had told the visionaries that she would appear to them there at ten thirty tonight, so all the pilgrims were going to walk up in a procession later on. The two women stayed at the door watching all the time in case there was a chance that they would be allowed up to the gallery now. One of them told how she had placed a stone she had brought home from Medjugorje under her bed. It had been covered in dirt and clay, but after a few months when she went to look for it, she noticed that all the dirt and clay had gone; it was perfectly clean.

The Australian priest to whom I had spoken earlier came to the gallery door. I put out my hand to attract his attention and he signalled me to follow him. I could come in. The two Irish women asked me to say a prayer for them. The priest let several others in and then closed the door, leaving the small crowd still waiting outside.

We walked up a narrow winding stair to the gallery, where about fifty people were praying to a painting of the Virgin with the words *Regina Pacis* – Queen of Peace – written beneath. There were flowers and envelopes and parcels on the floor. One dark-skinned man was kneeling near the painting. I presumed that he was the visionary and I watched him carefully as he knelt in concentrated prayer.

Time passed. Most people had rosary beads and you could see their lips move as they prayed. There were benches to lean on, so some people were hunched down low. Suddenly, there was a shout from near the door. It was as though someone was having a fit. I couldn't work out why everyone had turned in that direction, until someone close to me whispered 'Ivan' and I realised that the young man who had just come in was Ivan and not the dark-skinned man near the front.

Ivan was not what I expected. He did not look like a visionary. He was wearing a white embroidered shirt, a flowery tie, grey slacks and a light-green blazer. His hair was modelled in an American 1950s style. He was pretty and sun-tanned. He could have been a cabaret singer or a TV presenter.

He stood and examined the room, making clear that he wanted people to move so that he could walk towards the image of the Virgin without having to push his way through. He was obviously used to this. The style was polite and warm. He exuded a modest pride in his own authority in the room. I noticed his fancy tie-pin, and as he came closer I did not believe that the sun-tan was real. Most people carried a camera and they began to take photographs as he knelt down in front of the picture and joined his hands. This was show-business. A nun came and took a photograph of him, his face silhouetted against the painting.

Everyone knelt as he knelt. People handed him notes. It was hard to imagine that he had seen the Virgin; it was easier to feel that he had been in America, yet the prayers all around him were said with great fervour. He knelt there praying like a star among us all.

And when it was over he stood up and walked through the crowd like Moses through the Red Sea, touching hands, smiling, noting every face in the room. He motioned us to leave, including the people who had moved towards the painting of the Virgin and were touching it. I shook his hand. He spoke to the couple behind me in English, in an American accent, saying that he had been in Australia recently for thirty-five days. He had keys in his hands; they could have been the keys of a car, but it became clear that they were the keys of the door downstairs, which he wanted to lock when we had all left.

He had none of the unworldly innocence of the peasant touched by the shock of an apparition. And yet there was a sort of distance in his smile, a remote suaveness in his charm as he stood at the door and spoke to people, the grooming and the bearing impeccable. And then he walked away on his own.

As I approached the hill at about eight-thirty that evening, I could see torchlights halfway up as the pilgrims made their way to the top, stopping at appointed places for prayers, making the journey a sort of Way of the Cross. The scene with Ivan had lightened the day somehow; it had taken away some of the ferocity of the sermon and the interview with Father Pavich. There was, I supposed, a sort of innocence also in Ivan's dressing up in those clothes and playing the part of a star in a place which was so barren and rugged and poor that a tie-pin or a light-green jacket would seem like mini-apparitions in themselves. It gave him a dignity and set him apart, and this might be important if you were a visionary in a small village.

I had no torch, but I followed three young French people who had. The climbing was easy, and when we arrived at the top there were maybe a hundred people sitting around the enormous stone cross. There was a half moon in the cloudy sky and it was becoming bitterly cold.

I stopped to listen. I was sure that I had heard firing in the distance, which made other people stop talking and listen too. There was rumbling in the distant hills, faint sounds that could have been thunder but sounded more like gunfire. An American told me that Mostar was tense now and was ready to blow up, and most likely the firing was coming from there. But it stopped soon afterwards and there was no more firing that night.

A woman in the American group began to talk, as more and more pilgrims arrived. Our Lady had said she would appear for twelve years, the woman told us, so this would be the last year of apparitions, and this one, the one we were about to witness, this might well be the last apparition. Everyone in the group nodded. They all expected to see the Virgin. I had thought that only the visionaries could see the apparition.

I stood up and walked over to the cross. I heard someone speaking with an English accent and I asked him what time the apparition was due to happen. He knew as little as I did, and seemed as puzzled that everyone here actually expected to see the Virgin. He had driven a lorry-load of supplies from England to help out, he said, and he was staying with a local family. The shed behind their house, he told me, was a complete arsenal, full of anti-aircraft guns and long-range missiles as well as small arms. He was whispering now, and talking as though he had been desperate to tell somebody this. These people were fighting a war, he said. Most of the pilgrims did not understand this.

Just then, pilgrims began to move towards the cross, which had the dates 33–1933, marking the one thousand nine hundredth anniversary of the Crucifixion, etched on the stone. Most people kept their torches on, and there were prayers, while cameras flashed. Then word spread that the torches were to be turned off and no cameras to be used. It was time.

Everyone stood and watched the cross. There was a hushed silence. Once or twice there was a flash from a camera. It seemed colder now as we all stood there without speaking. The silence went on, and the concentration, as everybody stared into the sky around the cross. One minute went by. Two minutes. Maybe more. And then the prayers started, and everyone relaxed and word was passed around that there had been a message from Our Lady, and the message was: 'Mary says now is the time to decide for God.'

'Life or death,' a middle-aged Englishman close to me said. 'It's choosing life or death.' We were beginning to walk back down to the village. 'Have you chosen?' he asked, but I don't think that he expected an answer. I stayed close to him because he and his two companions each had torches and, being good Christians, they were concerned that the person with no torch should be looked after. All the way down they shone their torches on the ground for me to make sure that I did not slip. Some of the ground was difficult. They talked and then in mid-conversation one of them would start a prayer, an 'Our Father' or a 'Hail Mary', and say it in a loud voice while walking down the hill.

It was now past one o'clock. Most people were

waiting for taxis or mini-buses to collect them and take them to their lodgings. I decided that it would be quicker to walk, and as I neared the village I came across a bar which was still open. There were three tables of locals playing cards, and others were standing around watching the game, or drinking, or chatting. They were all men. This was a typical image of a village anywhere in Europe on a Friday night. It was all laid back and casual, except for the grumpy barman. He gave me a beer eventually, and I stood watching how serious these card games were, each card noted as though it was a rising price or a moral issue, and then the next card put down, with all eyes on it. A few men in the bar were drunk, but the men at the tables were sober, despite the fact that they were drinking as well.

When I was on my second beer an American priest and two young men I recognised as seminarians came into the bar, and succeeded in enticing a beer each from the barman. They, too, had been on the mountain, and they were friendly and cheerful. They presumed, I think, because I was Irish or because I was in Medjugorje that I was a practising Catholic, and I felt a bit uneasy about this. None the less, there was something I wanted to know that I had not asked anyone on the way down the mountain. Had they seen the Virgin? Had there been an apparition? I thought that it was all right to ask. The priest said that he had seen her. He smiled in a way which stopped me asking him to describe what he saw, as though it was too personal to describe, and perhaps a bar at this time of night was not the right place for such things. I asked him if he knew at precisely what point she had appeared and at what point she had left? He did, he said, he had witnessed that. The two seminarians, like myself, had witnessed nothing. One of them said that he was not ready. The card games were still going on as we left to go to our hotels. I felt as if I had been in Medjugorje for weeks.

I needed two nights sleep and when I woke in the tiny hotel room in the morning I could have stayed in bed all day. But I knew that Marija, one of the visionaries, was giving an audience outside her house at nine. I got a taxi there, just by saying her name; the houses of the visionaries are among the main destinations for the taxi drivers. The journey, which took a few minutes, cost four dollars.

There was a little crowd in front of her house, maybe thirty people, all English-speaking. She did not speak English, but would have a translator at hand. The house was a small, square, two-storey building, built perhaps just after the war. When she came out she smiled at us. Her clothes were plain, and her hair was straight. She was not like Ivan. She seemed much shyer, less self-possessed, more a modest woman from a small village.

She began to speak, telling us that Our Lady asked for strong faith, not just praying with words. She recited the 'Our Father' in Croatian, and as she did so a neighbour passed and she waved and smiled in the middle of the prayer, not irreverently, but as though she was including the person passing in her thoughts and prayers. 'Give glory to Our Father,' she said, 'and thank him for everything, for good and for bad, so that we know how to accept everything. You cannot learn to pray with your heart. You have to live it. Our Lady says: Dear children all of you have difficulties. You think Jesus and I are far from you. Our Lady says: we are near you. You must open your heart. She will not be happy unless we give up sin and not sin again. Our Lady would be most happy if we could renew family prayers, so Satan can do nothing to us. Our Lady says

Satan is very strong.

'Our Lady recommends that we wear something blessed on ourselves,' she went on, telling us about the importance of the Mass and confession, and the problems of young people. All the time as she spoke there was a real warmth and concern in the way she smiled. 'Our Lady wants us to be the carriers of peace,' she said. 'First peace in our hearts, and then in our families. Together we pray for peace in the world.' I looked around and wondered if the arsenal the Englishman had told me about was anywhere near here. 'When Our Lady appears I will recommend all of you to her,' Marija said as she ended, still smiling.

People had put petitions on small folded pieces of paper on the steps of her house, hundreds of them. Now more people came with more petitions as Marija stood in front of a couple and put a hand on each of their heads and said a prayer over them. We all waited in line for her to come to us. When it was my turn, she approached and she put her right hand on my head and her left hand on the head of the woman beside me. She gripped my skull, her fingers were strong and she put as much power into the touch as she could. She began to whisper prayers. I could feel her concentration. I tried to leave my mind empty, not to think at all. Although there were others waiting, she was in no hurry. We both stood there in front of her house with everybody watching as she held us. When she took her hand away I found that I was trembling and wanted to turn away and be on my own as quickly as I could.

12

Slovenian Spring

LATER THAT MORNING I spoke to the Franciscan Father Tomislav Pervan, who had come to Medjugorje first in 1982, a year after the apparitions had begun. He was a deeply serious, intense man in his late forties. He believed in the visions, he said, and, in his opinion, the early attacks on what was happening at Medjugorje were communist propaganda on one hand but arose also from long-running differences between the Franciscans who ran the parish and the local bishop, who had no control over them. 'All is the fruit of fraud, disobedience to the Church and disease,' the bishop had said.

It was easy for word of the visions to spread, not just through the tightly-knit and fiercely Croatian community, but through the powerful international network of the Franciscan order. Yugoslavia was open; tourists did not need a visa. Father Pervan watched the village change. Most men worked in Germany and sent money home; the local economy had depended on this. Now there was a total transformation in the parish. When pilgrims came they brought hard currency ('where there is money, there is Satan,' Father Pervan said) and this offered temptation to the people.

A few times I asked him about the war. He believed that the West should intervene to disarm the Serbs; only then could proper negotiations begin. What religion are the Serbs? I asked him. He laughed and then sighed. Not even 10 per cent of them are baptised in Orthodox churches, he said. Most of them are without religion and very superstitious, and the Church there now is closely connected to the government, it is the ideological leader of the occupation of Bosnia. Did he mean that the Orthodox Church was behind the war, or approved of the war? 'There is some kind of Old Testament attitude at work,' he said. 'The idea of ethnic cleansing comes from that, from the Book of Joshua, for example.'

He was living in Mostar now, where tensions between the Croats and the Muslims were high. The Muslims were not prepared to accept any of the agreements on offer, he said. 'For centuries, the Muslims were powerful and we were serving. My grandfather was the servant of a Muslim.'

Why did as many as five thousand people come to Medjugorje just two days after the original apparition on 24 June 1981? he asked rhetorically. It was on the feast of St John the Baptist, who prepared the path for Jesus and his coming, he said. It was 'prophetic', he said, as we live in a *fin de siècle*, as we move towards another millennium in which the western world is built on money and has no moral values. The visionaries are human beings, like saints, like apostles, he said. He never saw anything himself but he did not find it hard to believe. Medjugorje is like the Book of Revelation, Chapters Twelve and Thirteen, he said.

The previous day, in front of the church, I had bumped into an American reporter. She had been watching me taking notes and wondered if I was in the same business. We went and had coffee, and we talked about the shrine. She was bright and sharp, full of intelligence and curiosity. When I met her again after my interview with Father Pervan I had a lot to tell her: about Maria putting her hand on my head, about the men playing cards in the bar ignoring all these visions, about the lights going out on the hill the previous night, about the sounds of firing in the distance. She, too, had been working and, as we spoke, I was suddenly back in my own sceptical world. We talked for a long time. We didn't question the visionaries' sincerity, nor the pilgrims' faith, we questioned our own fitness to be here; and I did not know as I stood up to go how much longer I would be able to stay, remaining with these half-medieval beliefs, half-pretending that I shared them.

I had heard the night before that Ivan, the visionary whom I had seen all dressed up the previous day, would be speaking in English at five o'clock. At about a quarter to five I caught a taxi to his house, which was more remote than Maria's. We had to drive down a dirt track to a cluster of small houses. A woman standing outside one of them confirmed that this was Ivan's house and went inside to get him. When he came out he was still well dressed, still looking like a pop star. He explained that his meeting with pilgrims would not take place here, but at the church. He would be there in about half an hour. He turned and walked back into the house, like a man who was busy, who had been interrupted. I took the taxi back.

I met one of the American seminarians who was also going to see Ivan. Several times as we spoke he mentioned Our Lady or Our Lord in reverential terms. He had spent the afternoon praying in the church, he said. He appeared to think that I might have been doing the same, and I felt maybe I should explain to him that I hadn't prayed since I was a child and would not be sure how to go about it now.

We went into a modern building near the church and found seats; the room was filling up with English-speaking pilgrims. When Ivan arrived he was wearing a brown blazer and a light brown flowing tie with matching handkerchief. 'She appeared last night,' he said. 'She was praying for all of us. She said: "Dear children, tonight in a special way your mother will call you: you have to decide for God." And I think myself that it is a very clear message. All of you know that day twelve years ago Our Lady gave us a lot of messages, among them peace and prayer are the most important. Who is she? we asked. "I am the Blessed Mother. I am the Queen of Peace. Peace, peace, peace, dear children, peace within yourself, peace within families." These were the first messages to be sent to us in the whole world.'

He stopped and looked at us and then said that he was ready to take questions. There were hands up all over the room. The first question was: 'What does the Blessed Virgin Mary say about the youth of the world? And what about parents?' On the wall there were huge rosary beads, each bead the size of a large kiwi fruit. I found myself looking at it, concentrating on it because the question was so banal, and Ivan's answer came in the same tone. He talked about the problem of drugs and alcohol and mass media and moral issues and the influence of these on young people. He spoke about the need for parents to spend time with their children, and to teach them to pray. At the age of four, he said, you could begin with three 'Our Fathers' and one 'Hail Mary', at five increase this to four 'Our Fathers', at six to seven 'Our Fathers', at seven to a whole Rosary.

There was nothing wrong with young people keeping company, he said. He kept company himself, but sometimes, he added, it was worth staying at home.

He sounded like a mild young priest, as he gave us all advice, rather than a man who had seen visions.

Next an American explained the sense of negativity which emerged from the messages that visionaries in the United States received. Here there is hope, she said. And then she asked her question: 'Has the Blessed Virgin ever said anything about three days of darkness?' 'Nothing,' Ivan said. 'I don't know anything about this. I am not scared, maybe you are scared. We have to remove the darkness from our souls, that is the most dangerous, and let in the light.'

'When she appears is she crying?' was the next question. Ivan said, 'She was a little bit sad on Good Friday, for example, but usually she is not sad.' 'Does she appear in gold?' 'Yes, on feast days.' 'Were you taken to heaven, hell and purgatory?' 'Only heaven . . .' 'What was it like?' 'It's very difficult to describe heaven. Each word is too poor. That is what the Bible told us. You will see when you come to heaven. I also have to do my best like everyone else, no one has privileges.'

'Does she appear alone, or are there angels, or is Jesus with her?' 'On Christmas she has little Jesus on her lap, and sometimes with angels.' 'My three year old is very close to Mary. She says that angels have sparkling wings. Do angels have sparkling wings?' 'Yes, we could say yes . . . The child is a very good example to her mother,' he looked up and smiled gently at the questioner.

'Has Our Lady ever mentioned the condition of the Church?' 'If we are weak then the Church will be weak; if we are strong then the Church will be strong. We must strengthen our faith to strengthen the Church.' 'Are flash photographs disturbing?' 'During the apparitions we are in a state of ecstasy and we can't see everyone around us, or see flashes, but it is not a proper time to take pictures.'

He smiled again. He had taken his last question, even though there were still eager hands up all over the room. The young man in front of me kept his hand up until Ivan had left. I asked him what his question was. His accent was American. 'I wanted to ask if the Virgin had a message for seminarians.' He was totally sincere, and I could imagine the predictable sincerity of Ivan's answer. The young man was looking at me as though I was going to say something. But what was going through my mind, God forgive me, would be saved up for the American journalist. I would never have told the seminarian that Our Lady had sent a special message for him. 'She knows you're doing it. She's seen you doing it. And her message is: stop it.' As we walked out together, I tried to make sure that he would not know what I was thinking.

The American journalist had been at Ivan's question and answer session as well. We sat on the wall of the church grounds and compared notes; we both agreed that if the Virgin appeared to us we would be a bit more excited about it and our descriptions of it would be a bit more vivid. I told her what had come into my head when I thought of the Virgin's message for the seminarian. She fell around laughing. It was the devil, I said, it wasn't my fault. We both laughed more. And just then the Australian priest went by and stopped and looked at us and our irreverence with disapproval. We both sat up straight and stopped laughing. It was like being in school. We had been caught. He passed on and did not look back. We walked around to the gazebo at the back of the church.

The pale sun was going down in the western sky. There would be only another hour or two of daylight. The clouds, too, were pale. But there were crowds of people, most of them Americans, staring at the sun, pointing at it. 'Look at it, oh my God, look at it, it's really spinning,' a woman said in an American accent. We looked at it, but it did not move. It was a singularly undramatic soft sun in the hour before twilight. It was not moving. Or rather, for me it was not moving, nor for my journalist friend. But for those around us, it was spinning in the sky, and they stared at it and cried out in wonder and admiration. I looked at it again: it was emphatically not spinning.

I knew that there would be a special Mass this evening, that all these people would be here, that the seminarians so serious about their faith and their future would be here, that the two priests I had interviewed, so full of Croatian Catholicism, would be here, as would the priest I had met in the bar the previous night, as would the Australian priest who had caught us laughing. I decided I was going to leave now; I had been in Medjugorje long enough. I left the American journalist looking at the sky.

I went to the taxi rank and asked how much it would cost to go now to Split, about one hundred and fifty kilometres away. They discussed it for a while and eventually one man said that he could do it for a hundred dollars. It was more than I had expected to pay, but I wanted to go, and I agreed. He drove me back to the hotel. I checked out and we set off on our journey north. He spoke no English, but understood when I told him that I wanted to go to the airport in Split.

For miles there was only scrub and rock. Nothing grew in this land and there were no animals, just a fierce barrenness in the countryside and new houses and restaurants in the villages, where men were playing boules in the squares. But after ten kilometres or so there was a view of a long fertile valley. We were stopped at a check-point and told to drive back for about five kilometres to have papers checked and then return to this point. The driver did not argue. Later, we were stopped again and the driver was told to remove his taxi sign altogether, take it down and put it in the boot. After another fifty kilometres the land became rugged and desolate again. We were travelling along mountain roads in the twilight now. There was nothing growing; the barrenness was surreal almost, beyond belief. For miles and miles there were just fields full of rock.

I remembered the priest's remark that only Croats would inhabit this territory. It was this which gave the war in the former Yugoslavia its peculiar bitterness: there was good land, as in the fertile valley we had passed, right next to bad land. Thus any invader would leave the bad, intractable land to the vanquished, who would remain there. All of Europe had, at some point or other, been invaded and populations cleared. But here, as in Ireland, there was something un-European about the landscape which meant that natives could inhabit the high ground, becoming tough and resentful as they lived in miserable conditions, while the invaders, the English or the Turks, could use the good land. As a result mortal enemies could live close to each other. It created perfect conditions for a long and complex civil war.

At last light we came to the sea; it was a relief to escape from the unremitting poverty of the land we had been through. It was easier to feel lighter as we moved along this coast, climbing the corkscrew-shaped roads and then dipping again, and the car going fast, the driver sure of himself as he came to each turn, his headlights now on full. It could have been the Riviera, and I felt a surge of happiness at what I had left behind: I concentrated for a while on Maria's hand on my head and the feeling it had given me. But I was glad the rest of it was over.

For the last forty kilometres we were back in a Europe of motorways and dual-carriageways. The airport was still open when we got there at around nine-thirty, and I was able to book a ticket for a flight to Zagreb the following morning. The taxi driver made enquiries and discovered there was an hotel about five kilometres towards the city. He drove me there, and I paid him his money. He smiled as I counted it out.

The hotel was down a tree-lined avenue and seemed quiet and modest from the outside. Inside there was a long counter and a huge lobby-cum-bar. There must have been two hundred soldiers sitting in the bar and the lobby. All of them were in uniform, most were in their twenties, all of them had cropped blond hair and blue eyes, half of them were smoking, all of them were drinking cans of beer, some were playing cards, others were just talking. From a village full of pilgrims I had come to an hotel full of Teutonic soldiers. There were rooms to spare, they told me at reception. The soldiers were Belgian, the receptionist told me when I asked her.

I flew back to Zagreb in the grey, rainy morning. It was now Easter Sunday. At a turn in the street I passed a dark covered area, like a little cave. A middle-aged woman was reading a litany out loud from an old prayer book, using a magnifying glass to make out the words. Two older women were chanting the responses. There was a shrine in the corner with a statue of the Virgin; people were standing praying, facing the statue and the votive candles in the drizzly morning. There were names on plaques stuck to the walls all around, names of the dead, I assumed, whose loved ones had put up these small memorials to them.

As I walked down towards the cathedral I could have been in any city in central Europe on a Sunday morning. I felt that strange pleasure at not belonging here and being up and wandering around before most of the natives. There was no one on the street and there were no cars. There were crowds outside the cathedral, however, and loudspeakers relaying the Mass. They had been doing repairs to the façade which meant that there was only a long narrow entrance from the square. I pushed my way through. Inside, High Mass was being concelebrated, the lights were on all over the church, some people were still queuing for confession, and the aisles were full of people standing. I stood beside a man and his small son, who had his arms clasped around his father's neck as he watched everything; the thick pillars rising to the painted ceiling, the stained-glass windows; the organ, the choir singing the Kyrie eleison.

Close to the cathedral was a church which fronted on to the street. It was ringing its bells loudly, people were going in, but by the time I reached it there appeared genuinely to be no room. I could see icons and candles on the altar, but the door behind me would not close. A couple arrived behind me. 'Catholic?' I asked them, indicating the altar. 'Greek Catholic,' he said, and then he pointed towards the cathedral: 'Catholic,' he said. I stood out of his way and walked back.

It was a quarter to twelve and Mass was coming to an end. The organ was playing and the choir was in full flight; we could hear the music through the loudspeakers. In the next square they were selling daffodils and fruit and Easter trinkets; outside the cathedral people were greeting each other, they stood in groups or singly and chatted or looked around. Facing the church across the square there was a sight straight from an Irish village on a Sunday morning: men stood idly taking in the scene, hands in their pockets, looking at everyone, watching each move carefully out of the sides of their eyes. They were like secret police.

People walked down to the main square from the cathedral that Easter Day. Even in the drizzle the cafés had chairs outside. A children's trolley car was full of children and their parents, its toy bell announcing that it was ready to set off. They were all laughing and waving.

Suddenly, the city was empty again; there were just a few people walking home from Mass. The shops were all closed. The place felt desolate, shut-down, intensely private, as though people had learned over years to expect nothing from these streets and relied instead on remaining indoors. I went down to the city's art gallery. It seemed closed, which struck me as strange, since it was not yet one o'clock. I found a bell eventually and buzzed it a few times. A young man came to the door and explained politely that the gallery was closed. 'Why?' I asked him. 'Closed,' he said, 'the pictures have been taken down because of the war.' For a moment I was going to ask: 'What war?'

I walked to the Intercontinental Hotel and had a hamburger. Outside, in the car park, I had noticed UN and UNHCR jeeps. Inside now, there were only American voices in the bar. An American woman was talking to the waitress about her son: 'I hope that he wasn't too much of a pain in the neck, but thank you for making his sandwich just like he gets it at home.'

I knew that there was a train to Trieste at two o'clock and took a taxi to the railway station. I wanted to keep moving, leave Medjugorje further and further behind. The station seemed to be the largest employer in the city. There was one office for buying second-class tickets, another for buying first-class tickets. There were three people in the change money office: one to do the sums, one to handle the money and one in the middle to watch the customer and his two colleagues.

The train was almost empty and did not stop until it reached the border with Slovenia. A policeman came into the carriage and asked for my passport. He smiled when he saw Ireland and handed it back to me. I had become interested in Slovenia, because I had read the chapter 'Slovenian Spring' in Mark Thompson's book *A Paper House*. Thompson quoted a Slovenian friend: 'It's not how small a nation is, but whereabouts it happens to be small.' He added: 'Slovenia was small in the right place.' The country had fewer than two million inhabitants. 'In Slovenia,' Mark wrote, 'the Ministry of Agriculture has one telephone line, the football commentator on national television works from Monday to Friday as a family doctor. It takes half an hour to look at all the pictures in the National Gallery.'

There was no war in Slovenia then. And reading about the place made me feel it was a fiction, a country made up by Borges, perhaps, or a playful Central European novelist and miniaturist. It was a small place which had slipped away. But at the border between Slovenia and Italy three different uniformed Slovenians came to my compartment. Their uniforms were impeccable, as were their manners. They checked my passport, and my luggage and my ticket, but I felt that they were simply representing Slovenia, making sure that passengers on the train between Croatia and Italy knew that their new little country existed. I decided to go there.

Two days later, after a suitable period of rest and recreation away from the strangeness of Eastern Europe, big dinners in Trieste and long tours around its bars and cafés, I set out for Ljubljana by car with Nick Carter, a friend who lives in Trieste.

It was still rainy, the motorway between Trieste and Ljubljana was grim, and the city itself, as we parked the car in the main street, did not look promising either. The thing which made Slovenia unlike all the other new states which had emerged since the fall of the Berlin Wall was the banknotes. They were designed in the most odd and sumptuous colours. The back of the fifty tolar note was in shades of blue and purple fading into brown, with globes and aspects of the solar system in the background. The notes were hyper-modern, done with flair and imagination, full of visual flourishes and yet remaining discreet. Beside them, the Croatian banknotes looked not only dull, but with the Catholic cathedral in Zagreb depicted on the back of every note of every denomination, politically unimaginative, making clear that Croatia was going to be a state for Catholics. The Slovenian notes, on the other hand, suggested a world of infinite possibility.

We walked towards the river. The view from the main bridge was more like a scene out of Hans Christian Andersen than anything out of Borges. The river was narrow and flowed slowly, and the banks were lined with delicate willow trees. The bridge itself could carry traffic, but there were two ornate side-bridges for pedestrians. The houses had mansard roofs. Along the quays there were small bars and restaurants. The atmosphere was of civility and comfort, a world untouched by any of the wars which had scarred other European cities. It was nearly dark now and the lights of the castle above the city, and the lights on the river, made the bridge and the willows appear part of an illustration or a dream rather than a real city in the former Yugoslavia during Easter Week 1993, the worst year of the war.

I looked up at windows in the old city, trying to imagine the pleasures of waking up in the morning here. I started to picture myself here reading in a lamp-lit room and then turning to the window, as I could see a figure doing, and looking down at the soft river and the beautiful trees. We ate that night in the cellars of a former nunnery; there was a ceremony and a politeness everywhere we went which made the whole evening feel unreal, as if we were taking part in a movie. What sort of politics would such a city produce, or what sort of politics would produce such a city? I knew that Slovenia had seceded from Yugoslavia in a mild ten-day war, in which fewer than fifty people had been killed. It was as though it had shrugged the larger country off.

The following day as I wandered around, Nick having gone back to Trieste, the place seemed even more miraculous in the spring sunshine. There was a bookshop opposite the hotel with brand new translations of contemporary European fiction into Slovene. The books, like the banknotes, were superbly designed, full of light touches and technical skills.

There was any number of places to have breakfast. All morning people sat at windows eating cake and drinking coffee. There was nothing magnificent in the city; everything was perfectly to scale. If it were an imaginary city, then its imagined politics would have the same respect for scale, for the citizen as pedestrian; would prize the ordinary, the small civic virtues, order and tolerance. As I walked around I felt I was in a low-church Protestant Scandinavian city. I could not feel the weight of the Catholic Church, even in the churches themselves. In the airiness of the city, the lightness, it was hard to find any sense of religion at all. It was a city which had been constructed for the convenience of its citizens rather than as a way of establishing the authority of its rulers or its deities. I wondered about it. I re-read the chapter about Slovenia in Mark Thompson's book: 'Its population is more nearly homogeneous than that of any other republic. More than 90 per cent of Slovenia's 1.9 million inhabitants are ethnic Slovenes and 98 per cent of Slovenes in Yugoslavia live in their republic . . . The Slovenes used Yugoslavia to outgrow it, and they are the only certain beneficiaries of its ending.'

I rang Mark in Zagreb and asked him if there was someone here I should talk to; he gave me the name of Pavel Gantar, an assistant professor of urban sociology at the university, who spoke English and had been involved in the ten-day war. I telephoned him and we arranged to meet the following morning.

That night I found another Ljubljana, the city which had given us the punk-rock bands of the 1980s. Across the river there was a long street of cafés and bars. As the night wore on the bars filled up with pure counter culture. You defined people not by the expression on their faces or what they drank but the quality of their earrings. The atmosphere was sexually alive: in the way they drank a beer, or smiled, or found a table, people oozed sex. There was a sense, too, that no one was posing, that you wouldn't get away with posing here; people meant to look like that, talk like that, strut into the bar like that. It was another aspect of the city, a darker edge to the lightness of the architecture, which made the place seem even stranger, even closer to something poor old Faust might have seen in visions before they came to take him away.

I awaited the visit of the assistant professor of urban sociology with considerable interest. He came to the hotel at around ten o'clock in the morning. He was a tall man in his early forties, casually dressed in denims, with that vague distracted air which comes from time spent in libraries and classrooms. I asked him how he had imagined things would work out, say, a decade ago? He remembered being in a pub in London in 1984 trying to explain the future of Yugoslavia to a friend. He believed then that one part of Yugoslavia would follow the Westminster pattern: a market economy and a liberal politics. But he also believed that another part of the country was more oriented towards Russia.

After Tito's death, there was an attempt to pursue Tito's policies without Tito and that didn't succeed. Until 1988 and 1989 nobody expected that separation would happen very quickly or at all. Between 1988 and 1990 a lot of different concepts and solutions to the problems of Yugoslavia were put forward, all sorts of ideas, but the Serbs seemed to believe that Yugoslavia would never be allowed to break up.

Was he a Slovenian nationalist? I asked him. Did he feel an emotion about his country, his nation? He felt no personal emotion about Slovenia as a nation, he said. His tone was dry, matter-of-fact. Did he not want Slovenia to be a free nation? He never asked such questions, he said. He did have very strong national feeling about the Slovenian economy being run from Belgrade, but the idea of leaving Yugoslavia was proposed by very few. The idea of seceding from the federation was prompted, he told me, not by nationalist feeling, but by the desire to secure normal life. It became an imperative to leave.

Economists were doubtful, he said, about the advantages of leaving Yugoslavia. Half of all markets for Slovenian produce would be lost. But in the beginning of 1990, in a series of financial operations, Serbia, which controlled the economy from Belgrade, benefited at the expense of the other areas in the Yugoslav federation, and this was observed and noted by economists in Ljubljana. It was felt, from then on, that in three to four years Slovenia would have to achieve a sort of negative independence from Yugoslavia, simply in order to protect its economy.

So where was he when Slovenia declared independence on 25 July 1991? He was in Ljubljana, he said, and the following night he went out to dinner with friends to celebrate. His friends were all more or less rationalists so there were no really stirring speeches or emotional moments. He went home at two-thirty and fell asleep. He was woken up at eight o'clock by the telephone. The voice on the other end asked him to come immediately to the base from which he operated as a mobilising instructor in the local army. He turned on the radio and heard that Yugoslav troops were on the road. The border posts had been taken by the Slovenes and the Yugoslav army was under instructions to re-take them.

I asked Pavel Gantar if he saw any action. Not much, he said. He found a broken-down tank with three soldiers in it. People came to look at them, so he made sure they were given coffee and food and sent home safely. Did nobody want to kill them, or injure them? No, no, he said, absolutely not. There was no hostility shown to them.

It was a seven- to eight-day mobilisation, and there were only two cases of volunteers hiding or evading the call. Some people joked, he said, that if normal traffic had been on the roads more would have been killed in those days.

After the short war, then, there was politics. He was forty-three, Pavel said, but if he were in government he would be one of the oldest. There arose a new political élite, ministers aged thirty-four or thirty-five or even less. He smiled when I remarked on the beautiful banknotes; they were done by an Istrian, he said and they were printed in London. The printers were really surprised when they saw the design, they assumed that the designer came from another of those countries where people did not understand the technical problems of printing banknotes. But the designer knew exactly what could be done. Pavel smiled once more in satisfaction at this.

He went back to talking about independence: it might have happened differently, he said, the events which led to it were unpredictable; it was not a decisive, planned change, but a series of gradual actions coming from various angles. Now there was a legal mess; some of the old regime's legal arrangements were still in place, and there were serious problems with the mechanics of privatisation which allowed managers to identify one profitable aspect of a business and buy that, letting the rest of the business fall apart and putting a great number of people out of work.

What about the Church? I asked him. Was the Catholic Church involved in the process of independence? The Church, he said, was much more moderate here than in Croatia, much less politicised. Slovenians, he told me, have never been known as passionate believers. People attend Mass and follow routine Catholic procedures, but if the priests wanted the power of the Church to go further than that, if they wanted to impose Catholic teaching, most people would reject this, even though Slovenia is a Catholic country. Abortion and homosexuality, for example, he said, had become legal in Slovenia. Things were very liberal.

Now the country was culturally developed, especially non-institutional culture such as dance theatres and small theatres. But there were one hundred and twenty-five thousand people unemployed, and the costs of the new state had to be divided among very few people. With only eight hundred and fifty thousand people employed, there was real financial difficulty in running a state with its own foreign ministry, for instance, and its own bureaucracy. There was also what he called 'the density of political space', in a small state in which everyone knew everyone, there were too many friendships, and thus it was hard at times to implement a rational policy. He himself, he said, knew more than half the ministers in the government.

If your brother-in-law were in trouble with the law, I asked him, could you pick up the telephone and get him off? Not now, he said. In the previous government, maybe, if the charge was something like drunken driving, but not if there was an accident. But there were, he said, some advantages for those close to power, and there was an intimate connection between business and politics.

How had Slovenia developed in this way, I asked him, while Croatia, for example, or Ireland even, had been so hampered from approaching politics in the same rational manner he had described? First of all, he said Slovenes were not so very emotional about their nation. Second, from the mid-1980s there was a great deal of discussion about what a civic society would be, what democracy would offer. As long ago as the late 1970s, he said, the punk-rock and the hard-rock movement, really strong in Ljubljana, which I had glimpsed the previous night, triggered a debate; there was an alliance between the musicians, the intellectuals and the audience. *Mladina*, the radical magazine, was also deeply influential; when its editor and two contributors were imprisoned in 1988, its circulation had gone up to eighty thousand; the trial of the journalists was a focus for dissent. But there were other movements as well within the universities and among artists, within the gay rights movement and the peace movement, which were all ready to move into real politics once the opportunity arose.

The Church was not very important in this, he said, just as nationalism did not play much part. The Church was loyal to the state and was not overtly political at all. It made moral statements in favour of democracy, but priests came from rural areas and were not involved in the movements he had just described.

Why was Catholicism in Slovenia so different from Catholicism in Croatia? Why was it not an essential ingredient in the soul of the nation? What was the difference? Pavel spoke as though he had suddenly realised something, but he was none the less sure of what he was saying. It was easy to explain, he said. Slovenia had experienced the Reformation and Croatia had not. The first books in Slovenian were published by Lutherans in the sixteenth century; the rationalist spirit was brought in by the Reformation, he said. In places which experienced Lutheranism, religion doesn't try to creep into every corner of your life. He himself came from an area of the country, he said, where Protestantism was very strong, where the Protestant religion was maintained until the eighteenth century. The Counter-Reformation in Slovenia was more political than theological; it was agreed by treaty that the territory would be Roman Catholic. If that agreement had not been made, he said, then the area would certainly be half-Protestant now.

13

Velvet Voices

I TRAVELLED the next day on a train along a secondary railway line to Zidani Most and then changed and took a train to Zagreb. This time, there were no patrols at the border; in fact, I had no idea where the border was. The show of Slovenian strength was for the mainline only, it seemed. Along the way I could see the spiky spires of churches on the top of wooded hills. We passed small holdings with barns beside them in the shape of oversized abacuses for drying hay or wood. As we passed each station the station master would walk out on to the platform, perfectly dressed, and salute the train.

In Zagreb I left my bags in the station and bought a ticket for the night train to Vienna. I walked up to the main square, which was different on an ordinary working evening: there were crowds of people waiting for trams, it was busier, the shops were all lit up, and the cafés on the upper side of the square nearest the cathedral seemed more elegant now that it was not drizzling. I spent a couple of hours wandering around the square as though it were a little city in itself. Every now and then the general sense of ordinariness, the city at the end of the day, was disrupted by the appearance of soldiers in fatigues, big serious-looking fellows crossing the square, but no one else paid any attention to them. In one café, I watched as friends arrived at the neighbouring table and there was the ceremony of greeting and sitting down again and looking at the menu and talking to the waitress. A feeling that these people had money and had been doing this sort of thing all their lives. I watched from the plate-glass window of a café as the rush in the square slowed down and settled into silence for the evening.

There were a lot of desolate-looking people hanging around the corridors of the railway station, the only place where you could keep warm in the city if you had no money. I watched as one of them, a man in his forties, strayed into the bar. A Croatian soldier moved slowly towards him, to the amusement of his colleagues, ceremoniously caught him by the shoulders and steered him back to the corridor.

At the border between Croatia and Austria, a guard opened the door of my sleeping cabin and shone a torch in my face and asked me if I had any whisky or cigarettes. I told him I did not. The next guard wanted to see my passport. I fell asleep again and the next time I woke up the train was about to arrive in Vienna. Within half an hour I found a connection to Bratislava and arrived there around midday. It was now the Friday of Easter week. I booked into an hotel overlooking the Danube and rang a man called Juraj Mihalik whose name I had been given as a good guide to the recent changes in Slovakia.

As I walked around Bratislava I realised that it did not match Prague as a capital city, which must be difficult for the new state: everyone from outside would immediately start comparing it to the Czech Republic. Some of the old buildings were stately and dignified, but there seemed to be restoration and reconstruction going on in every street so that it was hard to look at the city as you walked around without seeing cement-mixers and lorries. I went into the new national gallery, and I tried to stop myself thinking of the national gallery in Prague up on the hill, the sheer grandeur of it, as against the modesty of this small building in a provincial capital on the Danube which had suddenly and unexpectedly become the capital city of a new state.

Close to my hotel was another gallery, which had obviously been restored in the 1960s: originally, there was an eighteenth-century building overlooking the river to which had been added a huge monstrosity like the sort of corridor which gets you from one terminal to another in an airport; this linked the upper storeys of the two wings. It was out on its own as a piece of interventionist architecture.

That evening I took a taxi to Juraj Mihalik's apartment, which was in a large cement-faced house on a hill not far from the city centre. He was in his early forties, a friendly, relaxed, open-faced character. The main room of his apartment was one of those rooms that you catch a glimpse of in foreign cities: full of shadowy, lamp-lit spaces, walls painted white, paintings and a sense of people at ease in the evening. Juraj's wife, Tana, was in the room, wearing jeans and a loose top and no shoes. They both exuded physical wellbeing; there was not an ounce of spare flesh on either of them; they could have been Americans in an apartment in Manhattan.

We had a drink and sat down. Juraj began to talk, moving back and forth over Slovakian history and recent political upheavals. Tana interrupted him often, making him explain things in more detail, or adding comments. I wanted to know their views first on what had happened in Slovakia during the war. I don't know why I believed that this was a good place to start. Slovakia was more or less on Hitler's side, Juraj said. The state of

Czechoslovakia was created after the First World War, but since the Czech Republic was richer, Slovakia was always treated as its little brother to the east; there was tension between the two all the time. Slovakia took its historical chance in the Second World War, he said, and agreed to play the role of a puppet state for Hitler. It was a free state, a fascistic state, with a Catholic priest for president. Sixty thousand Jews were deported to Poland in the first years of the war, but deportations were stopped in the later years, once it became clear that they were being deported to death-camps. But Slovakia had the same laws against Jews as did Germany.

There was no war in Slovakia until the main war was over; the country was liberated by the Americans and the Russians. In school, in the 1950s, the fascist period in Slovakia's history was completely ignored; instead, teachers concentrated on the uprising at the end of the war and the heroism of the communists. It was not illegal to go to church then, Juraj said, but if you went you were in serious trouble, you could lose your job, your children would not be asked to attend secondary school. In the 1950s older people, retired people and workers who had bad jobs went to church, people who had nothing to lose. The regime, he told me, tried to influence the church, and priests collaborated with the regime while others did not. He himself did not make his first communion but others did; many went out to villages and did it secretly. In 1971 his own sister got married and had a wedding in a church in a small village.

The Prague Spring was led by Dubcek, a Slovak who spoke Slovakian, unlike others who went to Prague and spoke only Czech. Later, he would get to know Dubcek and admire him for his sense of justice and his sense of humour. But the idea that he would travel one day to Washington with Dubcek was unimaginable in the dark years after the Prague Spring. It was always difficult being a Slovak in the federation, he said. Anyone in Bratislava who wanted to improve their career prospects moved to Prague. Only about 4 per cent of those working in the diplomatic service were Slovaks. Juraj himself had good friends in Prague: they had a common problem – communism.

There were only about seventy people killed during the Russian invasion, and in the immediate aftermath people were not sent to prison. Things were done slowly step by step. Since Juraj's parents were not communists he could not get into art school in Czechoslovakia; instead, he got a place in Krakow.

In 1975 he was invited by a family to visit the United States. It was always possible, he said, to get an exit visa, even though very few did. He loved New York. By this time he was studying at the Academy of Fine Arts in Bratislava, and, on his return he was expelled, told that he would have an imperialist influence on his fellow-students. The official reason was given as 'a sudden loss of talent'.

Even though he now views the election of Pope John Paul II as vitally important, in 1978 he viewed it merely as a big event for Poland. The relationship between Prague and Bratislava remained the same throughout this period. For everything important you had to go to Prague; Slovakia was for lakes and rivers and mountains. Slovakia was a poor primitive country; the industry and the wealth were in the hands of the Czechs. There were no embassies in Bratislava, and none of the connections to the outside world which the western embassies in Prague offered to dissidents. While there were a thousand Czech signatories to Charter 77, only fifty Slovaks signed.

But there was a dissident movement within Slovakia,

he said, operating through the Church and the environmental movement, rather than Charter 77 or foreign channels. In 1983 Juraj was permitted to make and sell flower-pots; in the looser atmosphere of the Gorbachev years he began to export ceramics to Austria, and this business grew throughout the 1980s. In 1989 he went to the United States once more, but this time was disappointed. In his subsequent book about the Velvet Revolution, *Velvet Failures*, he wrote: 'During this stay in the US I totally lost my illusions about this paradise on earth. I stayed with various people, particularly among the "lower class". I could not believe how hard the life was for some Americans. The driver on the New York bus line who worked ten hours a day could not afford to pay health insurance, let alone for a private flat in Manhattan. I was told that more than twenty per cent of Americans couldn't afford health insurance. I met an emigrant from Slovakia who worked as a shop assistant. In a pub fight he lost his front teeth, and because of this ugly hole in his mouth he lost his job next day. He didn't have the money to pay his dentist so he also couldn't pay his rent either and eventually became homeless.'

The first open demonstration in Slovakia against the regime was organised through the Catholic Church. It took place on 25 March 1988. People were asked to walk out of the churches and gather in one of the city's squares to ask for civil and religious freedom. They were asked to carry lighted candles and remain silent. The atmosphere was scary, Juraj said. The police surrounded the square, they had water-cannon and police dogs, but nothing happened. In November the following year he was driving back to Bratislava when he heard the news that the Velvet Revolution had begun. In Bratislava old friends of his, artists and actors, became the leaders of the revolution, and formed political parties in the new democracy.

At the beginning, Juraj said, Vaclav Havel was loved by everybody, and the problems between the two parts of Czechoslovakia did not surface. As he wrote: 'Before 1989 I did not have any strong feelings of nationality. I literally hated Slovak folklore, since it had always been supported by communists to the detriment of modern world culture, which was forbidden. I did not feel myself to be either Slovak or Czechoslovak . . . The only place I felt I belonged was Bratislava.'

In the days after the revolution there was talk that the capital of the federation should be in Brno, which is halfway between Prague and Bratislava. But there was a real sense that the Czechs did not understand Slovak sensitivities. The idea, Juraj said, that there was no time for such matters now, that the establishment of a market economy must come first, was quite shocking for him. He had been sure that Havel would understand the problem, that it could not continue under democracy as it had under communism.

After the revolution Juraj became a member of the Co-ordinating Committee of the Revolution, a twelve-member body. He spoke better English than the rest and worked on international relations. In February 1990 he became acutely conscious that there were going to be serious difficulties between Havel and the Slovaks. Havel had organised a trip to Washington and other North American capitals. The delegation consisted of two hundred and ten people, the second biggest foreign delegation to Washington in history (the biggest was headed by de Gaulle). Originally, there were to be eight Slovaks, but the new government rang from Prague and reduced the number to four, and then put it back to eight when there were protests.

This was followed by a trip to Israel. No Slovak politician was included; the two Slovaks in the delegation were representatives of the Jewish community. For Juraj, it was vital that a Slovak politician be present to apologise for what happened to the Jews in Slovakia during the war, and to make clear that the new Slovakia harboured no anti-Semitic feelings. In the end the actor Milan Knazko, a close friend of Juraj's and a leader of the revolution in Bratislava, went and made a speech.

'Milan Knazko's story,' Juraj wrote in his book, 'as Havel's Slovak adviser at the Prague Castle speaks for itself. He accepted the post with the original intention that he would later become a vice-president – a step that Slovakia would have welcomed, but it never came about. The opposite happened, since Knazko often disagreed with Havel and his team and strongly fought for Slovak interests. After several weeks in the Castle he lost direct access to the President and sometimes found himself waiting for days before Havel would agree to meet him.'

There were ten million Czechs and five million Slovaks; the ruling class in Bratislava came to feel throughout 1990 that they were being treated as nice peasants who lived in the mountains, who did not know enough to be part of the great velvet future, whose education out of their fascism and their Catholicism would take a long time. Prague was not even aware that there was a festering Slovak problem, as there was no Slovak newspaper available in Prague and no Slovak politician close to Havel. Slovak emigrants in the United States pointed out that as far as the western media were concerned, Slovakia did not exist.

In Prague, members of the old communist ruling class were slowly returning to positions of power, but in Bratislava, no one in the VPN (People Against

Violence) had any political experience. Juraj wrote: 'Our ideas about the world of politics, diplomacy and security were based on adventure novels rather than experience or logic. I remember my naivety when I agreed to go to the US embassy in Vienna, contact the CIA there and ask them to come to the VPN headquarters to check whether the building was bugged. They couldn't believe their ears when I asked them to put me in touch with the secret service and said there were no such people there. Eventually, a man responsible for security matters did see me. He might have been from the CIA but could naturally never say so. He gave me an address of an Austrian firm that provided this service, warned me it was expensive and saw me out the door.'

In the spring of 1990 discussion began over the name of the federation and whether there should be a dash between Czech and Slovak. Various Czech politicians openly made fun of the Slovaks and said that the dash could be used in Bratislava but not abroad. Slovaks, in turn, suggested that their state should be mentioned first, as in Slovakoczech. In Prague, this was viewed as a joke. Still, throughout 1990 Juraj believed that the federation could be preserved and he wanted to remain a citizen of Czechoslovakia, whether it had a dash or not.

But early in 1991 he began to change his mind. On 14 March a demonstration was organised in Bratislava to commemorate the setting up of the Slovak state in 1939. Between two and three thousand people attended, which was tiny compared to the huge demonstrations which had taken place at the time of the revolution when more than a hundred thousand people would turn up. There were two thousand wild Slovaks, Juraj remembered, a mixture of fascists, communists, anti-Semites and nationalists. For them, Vaclav Havel was the real enemy. Juraj noticed that there was a surprising number of foreign journalists and camera crews covering this demonstration and then he understood. Without informing the Slovak minister for the interior, 'Citizen' Havel, as Juraj called him, had arrived in Slovakia and begun a walkabout during the demonstration. The demonstrators attacked Havel, spat on him, kicked him and shouted abuse at him and the TV crews filmed all of this. They had, Juraj said, beautiful material of primitive Slovaks attacking the most loved politician in the world. Havel, he believed, must have known that they would get such footage. He blamed Havel for coming to Bratislava that day.

He was also outraged by the way friends of his who had become Slovak politicians had been treated; one, he believed, had been accused of being a police informer under the old regime because he opposed Havel's policies on Slovakia. He noticed that former friends now in power were becoming increasingly pompous. In his book he wrote of a former colleague: 'When I visited him in Prague and tried to explain something which he wasn't prepared to accept as valid, he asked whether I realised I was talking to the Federal Minister of the Interior. Another example: a director who was spontaneously greeted on the street by her friend's son lectured the boy "the times have changed and you cannot address me as Susanne any more." On holidays in the mountains, a minister's wife wanted us to "respect her husband's office".'

No one in the political mainstream in Slovakia had ever intended to secede from Czechoslovakia, he insisted, but when Havel announced, for example, that his country was not going to produce arms any more, he did so without considering that Slovakia was where the arms were produced, and a sudden shut-down of arms factories would have a devastating effect on the economy there.

Even after separation, Juraj believed, the campaign against Slovakia was still going on; the idea was being put out that the Czechs were good, progressive, smart, intelligent and the Slovaks were unstable, anti-semitic, old-fashioned, pro-communist.

There *are* differences between the Czechs and the Slovaks, he said. The Czechs are more eloquent, they have a stronger literary and artistic tradition, they are more secular, like Protestants, and they take ideology seriously. The Slovaks are more conservative, seventy per cent of them are Catholic, they are more down to earth and not so ready to be influenced by ideology. The way the Czechs have been treating us, he said, seems OK only because we are Catholics, but if we were Muslims it would be quite different, there would be war. In Slovakia, he told me, there has never been the same urge for revenge for what happened under the communists, they were ready to forgive; the Czechs, on the other hand, wanted to go through the files and blame people. They are more cerebral, he said, more interested in money; we are more emotional. The two nations did not have to separate; but, at the time, there was no better solution.

He himself decided to get out of politics and turned down several offers, including the Ministry for Culture and the ambassadorship to Washington. He wanted to build up his business and was glad, he laughed, that he did not have to get up in the morning for meetings.

He had been talking for hours, and I had been taking notes and asking questions, and Tana had been listening and adding details. We were exhausted. It was late. I felt that they still saw themselves as having a role in the new Slovakia, and talking to me, telling me about events from the Slovak point of view, was part of this. We had a beer. Juraj went to the phone and discovered that the KDH, the Christian Democratic Party, which had been in a coalition government after the 1990 elections but was now in opposition, was having its annual conference. It might be difficult for him to go there, he said, making clear that the divisions and splits in the years since the fall of communism had caused a good deal of personal bitterness in Bratislava. But he would take me there at lunchtime and see what happened. He and Tana discussed various characters who would be there, people they had worked with just a few years ago, and they laughed at what it would be like for Juraj to appear suddenly at the party conference.

It was hard to sleep after all this information. Juraj and Tana had talked as though all this had just happened to them, they had spoken with that peculiar intensity of people after an accident or a bereavement. I tried to think about it, work it all out, but when I saw them again at noon the next day, I felt as though I had not left their company at all. Juraj had a fancy car outside the apartment building, and I could see, as we sat in it to drive to his studio, that he enjoyed having a car like this. He put a tape on as he drove up through the city and then along narrow twisting roads, climbing all the time.

The studio was a house in its own grounds at the end of a lane. I had never really asked what sort of ceramics he made, and there seemed to be no examples in his apartment. But, here I could see what he did and why it was so successful. His pieces were elaborate jokes: his tea-pot, for example, was not completely useful, but it would be a good souvenir, or present; it looked well made and funny at the same time. I could see how it might be more fun making these and marketing them than being the Slovak Ambassador to Washington.

Juraj was thinking about the Christian Democrats, going through the names of people who might be there, wondering whom I should meet. 'The Christian Democrats feel so bad about being out of power,' he said and chuckled. We drove back down to the city centre; he parked outside a modern building where the conference was going on. It was now lunchtime, so there should be people free, he said.

As soon as we went into the main hall I could see why Juraj was not a member of the Christian Democrats. There were groups of men standing around; those who were not middle-aged looked as though they soon would be. They all had that slightly worn, cautious appearance of men who join centrist political parties. Juraj might have been the wayward son of any of these men in suits, although he was the same age as some of them. He was dressed confidently in casual clothes, his hair was styled. He stood out in the hall. He greeted a few people and then spoke to a man who moved quickly away. A few people looked at him. I was standing close to the door. He came over and said that this wasn't easy, but he thought he might be able to get me a senior figure who spoke English. One man, with whom he had worked, had moved away from him, he said. I told him that I had seen this happen.

After a while we were ushered into a long office which was comfortably furnished. I felt that Juraj was excited being here and was looking forward to what the politician, who was called Jan Carnogursky, was going to say to a foreign journalist. Carnogursky was in his fifties. He was a thin man with a cautious and serious appearance. His parents were both teachers, he said, but his father had been a political activist before the war and had supported the Slovak state during the war. After the war he had tried to establish a Catholic party, and was imprisoned.

Carnogursky was brought up as a Catholic. He went to Mass on Sunday. Everyone around him, he said, was anti-communist. He didn't think that anyone in Slovakia was pro-communist, although some people joined the party. But there was only one youth organisation, which was communist-run and he was a member; almost all young people were members. He lost three years of schooling because of the political activities of his father; he wasn't allowed into secondary school. He got a secondary education simply because his father had friends in the north of the country and he went to school there; the communists were not well-organised enough throughout the country to know who he was and prevent him.

He did not support the Prague Spring. His family remained anti-communist, and the fact that this softening in the regime was run by communists was enough for him. He managed to study to become a lawyer and specialised in labour law, representing, for example, teachers who had been seen at Mass and fired, or teachers who had sent their children for religious instruction and been fired, or a senior doctor who had attended Mass and was fired. These were all unwritten rules, he said, and thus could be challenged in the courts.

Later, he defended people who had signed Charter 77, but in 1981 he was banned from practising as a lawyer. He drove a factory jeep for a while, then worked as a lawyer for the factory, then for a farmers' co-operative. From 1987 he was unemployed again and the following years he started secretly to edit and distribute Christian Democratic propaganda. The second half of the 1980s, he said, saw the rise of the organised Catholic movement in Slovakia. There were pilgrimages to holy shrines.

In 1987, for example, he told me, about six hundred thousand people took part in pilgrimages in Slovakia, and through this a self-conscious Catholic movement took shape. The state allowed and, in certain respects, encouraged an official church, but this was organised by a secret church, and it was the secret church which planned that first demonstration in March 1988, a secret church made up of priests and lay activists.

In 1989 he was imprisoned; in November when the revolution began he was sharing a tiny cell. He knew that the Berlin Wall had fallen, and he knew there were demonstrations in Prague and Bratislava, but one night he could hear clapping and shouting, he could hear the crowds outside. That was 23 November 1989 and there were five thousand people demonstrating in front of the prison. ('I was there,' Juraj interjected as Carnogursky described the scene.) Two days later he was released, let out into the street alone. He took a tram home. A few days later he was a member of the delegation which negotiated with the government, demanding the participation of the opposition in a new government, followed by free elections. He was the only Slovak in the ten-person delegation, but that was not an issue then; overcoming communism, he said, was the aim, everyone's overwhelming aim.

On 10 December, two weeks after he was freed, the government caved in. Suddenly, he was deputy prime minister of Czechoslovakia. He had cars, telephones, a secretariat. After twenty-five years in opposition all at once he had to become engaged in all aspects of the state. He just changed his point of view, he said, as if it all had really been very easy. He was in charge of new legislation, passing, for example, a law governing the freedom of the press. Although he was based in Prague he started to organise his party in Bratislava.

He had always been aware, he said, of the problems between the Czechs and the Slovaks and he gave me precisely the same definition of the difference as had Juraj. The Czechs were more rational and western; the Slovaks more emotional.

In ways, he said, the difficulties between the two nations were caused by Czech lethargy in relation to Slovak grievances. He was not a Slovak nationalist; for him anti-communism was more important. Nationalism, he said, is always quite easy to misuse, as a means of mobilising people. A good number of former communists, he told me, quickly became nationalists. He himself wanted the relationship between the two states to be modelled on states of the European Union.

I asked him about the war years. During the war, he said, Slovakia was formally independent for the first time. The Slovak state was quite successful, he said, economically, culturally, politically. Its president was a Catholic priest, Dr Josef Tiso, and there is, he said, a positive feeling among Catholics about this state. At the time, Carnogursky believed, Slovakia had two options: to be divided between Poland, Hungary and Germany, or to become a puppet state under Hitler. The period is controversial, he added.

I merely asked questions. I did not argue, I underlined what he had said in my notebook: The Slovak state was quite successful, economically, culturally, politically. I had expected him to hedge his bets, fudge the issue, but he seemed to have no idea how important this was.

It was the same problem as the Croatians had: how to deal with that period when Hitler offered them a quisling state and they accepted, how to deal with history that was still remembered by others such as Serbs and Jews as dark and murderous, but by Croats and Slovaks as the first time they had a state as well as a nation.

No one in the West now in a Christian Democratic party would admit to seeing the Hitler period as anything other than disgusting. Carnogursky was naive; he was just beginning. But I felt, all the same, that he needed to know, as other countries had learned in the years after the war, what the word Hitler meant to Jews, gypsies and homosexuals in Europe; and how the quisling states bear a guilt for what happened. As we left the building I presumed that Juraj had similar feelings and I spoke to him as though we shared a political outlook. But he did not understand what I was talking about. The war years, he said, we have nothing to do with them; and we still don't know enough about them. I walked to the car with him and we drove back towards his studio.

I spent that afternoon in a house close to the studio which had a big garden. Friends of Juraj and Tana's were hosting a barbecue. People dropped in for a while, had a drink and left, and then others came. Juraj and Tana went to do some work, but I stayed on. Everyone was bright and well-dressed and thirtysomething. The food was good, and the air was warm enough for us to sit out on the veranda, even though the sky was full of pale, low cloud. An American couple working as volunteers in a local bank told us how Prague was full of Americans now, Bratislava was a much better place to be if you want to mix in the society.

At the first hints of twilight a couple came to collect their son who had been playing in the garden. They were different from the rest, taller, much more glamorous, a bit older; even when they didn't talk – and the man said nothing most of the time, merely watched everything and smiled – they appeared to be the centre of things. I wondered who they were and what they did. He looked like someone I had seen on television. He was in his early forties and dressed in black; his wife was elegant with long blonde hair. He seemed half bored, sitting there nursing a beer, as though his mind was elsewhere; he exuded a restless sort of contentment.

It was only when Tana returned that I learned he was Milan Knazko, the actor who had led the revolution in Bratislava, who had addressed all the meetings in November 1989, who held the crowd in the power of his presence. He was the one who used to shout 'Make a corridor' if someone was ill at the front of the crowd and needed to be carried to the back, until the phrase became a catch-cry. And he was in power in the days after the revolution, and lost power in the intricate political machinations in Bratislava in 1990 and 1991, but there was talk now that he might return to politics, no one knew. I thought of how hard it must be to have known those days when you could lead your country, hold the crowd, realising that the days would never come back, that afterwards everything would be dull and distant. People who get a taste of power always find it hard to do without it. He asked me what I was writing about.

'Catholic Europe,' I said.

'I'm Lutheran,' he replied and smiled, as if to say that he was sorry he could not be any use to me. He stood up to go. As they collected their son, it struck me that they were going home and would not go out again, but would sit in tonight: something a politician would never have to do. Just a few years ago the phone rang for Knazko day and night.

It was cold now and the party was breaking up. Tana and I agreed to walk into the city, but as we left I noticed a sort of quarry in front of the house. It was a grotto, and there were a few candles lit in front of the statue of the Virgin, and a woman kneeling praying. There were trees all around offering shelter, and they rustled suddenly in a gust of wind. I saw a woman standing behind a tree, like a shadow, praying. There were plaques stuck to the stone in German, Hungarian and Slovak, with names and dates from the early years of the century, some of them – Tana translated for me – thanking the Virgin for recovery from an illness. It was strange standing here, having been so close all afternoon without knowing that there was a grotto nearby.

As we walked back up the steps to the road I could hear shouting in the distance, as though there was a football match going on. Tana said it was a bar. It was still open. All the clientele were sitting outside at tables, most of them were young and many of them were seriously drunk, roaring out songs and slogans and queuing at the hatch for more big glass tankards of lager. The beer was strong, Tana said, it made you drunk easily. It was freezing now that darkness had fallen, but this put none of the drinkers off. We had beers and tried to talk despite the terrible, loud singing coming from the other tables. I was not entirely sure that this scene and the scene at the grotto with the woman praying in the shadow of the tree were not from a dream, or a movie, or something imagined. But the cold was real. And we went back to talking about politics.

Knazko was a popular film, TV and theatre actor, Tana told me, and after the revolution he moved to Prague to become an adviser to Havel. Once he grew disillusioned with Havel, he became a member of the Slovak parliament and Minister for Foreign Relations, but he had lost power in the many splits and personality clashes which had arisen since independence. He was good during the revolution, she said, brilliant with the crowd, but he was not so interested in the systems and structures you have to apply when you are running a country.

I told her how amazed I had been by Carnogursky's response to the question about the war years and the quisling Slovak state. She shook her head and said that no one in Bratislava now knew much about the period; they were not sure what was communist propaganda and what was truth. Historians would have to do more research, she said. I did not know what to say.

We went back to Tana and Juraj's apartment. Friends called around, people they had known for years who had nothing to do with politics, and they sat around talking for the evening. I asked them if they knew a good bar in Bratislava that was open late, and they gave me an address which was near my hotel. I went back to the hotel and read for a while and had a shower. It was nearly midnight and the streets were completely deserted. It was platonic Eastern Europe, where everything happened indoors, where nothing moved at night. The world had closed down. I followed my directions until I arrived at one of the many small alleys in the city, but still there was no sign of life. This was, none the less, where they had told me to come. I noticed an open doorway with a light on and I peered in: there was a stairway to a cellar. I walked down. I could hear the drum thuds of rock music in the distance somewhere. Suddenly someone opened a door and the music became loud and I knew I was in the right place. I walked into a cellar which had been done up into a disco and bar. It was full of well-dressed, trendy-looking people. I went up to the bar and had a beer.

It was Sunday morning in Bratislava. I had a vague hangover as I toured the streets, comforting now in their lack of grandeur. Juraj had told me how much the city had been destroyed by a motorway cut through the old quarter. The new road had barely spared the cathedral, almost grazing it as it sped past. There was thus no great square in front of the cathedral, and there was no easy access to the old quarter or the Jewish quarter across the motorway. The Danube always seemed distant from the centre. They would never have done this to Prague, I found myself thinking.

I was ready to go home now, wandering around, killing time before my train was due to leave. In the city centre, near one of the old churches, as people came out of Mass, preparing to disappear once more into the hidden domestic life of the city, there was a stall selling books by and about Dr Josef Tiso, who ran Slovakia for Hitler between 1939 and 1945. The books looked dog-eared and badly produced; they were cheap. Two elderly women sat on chairs beside the stall, a few men stood behind them. They watched as the crowds streamed out of the church. No one paid any attention to them, no one stopped at the stall, or bought their books. They had the air of people who belonged to an old world, a time gone by. And on that Sunday morning, the First Sunday after Easter 1993, the works of Dr Josef Tiso did not seem to interest the people of Bratislava on their way home from Mass.

14

England, Their England

IN THE MID-1980S I was sitting in my living room in Dublin with an Englishwoman whom I liked and enjoyed working with. We were going through a book of photographs, and I showed her pictures of Irish Catholics praying at a shrine, taken in the previous few years. The people had been caught in a state of reverie; they knelt close to statues, or with rosary beads in their hands, intent on prayer, completely unselfconscious. I pointed at a face.

'Yes,' my English friend said. 'Vile.'

Vile? These were the people I had grown up with, the world I came from and lived in. I had shown her the photographs because they were ambiguous and disturbing. And she had misunderstood me, assumed that I shared her distaste for Irish Catholics; a distaste I came to see, perhaps wrongly, as a fundamental aspect of Englishness.

She was born in a country where the heir to the throne was prohibited from marrying a Catholic, where the monarch was head of the established church, where the prime minister had a say in the appointment of bishops, and where changes in the state church – such as the 'ordination' of women priests – were debated in parliament.

Catholics, like Muslims or atheists, had a right to feel strange about official England. The Church of England, viewed from Ireland, seemed like the English class system, or the House of Lords, or the monarchy itself: part of a dream of England, part of something devised long ago; stable and old-fashioned, and oddly admirable in its own cold way, but, in its constitution, its actuality, beyond belief.

And distant from a world where people brought up in poverty prayed to favoured saints, statues and relics for material things, and accepted the authority not of the Bible but of the local priest, and used the sanction they received from Rome and from heaven to justify violent rebellion and treachery against the civil power and the monarch, and constantly grew in number, and emigrated and behaved fecklessly.

In other words, traditional Irish Catholics.

One day in London in the late-1980s I was having lunch with a journalist who told me how much she enjoyed collecting rosary beads. She had some converted into bracelets and necklaces, she said, but others she just kept as antiques. The problem was, she went on, that old ladies in Ireland insisted on being buried with their beads, which was a nightmare for the serious collector.

All Catholics, I told her, are buried with their fingers entwined around rosary beads, and anyway, I went on, these are blessed objects, they are sacred, and they cannot just be collected like jewellery. Suddenly, I found myself defending the idea of rosary beads and resenting my English friend's fascination with Catholic objects. Catholicism and all its trappings, somehow, belonged to me. Englishness and Catholicism, I seemed to feel, did not go together. It was something that they would never understand.

English history from the sixteenth century is haunted by the threat from Catholics, from their disloyalty and ability to pact with foreign powers. The figure of Guy Fawkes remains a central presence in English fear and suspicion of Catholics. On Guy Fawkes' night in 1993 I went to Lewes, near Brighton, to watch the commemoration, the parade and the bonfires. The guide-book to the event explained its origins: 'At two o'clock in the morning of 5 November 1605 Guy Fawkes was arrested in a vault beneath the House of Lords while guarding thirty-six barrels of gunpowder hidden under faggots of wood. A member of a group of Catholic conspirators . . . it was Fawkes' task to light the fuse which would destroy the Parliament killing James I and all those gathered for its opening. In the ensuing chaos a Catholic uprising . . . was to seize the organs of power and instal a Catholic monarch.

'The Government of James', it continued, 'reacted swiftly and punitively against the co-religionists of Fawkes, two Acts being passed imposing restrictions and exclusions on Roman Catholics that separated them from other Englishmen. The outburst of anti-Catholicism that followed the Plot was also given legal expression by the passing of a third Act entitled "An Acte for a publique Thanksgiving to Almighty God everie yeere of the Fifte day of November" in January 1606. The Act proclaimed that the discovery of the Plot should "be held in a perpetual Remembrance" and that the 5 November be "a holiday for ever in thankfulness to God for the deliverance and detestation of the Papists" . . . In the popular mind patriotism and anti-Catholicism were inextricably intertwined.'

The parade to thank God for deliverance endured in Lewes, while it died out elsewhere. 'In the period leading up to 1913,' according to the guide, 'the effigies of Pius IX . . . and that of his successor Leo XIII were burnt.'

Over the years, while most groups taking part seemed to want to abandon the overt anti-Catholic symbolism, one group insisted on maintaining it, and marched behind a 'No Popery' banner every year.

It was a clear winter's evening in Lewes; the moon was almost full. As soon as I arrived in the main street, at around seven o'clock, I saw a plaque which said that ten of the seventeen Protestant martyrs burned at the stake between 1555 and 1557 had been held in the vaults beneath this building. I had seen a photograph of the memorial to the martyrs, which was as big as a normal war memorial in an English village. Clearly, they took their Protestant martyrs seriously here in Lewes.

Crowds lined the High Street to watch the parade. Men went by dressed as American Indians and then others wearing African masks, feathers and jewellery and leopard-skin tunics. One man had a fake bone through his nose. It could have been a pageant or a parade in any town at any time of the year. There were police and organisers everywhere, and a sense of order and care.

Lewes is one of those beautiful, well kept and rich towns in the south of England; the old buildings are meticulously preserved and the shops, restaurants and pubs along the High Street are carefully designed. There is always a randomness, an untidiness and an air of poverty about Irish towns that made me wander up the High Street of Lewes with a feeling of mild wonder.

Men passed wearing Mexican hats, and women in seventeenth-century costumes carrying torches; others pulled half barrels on wheels full of fire. 'Death or Glory', proclaimed one banner; 'Success to Waterloo', another. There was military music and a band playing 'Spanish Eyes' and more Apache Indians and a smell of fire and sulphur. The street was full of smoke. Some were dressed as Confederate soldiers; one in the robes of a Protestant bishop; another carried an effigy of Guy Fawkes on a stick.

Only one sign said 'No Popery'. I was watching for it, but I don't think that anybody else noticed it. People were more interested in the rolling barrels of fire and the torches and staves left burning on the street. There were clowns and banners and a band playing the slow movement of Dvořák's New World Symphony. It was a night for tourists, for young people down from London, for all the family. It bore no relation to Orange parades in Northern Ireland. Bands played 'Quando, quando, quando' and 'When I'm Sixty-Four' rather than sectarian hymns. No Catholic could be offended by the parade. It seemed to me that, despite the 'No Popery' banner and the bonfires, all the original meaning had been removed from the commemoration, that we were in post-industrial, post-imperial and post-Protestant England.

Outside the town near the cliff there were enormous bonfires. Fireworks echoed against the cliffs as they exploded, spilled out in various colours. An enormous cross was set on fire, the flames licking it and then beginning to burn the wood. The crowds came to watch as effigies were pushed into the bonfires and burned.

That night law and order prevailed in Lewes, there was a sort of deadness about everything that happened; everything was controlled and careful, part of the heritage industry, part of a society that had ceased to bother about history. But I still wondered afterwards what it would be like to be Catholic in England, and I went and spoke to a few English people who belonged to the Church of Rome.

I had never lived in England, or spent much time there. I used to joke about London, about how beautiful it was, how fine its buildings and squares and high streets were, how efficient its transport system was; and how right we were, as Irish people, to have built it, how wise our navvies, labourers and emigrant workers were to become involved in such a grand project. But in the spring of 1994 when I went to Oxford for the first time to meet Terry Eagleton in a bar where one of the earliest performances of *Hamlet* had taken place, I realised that we had nothing to do with the building of Oxford. I was impressed by the splendour of the place. It came from a time before England had ever set its sights on Ireland, when surplus capital was employed to build centres of learning rather than to expand empires.

Terry Eagleton is professor of English at St Catherine's College in Oxford. He seemed, when I met him in the bar, an unlikely professor; he was not pompous and I did not notice his English accent. He was dressed casually and he smiled a lot as he spoke. I imagine he was aware that we had political differences – he is, I think, further to the left than I am, and he is an Irish nationalist, which I am not – but we didn't talk about our political differences.

His grandparents had come from Ireland, he said, had emigrated to a mill town in Lancashire, then moved into Manchester and become part of the Irish semi-ghetto there. On his mother's side there was a tradition of Irish republicanism. He could sing the Irish rebel song 'Kevin Barry' ('Another martyr for old Ireland, another murder for the Crown/ Whose brutal laws may kill the Irish, but can't keep their spirits down') at the age of seven, and his family viewed Ireland as sacred soil.

They were pretty devout Catholics, and he was taught by De La Salle Brothers; all seven hundred children in the school had Irish names, but there was no emphasis placed on their Irish heritage. They were being equipped for English society; their teachers, who were mainly Irish, were educating them to forget their Irish roots. They did it very well, he remembered.

Did he feel he had full rights in England, I asked him. No, he said, he never felt completely English, because he was Catholic, and that left him at once marginal, as he was in a minority, and superior as he felt that he was in possession of the truth. England wasn't really your country, he said, the Queen wasn't really your Queen; but at the same time you shared the accent with the English and you mocked teachers with Irish accents. You associated Catholicism with persecution and you sang the anthem of English Catholicism, 'Faith of our Fathers'.

I had always thought that this was an Irish hymn. We had sung it in Enniscorthy during the annual Blessed Sacrament procession. ('We will be true to Thee till death.') If we had known it was English, I'm not sure that we would have sung it with the same gusto. Terry Eagleton recited a verse of the hymn and then wrote it in my notebook: 'Faith of our fathers, Mary's prayers/ Shall bring our country back to thee;/ And by the truth that flows from God/ England one day shall be free.' In Ireland we had left this verse out.

They sang it in Manchester at Whitsun processions when the clergy wore top hats and frock-coats, when the schoolboys filed past the Bishop of Salford and raised their schoolcaps to him.

There were Italian, Ukrainian and Lithuanian Catholics as well, but the Irish felt different, because they were somehow English, or more English than their fellow Catholics from Europe. There was a great desire for learning; parents wanted their children to use the education system for advancement. And the vast majority of those seven hundred school children, his schoolmates, became assimilated into England; they had Irish names and a Catholic education and memories of parents talking about Ireland, but they had become part of the English mainstream.

He went to Cambridge in the early 1960s where there was a great ferment of radical and trendy ideas. He became involved in the Catholic left, which was led by the Dominicans in Cambridge, working on a magazine called *Slant*. If you were Catholic then you were working class and you never really understood English liberalism, and the system in Cambridge was based root and branch on the English middle-class liberal tradition. His tutor at Cambridge was able to say 'Well, I don't know' at the end of class, and this for Terry Eagleton was strange, this agnosticism; all his own training was to know, because there was something at stake in knowing.

This was clearly a matter he had been thinking about and writing about in recent years: being a working-class Catholic of Irish origin in England. The working-class bit gave you an innate lack of confidence, he said, but this was counter-balanced by the intellectual arrogance conferred by Catholicism. As a Catholic, you believed yourself equipped with the truth, and there were many ex-Catholics like himself on the left in England at that time, who, early on, had been trained in the intellectual habits of rigorous and systematic thought in religion classes and were now catapulted into an English society that was open-minded and unsystematic.

I remembered religion classes as a bore, always half-hearted. I learned nothing. But in his school, he said, they studied St Augustine and Church Doctrine. I wondered if religious instruction was taken more seriously in English Catholic schools, where religion cannot be taken for granted.

It seemed easy to move from Catholicism to Trotskyism without going through a liberal phase, he said. It made some weird sense. To be a Catholic or a socialist is to be at odds with conventional wisdom in England. *Slant* folded in 1970. The Troubles in Northern Ireland and liberation theology had both begun, and a left-wing intellectual Catholic magazine produced in a suburb of Cambridge seemed the wrong project just then. He moved away from the Church.

But his background stayed with him. He had never gone through the Oedipal rage and revolt so common at the time, he had never fully walked away from his Irishness or his Catholicism. As the Troubles continued in Ireland, he believed that he knew more about the country than English people did, even though he had been assimilated into England. Ireland became increasingly important for him. There was, first of all, what he called the nostalgic impulse to find an identity in a Thatcherite post-Modernist universe. It took him a long time to tackle it intellectually. He felt that he was able to bring to bear on his Irish background the sort of things which an English education had taught him.

In the Bodleian Library now he was reading obscure works from the nineteenth century, books and pamphlets – many produced in Ireland and sent to Oxford to fulfil copyright law – about the Irish Repeal Movement and the Famine. Books whose pages have never been opened before, which have lain there untouched, unread. In England, he said, they know nothing about Ireland, they don't want to, they are deeply uninterested. He was writing a play about the Famine and we talked about that for a while. I couldn't imagine writing about Irish history. But he was trying to rediscover an Ireland which I knew too much about, maybe. Maybe I had lost something by living there day-to-day, just as he had lost his country by his grandparents' exile. I half envied him having a place to dream about.

He was Thomas Warton Professor of English Literature at St Catherine's College, Oxford. There was no dreaming in that title. And he was surrounded by England at its most liberal and wonderful. But still, emotionally and intellectually, he felt that he lived outside the mainstream. He believed that this was inherent in being a Catholic in England.

In London two days later I went to see Piers Paul Read, the English novelist who has remained a Catholic, and whose articles in English newspapers expressed what I thought I could call right-wing views. He lived in a large, bright house in a good part of central London. Like most Irish people, I always feel socially uneasy knocking on the door of an English person whom I don't know well. There is a sense of not belonging in this country, so that everything is open to be watched and noted (and laughed at later, or at least discussed). Nothing is taken for granted, not even the notion that you have the smallest right to be standing there. At the back of your mind there is the idea that someone will call for the police. Also, English people use language in a manner which is precise and clipped and they have a very special way of making a nervous and slightly stammering Irishman feel most uncomfortable.

Some of this went through my mind as Piers Paul Read opened the door. He was a neatly dressed, self-possessed man in his fifties, and he led me to a room in the basement where we could talk without being interrupted. His father was the art critic Sir Herbert Read; his mother, who was a mixture of Irish, Scottish, German and Italian, was a convert to Catholicism. Read was brought up in Yorkshire and went to Ampleforth, one of the leading Catholic public schools in England, where Cardinal Hume was Abbot. The ambiguous position of English Catholics was understood, he felt, and in the school they went out of their way to prove loyalty to the crown. Ampleforth tried to be more of an English public school than a Catholic school.

His mother was superstitious in her religion, he recalled; his father worshipped at the shrine of modern art, but couldn't take pop art and other movements of the 1960s. He himself never doubted the truth of the Catholic Church. He went to Cambridge; he was there just before Terry Eagleton, and remembered *Slant*. He was more interested then in politics than in religion. He looked out of the window for a moment in silence, and then he turned and spoke quietly: when your faith deepens, he said, you realise that it's more about eternal things and less about social things.

Somebody commented to him that as he became richer he became more right wing, but he thought that this was unfair. He did not smile or laugh as he said this; all the time as he spoke he maintained an even, po-faced expression like a mask on his face. At times it was impossible to know whether he was being entirely serious, or whether he was setting out to shock or disturb me. He had once supported the Labour Party in Britain, he told me, but had become disillusioned with Labour over Europe, as he was rather pro-European. In Yorkshire, the Conservatives were the local snobs, the arrogant Etonians, people who had butlers; but when Thatcher and Tebbitt came along, he admired them, considered them populists who said things such as it was ridiculous to have a plumber's mate when you could have just a plumber.

He still believed that they had had an energising effect on England. He agreed that it was hard to imagine

Thatcher as a Catholic on her knees confessing her sins to a priest, that her Protestantism was essential to her appeal. Yes, he felt that there was an ingrained anti-Catholicism in England, and it was tinged sometimes with anti-Irishness, with visions of people having lots of children and getting drunk and getting into quarrels. But there were posh Catholics in England too, he remarked.

Some people had said that you could not be a proper Catholic unless you had lapsed, but he did not share this view. His novels had a Catholic perspective, he said. He had become very alarmed by liberation theology; he was desperately against it, and against other movements which were trying to pervert the teaching of the Church from within, which sought to erase the supernatural dimension. I asked him if he believed in transubstantiation. 'I do, don't you?' he said and looked at me. I shook my head.

He believed in it, and in the veneration of the Host in the monstrance at Benediction, and in the Mass as a sacrifice, re-enacted. He believed in grace and its power to change you. He really could not imagine himself praying for things, for a book to be a success, for example, or for film rights to be sold, but maybe for a child to pass an exam. He thought about it, and shrugged: there are people who pray for every little thing, it's hard to know.

And he believed in hell. There must be a possibility of hell, he said. If Christ died to save us, he had to save us from something. What about *Humanae Vitae*, the Church's teaching on contraception? He had always taken the view, he said, that the Church knows best. He found the teaching on birth control hard to accept, although he was against what he called the contraceptive mentality which, in his view, caused the break-up of marriages and boys being brought up without a father. He believed, he said, in strong faith and authority.

But he had difficulty in understanding the Marian cults which were so popular in Ireland and in Europe. He was puzzled at so many of the Irish remaining Catholic. They were born into Catholicism, he felt, whereas he had chosen this, he was a Catholic by conviction and faith. Taking it on in England as he had done, made it different. It belonged to him rather than to his race.

In his forties he had kept his head down as a Catholic novelist, he said, but now with feminism and homosexuality he considered that he had a duty as a Catholic layman to speak out. The Church had no Catholic intelligentsia in England. The bishops and clergy were not noted for their intellectual acuteness: the religious orders creamed off the best minds.

Did he think he could change? Become more liberal, perhaps? No, he was sure that he could not. He felt that the Pope, in certain respects, was too liberal. Liberalism in moral teaching, he thought, had done a great deal of harm and he admired old Irish priests talking plainly about old-fashioned moral questions. In London now, he said, there was a new wave of orthodox priests and the 1960s radicals had been discredited.

I asked him if his interest in authority, the authority of the Church of Rome and of the Tory Party and of Margaret Thatcher could come from something personal, some need within himself. He held my gaze as I asked the question. He looked into the distance and nodded. Yes, that was possible, his father had been a very powerful and authoritarian figure. He returned my gaze again. He had obviously considered the idea and it did not seem to disturb him. As I stood up to leave I asked him if he felt isolated. No, he said, he was a member of the Catholic Writers' Guild, and a third of his friends were Catholic, and there was a big Catholic middle class now in London.

In the early 1990s, the English newspapers ran articles about the new wave of converts to Catholicism. Some joined, it appeared, for the smells and bells, the strict rules, the security. Others felt pushed out by the changes in the Church of England. Somehow, it became fashionable in England to be Catholic.

On 13 March 1994 the *Sunday Telegraph* published a piece by Charles Moore, its editor, on why he was about to become a Catholic. As a child, he wrote, he had seen 'the local Catholic church, a characteristically ugly red-brick edifice, and I knew that we didn't believe in it and had heard that Catholics were slightly separate from us and thought funny things about the Virgin Mary and pieces of bread . . . But as I began to read history and travel on the continent of Europe, I could not help noticing that these Catholics, who in my own lifetime seemed marginal, were clearly the chief expression of Christianity, that they, more than any others, had shaped the civilisation of which I was a part, and that they seemed to pray more than we did. I was struck by the fact that poor people would go into a church when no service was in progress, light a candle and pray. I had never seen that in the English church.'

Yet Moore was content as an Anglican: 'I still think the Book of Common Prayer is the greatest of all liturgies written in English . . . I liked the good order of the services, the gentle temper of Anglican parish life and intellectual manners . . . over the past ten years or so it became clear to me that the Church of England was deep in the thicket. Its traditional *via media* had degenerated from an intellectual position to mere weakness of mind.' The ordination of women priests became an important matter for him. 'I was not sure – I am still in no position to know – that women could be priests. But I did know that such a decision could only be made by the general assent of the universal Church and not by a two-thirds majority in a meeting of the English middle classes.'

Moore decided to become a Catholic. 'It feels sad', he wrote, 'to leave the church of my ancestors, my family and my country . . . What I am about to do seems necessary. I am accepting the most perplexing thing of all perplexities that surround the Catholic faith: that it is true.'

A short time after his article was published I went to London and spoke to two women who had converted from the Church of England to Rome, to find out what it was like to leave the church of your ancestors, your family and your country.

Jill Lusk, who worked on the magazine *Africa Confidential*, was born in the English midlands and brought up in the Church of England. The village school was controlled by the Church of England and she was sent to church every Sunday even though her parents didn't go. Over the years, as she became an adult, she drifted way from the Church of England. In the mid-1980s, however, when she was living in the Sudan she felt drawn to religion, and when she came home on leave would go into bookshops and look at religious books. She started collecting them, heavy works of theology, though she didn't read most of them.

She slowly began to entertain the idea of converting to Catholicism. She was attracted by the explicit moral and religious basis for what went on day by day in the Catholic Church; she was drawn also by the level of commitment and involvement required. Did she never consider going back to the Church of England, since her initial religious feelings were vague? I asked. It simply didn't occur to her, she said. The Church of England, she felt, was the middle classes at prayer. The Catholic Church was more universal and international. She used to lurk at the back of Westminster Cathedral taking in the atmosphere of holiness and sanctity, she loved the candles and the incense. And in 1987 she decided to go for instruction. I knew as I spoke to her that she was not someone who would ever be amenable to authority and taking orders. I could not understand how she could convert to Catholicism and its doctrines with such ease.

Once she converted, she said, she went to Mass and communion every day. But she hardly ever went to confession. I asked her about the Virgin Mary, but she said that devotion to the Virgin didn't really figure in her Catholicism. Did she believe in transubstantiation? She didn't think that it was an issue since God was present in everything. She had always communicated directly with God, never through the intercession of saints.

The history of the Church in England and its status were important for her. She liked it being a mainly working-class Church, with an element of rebellion, a history of being the underdog in England. That appealed to her, whereas the Church of England was bound up with British Imperialism, the churches were full of flags and shields and war memorials. It never occurred to her, she said again, to go back to the Church of England. It would have been dull and ordinary, and she was looking for something new.

She went to Walsingham, the shrine near Norwich which is run jointly by Anglicans and Catholics. She went with a nun; she drank the holy water and was very moved by the outdoor Mass, the beautiful robes and the eight priests at the altar. She was annoyed that when it rained most of the congregation fled back to the coaches.

Over the past few years, however, her interest in

Catholicism had waned. Having made one change, she could make another. She still loved the Catholic churches, how there were always people in them, how the church was part of the community. And she could still talk with dismay about the routine manner in which many priests said Mass as though she belonged to the fold. She spoke as if she had not fully decided what to do about her conversion but I did not feel that she would stay within the confines of the Catholic Church.

She felt a bit let down, she said, by the Church, a bit disappointed. She disliked the way enormous intelligence was applied to angels and pin heads and not to the meaning of life. She thought that the Church sidestepped major questions. The universality of the Church took her in, she said, and she wondered if she had been a bit starry-eyed.

When I telephoned Ann Widdecombe's office at the House of Commons, I felt like a latter-day Guy Fawkes. Even dialling the number and holding for her secretary made me uneasy, as if I would soon be found out. I left a message and my number in Dublin and waited. Later that afternoon, my phone rang and I was told that the minister would see me for thirty minutes in her office a week later.

She worked in a large modern block near Westminster. I arrived fifteen minutes early, but she agreed to see me immediately. Her tone was friendly and businesslike. She clearly enjoyed being brisk and using language precisely, and whatever arrogance she exuded came from the pleasure she took in her own cleverness rather than any desire to undermine her interviewer. We sat opposite each other in old style armchairs.

She came across the Catholic Church when she was

quite young, she said, having gone to a Catholic school because it was the best in the area. All the teachers were Irish Catholics. She was very definitely a Protestant then. She did not accept the superstition in Catholicism, she said, she rejected transubstantiation and the Virgin Mary and the paraphernalia with which the Catholic Church surrounded worship. She disliked the oppressive nature of Catholicism in the 1960s when Catholics could not go into non-Catholic churches. She admired the legacy of Hugh Latimer and Cranmer and Ridley in the pantheon of English Protestantism.

How did she feel about the Church of England being an established church? She spoke all the time with great certainty. She was in favour of it. Having an established church was, she thought, England's only remaining claim to be a Christian country. She was an extremely happy Anglican, she said. Her first problems arose when Canon Hugh Montefiore in 1967 or 1968 went public and declared that there was no reason to assume that Christ was not homosexual, and then three weeks later was made a bishop. She was at Birmingham University at the time and this was her first realisation that the Church of England was compromising. She was most distressed and disgusted. However, for her, the 39 Articles and the Book of Common Prayer and the traditional Church of England continued to be vital, though she began to loathe the banality of modern worship.

She was appalled when the Bishop of Durham, whom she constantly referred to as 'Durham', questioned the resurrection and the Virgin birth, and more recently the immortality of the soul. She felt that the Church of England was not playing a substantial role in the Pro-Life Movement for example, and was equivocal on divorce. She was agnostic for some years, but very slowly in the 1980s came back to the church and started to worry about what was happening.

I asked her if she had ever changed in her politics as she had in her religion. Had she ever thought of, say, joining the Labour Party rather than the Tory Party? She sat up straight in her armchair and became even more brisk. Never for one moment in her whole life, she said, had she identified with the suppression of the individual which is socialism. That seemed to settle the matter, and she looked at me demanding the next question.

I asked if she had come across Irish priests in her instruction, as there were many in London, and how she felt about the sort of Irish Catholicism she had encountered at school: the blind obedience, the superstition, for instance. Yes, she knew what I meant, but in the period of crossing over she had dealt only with the priests at Westminster Cathedral. She did not want to sound snobbish, she said.

She had always known that if they ordained women in the Church of England, she would leave. It would be the last straw. You might as well have a man playing the Virgin Mary. No doubt, she said, the Church of England would do that too. But if you believed in priesthood, then you could not accept the idea of women priests. And if the debate had been theological instead of secular, if it had been argued, for example, that the essence of Christ was his humanity rather than his maleness, it would have been different. She knew that she was going to lose. Some people advised her to stay in and fight. But she said she was going, and she left the church within five minutes of the decision being made, then spent four months deciding what to do.

When she decided to convert were there doctrines which she did not accept? Yes, she said, and listed transubstantiation, the Virgin Mary, purgatory and the paraphernalia surrounding worship.

She had a series of conversations with a priest about doctrine. And she came to have real difficulty with the notion of purgatory. She believed that there was nothing to add once 'full, perfect and sufficient sacrifice' was offered. For three or four months this was the real stumbling block.

She went to see the Cardinal and got his reaction on the numbers who wanted to cross from the Church of England and how they would be facilitated. In the last five minutes she spoke about her own problems. You don't have to be one hundred per cent convinced in your mind about everything, he told her, if you are prepared to believe certain truths.

She decided that she could convert. She realised that within the Catholic Church it was possible for each person to have a different emphasis. Some people who are devoted to the Virgin say the Rosary, for instance, but she didn't. She did not devote much time to the Virgin, but rather to Christ. And the saints, I asked her? 'They hardly get a look in,' she said crisply.

What about confession? It should not be the case, she said, that it is a greater deterrent to sin to have to tell a human being than to have to tell God.

Would she pray for something material that she wanted? No, she said in horror. Would she pray to win an election? She would pray, she replied, that she might not be confounded by her enemies. She did not smile or bat an eyelid when she said this, and even when she added, 'It worked splendidly', she remained deadly serious. But she would pray every day for the prime minister, she added, who is a very decent man beset by an awful lot of ill-informed criticism. She would pray that he might have strength. She would pray for the Queen.

Would she really not pray to win an election? She

did pray, she admitted, that the Tories would win the last election. The Labour Party was led by an atheist, she said. What about St Anthony? If she lost something, would she pray to him to help her find it? She had never said a prayer to St Anthony for anything, she said emphatically. But recently, she went on, she was suing someone, and while she didn't pray to win, she prayed that justice would be done, believing that justice was on her side. Her tone was factual and sardonic.

So you didn't join the Church for the smells or the bells or the saints, I said. She laughed and said no. But she was not prepared for the extraordinary irreverence of the whole thing. Anglicans form an orderly queue, she said, sometimes you could hear a pin drop during a service. But in Catholic churches there was such shuffling – she spoke with great distaste – during the collection and then people criss-crossing and falling over each other during communion. It was a shambles, bedlam. It was difficult to explain to someone who is a Catholic, but it was an enormous shock to the system. I told her that I found this funny, the idea of a Tory Junior Minister at the Department of Employment trying to clean up Catholic services, and I realised that she found the idea funny too, and her account of her distaste was a performance she had tried out on groups with whom she had discussed her new religion.

She considered the most recent papal encyclical a wonderful document, emphasising that there is right and there is wrong. In fact, she had seen a copy the day before it was released. She believed, when she was with the Cardinal, that she was speaking to one of the successors of the Apostles. She liked that link to the early Church.

She had applied to be a Catholic in mid-March 1993 and was received into the Church on 21 April. The ceremony took place in Westminster Cathedral at eight o'clock in the morning; the press and the cameras had been allowed in, but afterwards in the crypt of the House of Commons there was a private service.

While she believed that the ordination of women was wrong, she did not rule out the idea of married priests. She felt now that her earlier views on Catholicism were based on what she saw of Irish Catholicism at her school. There was now, I said, a large number of priests and laity who wanted to follow her from the Church of England into the Church of Rome; did she feel that she had any influence over them? No, no, she insisted. She simply showed that it could be done quickly and individually.

But others who wished to convert were having problems. They were being put through courses run by Catholic lay people who knew nothing about Anglicanism, and who did not know enough to instruct priests and sophisticated lay people in the new religion. People were being put off by their ignorance, Ann Widdecombe said. None the less, there was now a major realignment in Christianity in Britain. She saw the Roman Catholic Church as the natural choice of Christians in this country ten years hence, she said, as the Church of England swayed in the wind.

She was sure she was right in religion as well as in politics. I wondered if she would be able to survive the shuffling crowds and the Roman rules. Her tone was so British; so full of the establishment. Now she had joined the religion of Guy Fawkes and various other treacherous forces. She walked with me to the outside office, where her staff looked up when she entered the room. 'I'm trying to make her an Irish Catholic,' I said to them. She smiled, for once. 'I'm much too reserved and British for that,' she retorted.

15

Forza Italia

IT WAS PALM SUNDAY in Palermo. At nine o'clock in the morning along the Via Roma two boys speeding on a run-down scooter were pulling a donkey behind them. The donkey was dressed up for the Palm Sunday ceremonies with a red bow on its head and red cloth over the saddle. The passenger on the scooter held the rope which dragged the poor animal along, the donkey's hooves slipping and sliding on the smooth surface of the road.

There were palm fronds for sale outside all the churches in the city centre. The green was faded, as though it had been washed or left in the sun. Some had been coated in silver. The people who walked behind the priest in procession down Corso Vittorio Emmanuele to the church of San Micaele each carried a frond of palm. I had just come from Dublin, having spent three or four months under the low and threatening northern sky, with constant rain and wind. This, then, was pure pleasure: the sky blue, the air clear and warm as I walked up towards the cathedral and sat in the sunshine looking at the mixture of styles – Norman, Catalan, Turkish, Italian – that made up the great building. Soon, a procession would begin here too, it would be led by the Cardinal who would preach to the congregation about faith and sin.

But there were other things going on in Sicily that day which were harder to notice, which did not properly belong to the colourful rituals and traditions of the week before Easter. It was election day – the most important election in Italy since the war. The old Christian Democrat Party, created after the war with the full support of the Church to combat communism, had become corrupt; most of its leaders were discredited, some were in jail. A strange phenomenon had crept into the vacuum left by the Christian Democrats. It was hardly a political movement at all. Its title, Forza Italia, was a football slogan rather than the name for a political party; and it had had no time and not much inclination to outline its policies.

The leader, the guiding force, was Silvio Berlusconi, a self-made magnate, who owned three of Italy's six television stations, along with magazines, a newspaper, a huge publishing house, a soccer team, a cinema chain, an advertising agency, an insurance company and numerous other interests. During the campaign he had used his television stations shamelessly to promote his political party. He had failed to attack two of the main dangers to public life in Italy – the mafia and the neo-fascists – and had held no press conferences. Nobody seemed to bother too much about allegations that he had been involved in some of the shadier aspects of Italian life.

Berlusconi was big brother: rich, mysterious, powerful and strong. In post-war Italy, politics had meant polarisation and corruption. Berlusconi came from outside politics, he came from something that people preferred to politics, he came from money. And he represented glitter and glamour, success and vulgarity. In the last two weeks of the election, no polls were allowed, so on this Palm Sunday it was still unclear whether he would win enough seats to form a government.

All over the island the rituals went on, the preparations for Easter. But there was one building in Palermo owned and controlled by the Church where there were no palms for sale that day, or Palm Sunday processions, or sermons about faith and sin. It was a modern building, and until recently it was protected by the army. But on Palm Sunday morning there was no army presence in this street called after the composer of *The Merry Widow*, Franz Lehar.

I rang the bell with the name Gianni di Genaro on it. I spoke through the intercom and then a buzzer was pressed which opened the gate. He stood at the door waiting for me, a man in his late thirties wearing a pullover and slacks. He had joined the Jesuits when he was nineteen, he told me, having come from a middle-class family in Naples. He had worked in Italy and then in Colombia with native Indians and had arrived in Palermo five months ago. He did not come to preach the gospel, or lead processions, or hear confessions. He came to join the other Jesuits in their mission – which began in 1986 – to confront the mafia.

What was this building? I asked him. As he spoke he moved between English and Spanish – he was fluent in both. This was, he said, the Jesuits' school of politics. It was their ambition to educate lay people in Palermo about political and social issues, hoping to encourage political commitment. There were five Jesuits based there full-time, and each one had a specific role; outside experts were used as well. They sought to remove the mystery which was a central part of the mafia's power.

It was important, he went on, that people should understand the culture of the mafia, that this should become a centre of information about how the organisation operated, what it did. The centre existed to study the mafia, but it had other functions: to publish articles, to arrange conferences, to provide analysis. It was in touch with institutions which worked against the mafia, such as the magistrates in Palermo. 'We are very close to some of them,' Father Di Genaro said.

The Jesuits in Palermo had no public church, no parish and no direct contact with the people of the city. Instead, they served the whole administration of Sicily, and were open to any non-religious person. They offered more than moral support against the mafia; they offered an understanding of mafia strategy. Politicians came to the centre for real information and guidelines for action. The Jesuits had begun to analyse the mafia's involvement in the local economy. 'Our aim is to train people. Our expectation is for the long term, the new generation,' Father Di Genaro said.

There had been difficulties. One of their number, Father Pintacude, had left the centre two years earlier. Leolucca Orlando, the mayor of Palermo, had been Pintacude's student when he taught theology and Pintacude had supported him for mayor and continued to support Orlando's La Rete party, which, in the opinion of the Jesuits in Rome and his colleagues in Palermo, endangered the neutrality of the centre, and he was suspended. It was very hard, Father Di Genaro said, as he was so strongly associated with the school and so well known in the city.

'What you are doing then in this building,' I suggested, 'is trying to re-create the ruling class of Palermo.' He nodded. What did this have to do with his function as a priest? The Church, he said, was committed to fighting poverty and criminality; the Jesuits were examining the causes of criminality and the consequences of capitalism.

The Church, he said, had various levels of involvement in society. The traditional Church in Sicily was very strong, was a central point of reference for many people. But people could express their faith in different ways.

As we spoke, bells began to ring all over the city. We could hear them through the window. Father Di Genaro remained undistracted by them as he discussed development and change among Catholics in Italy, who saw no reason to vote for the Christian Democrats or against abortion and divorce simply because the Church favoured such votes. Now, too, in Sicily, the authority of the mafia was, he thought, slowly being eroded. Three or four years ago, he said, it was impossible to talk about the mafia – the word itself could not be spoken publicly; now there was open talk about the mafia and justice.

It was a strange time, he said. There were still groups who controlled old families, there was still an organised mafia, but not like fifteen years ago. A great deal was known, because of the trials which had taken place, about operations and structures. The Jesuits would go on working here indefinitely. Things could change very quickly, he said. The social climate now in the period before the election was different from that of three or four months previously. It was more free; there was less danger, less need for a military guard at the gate. But he made it clear that this, too, was something temporary.

He saw me out and we stood at the door, both perfect targets for a sniper in the adjacent block of flats, whose balconies overlooked the front garden. Judge Falcone, who was murdered by the mafia, had begun the new wave of investigations against them; he had, Father Di Genaro said, become a symbol of conscience and justice, a symbol of commitment for many young lawyers. There was a tree decorated in his memory nearby outside where he used to live. I should go and look at it.

In his book *Men of Honour*, Judge Falcone wrote about returning to Palermo, after an absence of thirteen years, in 1978, and finding the city transformed: 'The centre had been almost completely abandoned. And the splendid villas of the Liberty quarter of Palermo [built at the end of the nineteenth century and the beginning of the twentieth] had been demolished, their place taken by ugly apartment blocks. I found a disfigured, vulgar city, which had partly lost its identity. I went to live in Via Notarbartolo, a street that descends towards Via della Liberta, the heart of Palermo . . . One day as I arrived home with my usual regrettable escort of wailing sirens, police cars and bodyguards with guns drawn, I overheard a passer-by whisper, "To be protected like that, he must have committed an outrageous crime!"

'Talking about the mafia with Sicilian politicians,' Falcone observed, 'I have often been amazed by their ignorance on the subject.' He describes their rituals in his book. 'Then the swearing-in ceremony takes place: each man is asked which hand he shoots with, the index finger of that hand is pricked and a drop of blood taken and spread on to a sacred image: often a Virgin Mary at the Annunciation, whose feast is celebrated on the 25 of March and who is considered the patron saint of Cosa Nostra. The image is then set alight and the candidate passes it from hand to hand, trying not to let it go out, and solemnly swears never to betray the code of Cosa Nostra, and if he does so to burn like the image.

'I have learned,' Falcone wrote, 'that the logic of the mafia is never obsolete or incomprehensible. It is nothing more than the logic of power . . . At certain moments, these mafiosi seem to me the only rational beings in a world populated by madmen.' On the last page of the book, he wrote: 'One usually dies because one is alone, or because one has got into something over one's head. One often dies because one does not have the right alliances, because one is not given support. In Sicily the mafia kills the servants of the state that the state has not been able to protect.'

The mafia blew him up, with his wife and three bodyguards, on the road from the airport into Palermo on 23 May 1992. He had returned from Rome on a secret, unscheduled flight. A month after his death a hundred thousand people marched in protest against the mafia in the streets of the city. In the local elections in October 1993 Leolucca Orlando, leader of the anti-mafia party La Rete had been elected mayor. People were now watching to see how Orlando and Berlusconi would fare in Sicily in the general election.

On the afternoon of Palm Sunday 1994 I walked around the abandoned centre of Palermo, 'the disfigured, vulgar city' described by Falcone. Almost every building in the narrow streets and the small squares was crumbling and faded beyond any possibility of repair, even though some had signs up saying that they were being restored. Everything seemed poverty-stricken and desolate. The area between the port and the Via Roma, one of the straight streets added to the city in the nineteenth century, had once been full of churches and palaces. In other Italian cities and towns the old centre had been re-built and lovingly preserved. Here it was run-down and depressed, with no bars, nowhere to sit, a few watchful figures standing about, and an overwhelming sense that nothing was going to change.

The next day I went to look at the tree which grew in front of Falcone's former apartment. It was one of those strong trees that grow out of a tiny bit of dry soil on Mediterranean streets. It was guarded by two young soldiers with machine-guns. There were flowers in the soil below it: gladioli, chrysanthemums, fuchsia, winter jasmine, cyclamen. And there were all sorts of strange mementos: posters, photographs, a carved icon, dried flowers, poems, pieces of clothing and paper. Some of these were pinned to the tree; some lay on the soil. One note pinned to the tree said that Falcone died for us, gave up his life for us against the mafia. It was a mixture of a religious shrine and a more primitive memorial. As I examined the tree the two soldiers stood there watching the street. The general election was taking place over two days, and this was the second day.

I flew to Rome that afternoon and watched the election results in a friend's house in a village outside the city. The exit polls favoured Berlusconi, and the results, as they came in, confirmed this. If he could make a deal with the Northern League, who wanted to give political status to the north/south divide in Italy, and the neo-fascists, whose leader would say that Mussolini was the greatest leader in twentieth-century history, he could become prime minister. He had won a landslide victory in Sicily. Forza Italia could effectively replace the Christian Democrats as the mainstay of centre and right-wing politics in Italy. Just as the Catholic Church was the bedrock of the Christian Democrats, the television set was the basis for Forza Italia.

We watched our set for Berlusconi to appear. When he came on his face was like a mask: it was hard to tell what age he was, whether he was good looking or not, whether he was smiling or not. He held a microphone and began to speak. We flicked from channel to channel; all six covered his address. After a while it became clear that he was saying nothing new and did not seem about to stop. He was uttering political platitudes, vague statements about Italy and its future. Two of the state channels went back to reporting on the election results, the third ran the film of Berlusconi speaking in the background but continued with a studio debate. But his own three channels covered him until he was finished. The cameras did not move, the angles did not change, there were no close-ups. The camera remained distant from him, filming the top half of his body only, as though he were an Eastern European dictator in the early days of television. It was like something out of science fiction, or a dream about television, or a new version of *Nineteen Eighty-Four*. We watched it in a state of wonder, the brave new world of post-Christian Italy: the media magnate as god, the prime minister who owns three television stations. Elsewhere, in the Piazza del Popolo in the city, the neo-fascists were holding a rally, roaring and cheering 'Viva il duce!'

On Holy Thursday I flew to Bari in the south and then took a train to Taranto, a port city on the instep of Italy. The *Michelin Guide* had a map of the city which looked promising. The old quarter was on an island connected by a causeway to a new city. It was a glorious day, the sky a pure, rich, summer blue over the sea. I walked on to the island and along the seafront, glancing down the narrow streets which led into the heart of the old city, which even from a distance seemed shadowy and down at heel.

I made my way to the modest cathedral, which had scaffolding on the front. I had a coffee in the small stand-up bar beside it, looking out on the run-down square where a hearse was waiting. When the mourners came out of the cathedral the owner of the bar moved quickly to pull the iron grille in front of the door halfway down as a mark of respect. He stood outside. I watched through the window.

It was a child's white coffin which a man held cradled in his arms and then placed in the back of the hearse. The mother was in her thirties, a strong-looking woman with unkempt hair and an open coat. She was distraught. Two other women supported her as she shouted and sobbed. Her voice was low and strong and echoed in the square. Her husband, as far as I could make out, was the dark-skinned man to her left. He held a handkerchief to his face and cried. The back door of the hearse was closed, and the hearse moved off through the narrow streets. The mourners walked slowly after it; they had no transport.

I waited for a while and then finished my coffee and followed the route the funeral had taken across the bridge towards the new city. The long winding street which led to the bridge had obviously been important in the eighteenth and early nineteenth centuries. Now, you could smell the poverty in the dark doorways, the graffiti was about heroin and the sense of misery was complete. This island, which seemed so appealing on the map in the guide, was a new ghetto.

But once I crossed the bridge I was in a new Taranto. As the afternoon went on, this city with wide, airy streets leading down to the port grew busier as shops reopened after lunch. It was easy to see why the old quarter on the island had been abandoned for order and fresh air.

It is common in Italy to see posters bordered in black on the wall announcing a death. Here this was done to announce an anniversary as well, giving the name of the dead person and below, in smaller print, the names of the relatives. There were four or five of these pasted to the wall in every street. I passed a coffin shop in the city centre, with different types of carved coffins in various colours on display. Holy Thursday was, I suppose, a suitable day to be confronted with so many images of death.

At eleven o'clock that night in the Piazza Giovanni XXIII shrouded male figures began to appear in front of the church. They wore blue big-brimmed hats tied with string around their necks and medals and rosary beads hanging from belts around their waists. All of them were in bare feet, and their heads were covered with a white sheet with tiny, round slits for their eyes. These strange, ghost-like figures moved in twos across the square towards the church, swaying as they walked, as though they were on a boat.

Earlier, because of the grid-like pattern of the streets, I could not work out which direction I was walking in, and I asked a couple to guide me to the old city. It's dangerous there, the man said to me, especially at night. What about tonight, I asked, are there not processions all night? He shrugged to signify that it was still dangerous, and then he pointed me in the right direction.

The cathedral was still open. People milled in through the front door and walked up the aisle, visiting the frescoes underneath the altar, queuing to look at the rich baroque side chapel with its gilded walls and painted dome, and then leaving by the side doors.

The church of San Domenico was at a narrow T-junction beyond the cathedral in the old city. At a quarter to twelve the statue of the Virgin had already been carried into the street. There were double steps leading to the church door, braziers had been lit all along the parapet at the top and were burning fiercely in the night wind. The statue of the Virgin had been placed on a float. She was dressed in black with a black veil ringed in gold, a handkerchief in one hand and the

Sacred Heart in the other. She was old and there was a frown on her forehead. There were nineteenth-century lamps at her feet and some flowers. Of the four men in front carrying the float, two were in military garb, and two behind them were in dinner jackets. All four wore crowns of thorns on their heads. In Taranto it was the custom to bid money for the right to carry the float.

There was a huge crowd in the street, people watching and trying to push their way forward. From a temporary stage opposite the church various television crews filmed what was happening. Everything was bathed in the hard television lights, which gave the scene a lurid significance, as though we were witnessing a piece of important current affairs, as though something momentous was about to occur.

I managed to make my way on to the steps of the church so I could see the brass band behind the float and another band in front being led by two dozen figures in white cowls with crowns of thorns and black tunics, and black hats tied around their necks. An hour went by and the procession hardly moved; some people had video cameras and were busy finding new angles; others carried large, thick candles maybe three feet high.

We waited. I could not work out what we were waiting for. I asked somebody what was going to happen and he wrote the word 'nazzicata' in my notebook. When the bands played, he said, the statue swayed. Had I not noticed? I had watched the bands playing the sad café music, but noticed nothing. Watch the next time, he said. When the band struck up again, the float swayed as though it was blown by the wind, and everyone gave it their full attention, as though a miracle was about to take place. But this seemed to be the miracle: the statue of the grieving Virgin swaying to the music. And when the band stopped, people went back to talking to each other or refocusing their video cameras or, if they were young, fondling and kissing each other.

The procession began to move now, and people lit their candles and followed it. But progress was slow. By two-thirty the float had still not made it to Via Porto, which was less than a hundred yards away. The crowd remained in the square. All the buildings around were derelict and uninhabited, as though they had been bombed and then abandoned. The men in cowls walked by barefoot, and a man carried a cross which was strangely decorated with a miniature hammer, spear, whip, chalice and crown of thorns. But even when the music played and we could see the Virgin swaying in the distance, people continued to talk and laugh. People were having a late night out; there were still children walking about.

At three o'clock in the morning in Piazza Fontana, close to where the procession had halted again, there was cold beer for sale from vans, and popcorn and other refreshments.

By now, the crowd around the procession had thinned out. It was cold. The television lights had been turned off, which removed all the glamour from the procession and left the street dark and desolate. The group of women with lighted candles had grown in number. Now there were perhaps one hundred women standing patiently behind the float. Some of them were well wrapped up; they were going to stay out all night. They looked different from the crowd who had been around the church, or the young people in the square. They seemed serious, stoical, prepared to wait, and there was something dramatic and primitive in the way they stood as though they were a women's chorus from a Greek play. They did not look rich, even though they were well dressed. I noticed when I looked down that all of them had bare feet.

In the morning in the modern city, all the shops were open, even though it was Good Friday. On one of the long main streets, the same statue, the frowning Virgin in black with the Sacred Heart in one hand and a handkerchief in the other, was still being carried along. I recognised some of the faces of the men in the brass band and men carrying the float. They had been going for twelve hours. People stood on the side of the street to watch; some had video cameras, others had been shopping. The women I had seen in the old city were not here now, nor anybody like them. The band struck up and the statue began to sway. But business went on as usual, people walked in and out of posh shops. I realised that I was watching a pageant from Berlusconi's Italy, Catholic and conservative, but deeply materialistic too, excited by the possibilities of glitter and wealth which Berlusconi and his empire offered, but holding on to traditions and processions on feast days, taking part in the great balancing act between the traditional and the venal which Berlusconi had organised.

That morning the swaying statue in broad daylight seemed just another spectacle to be videoed, a mild distraction rather than a thing of mystery or primitive wonder, as it had been for a while the previous night once the television lights had been turned off in the old abandoned city. And now in the bright new Taranto the band stopped and the procession moved forward, then came to a standstill again. It would take another hour for it to get back to the old city.

On Saturday night at eight o'clock I joined one of the queues for Midnight Mass at St Peter's in Rome.

Here, too, as in the rest of Catholic Europe, Midnight Mass had been moved to nine o'clock in the evening, which meant in certain places that there was no drunken shouting or brawling any more, and here that the ceremony could last for three and a half hours without people seeing the dawn on the way home.

Some people had a ticket, but you did not need one. Each person was searched and anything which was considered dangerous was removed. At eight-thirty there were still empty seats in the vast basilica. Just as I was seated, a small man who was an official of the Church, with all the busy and bossy watchfulness that characterises the layman put in charge, motioned a group of us to come further up the church where he found us seats. For the rest of the ceremony he and his colleague found more empty places and suitable people to fill them, and watched us all in case we thought of behaving badly.

This, it was explained in Italian, English and Spanish, would be the liturgy of the light. 'On this night death passes to life,' the voice from the loudspeaker said, and then warned us not to use flash cameras when the lights were turned off.

Everybody turned to look as the tips of the cardinals' mitres appeared at the back of the basilica; people around me stood on their chairs to get a better view of the Pope as he walked up the centre aisle after the bishops and the altar boys. People flashed their cameras at him. He seemed worn and distant from us as he walked slowly up the church.

It was time for people to light the candles they carried in plastic tubes. Soon the lights began to dip in the basilica, but the place was too big and there were too many people for any real atmosphere to develop. 'Lumens Christi,' a voice from the loudspeakers intoned and the congregation replied: 'Deo gratias.'

Suddenly, when this was over, the lights came up. It had all happened too quickly; people blinked and looked around in surprise. The Pope sat on St Peter's throne under the black and gold canopy with curved columns, and singing began in Latin, soothing sounds that I knew. I noticed a man moving along a ledge just under the dome of the basilica. He was tiny up there, otherworldly; down below, the readings told of Genesis, Moses parting the Sea, Abraham and Isaac and the Exodus, the elemental stories.

The Pope prayed in Latin. I looked up at the ceiling – it was gold and white. The Epistle was from St Paul to the Romans. Bells began to ring. It was only when the choir and the congregation began to sing 'Gloria in excelsis Deo' that I realised that if I closed my eyes I could be right back in Enniscorthy Cathedral in the early 1960s. The arrangement of the 'Gloria' was exactly the same as the one we had used. It was, musically, so ordinary and dull that I had always imagined it belonged to provincial towns in Ireland, but it must have belonged here in Rome too.

Nothing had changed: 'Dominus vobiscum' was followed by 'Et cum spiritu tuo.' I had not heard the phrase 'Sursum corda' for thirty years. It had been replaced by 'Lift up your hearts' in the English Mass. But more than anything, standing and sitting through this ceremony in St Peter's brought me back to the half boredom, half attention of long childhood sessions in Enniscorthy Cathedral, where anything would distract you – the ceiling, the bells, a man on a ledge – and then the prayers and the ceremony would pull you back again; where you had time to brood about anything that came into your mind without any adult knowing what you were thinking.

The choir in Enniscorthy always sang the 'Alleluia'

with great gusto. The Pope sang out the word in a harsh, nasal voice. Then the organ played and he put his hands over his face. All the other church dignitaries and the altar boys left the altar, left him alone there. We listened in Italian to the story of the Resurrection.

I knew that there would be baptisms now, and I presumed that Romans carried newborn babies to the Vatican to be baptised by the Pope. I expected the sound of babies' crying to break through the prayers, but there was no such sound. I asked the man beside me where the bambini were. 'Bambini no,' he said, 'nuovi cristiani'. All those to be baptised were new Christians, adults, converts, from outside Italy. They waited as we renewed our baptismal vows and articles of faith. Some of the women, the Koreans and the Japanese especially, were dressed in colourful costumes, and each approached the Pope with a sponsor who handed a piece of paper to the priest behind him. Everyone in the church could see them, speculate about their nationality and look at their clothes, as a women's choir sang beautiful soaring music. The converts crossed the main altar three times; they were getting value from their trip to Rome.

Now it was time for Mass. The Pope's throne was taken away and a number of cardinals and bishops joined him at the altar. Once more, the Sanctus was the same setting as in Enniscorthy thirty years ago. I knew the words of the Consecration off by heart in Latin, so did most people in this congregation who were more than thirty-five years old. Listening to it now was like walking back into the living room in my parents' house as it was in 1960, lino on the floor, red brocade curtains, a wireless in the corner; like suddenly seeing a stain on the table in that room, or a piece of wood chipped from a chair, or the old clothes-horse that was always around the fire on Saturdays. Or looking at old photographs, old hairstyles, cars from thirty years ago. 'Hoc est enim Corpus meum,' the Pope said as he raised the Host and the congregation looked up for a moment and then down again, as we all had been taught to do in our Catholic schools all over the world. At that moment adults, middle-aged women particularly, always appeared at their most demure, most serious and solemn.

I was told, beforehand, that the new habit of giving out a communion wafer into the hand – rather than directly into the mouth – was not followed in St Peter's because of the possibility that certain profane tourists would take the Host home as a souvenir. But this turned out not to be true. I watched the priests giving out communion, and they did, in fact, allow the faithful to decide which method they wanted to use.

The ceremony finished at twenty past twelve: the Pope and his entourage, including some Swiss guards, made their way down the centre aisle. This time the congregation applauded, stood on chairs to get a better view and took photographs. The Pope seemed tired and in pain, as he walked slowly carrying his silver cross.

I went back the next morning at eleven o'clock for Easter Sunday Mass and the Urbi et Orbi blessing in St Peter's Square. I had a special pass which meant I could sit on a chair close to the altar, while the crowds, thousands of tourists and Romans, stood in the pouring rain. But soon this did not matter much as the chair became so wet that I had to stand like the rest. Once more, there was nothing by any of the great composers – no Palestrina even; it was the Latin Mass with the choir singing the tunes I had always known.

This was not what I had wanted or expected. I had

expected the crowds in the vast square, the Pope on Easter Sunday morning and the great city to take me somewhere I had not been before, to give me a sense of what it is like to be at the centre of things. Instead, it had taken me home, and made home seem like the centre of things. Close by was the restored Sistine Chapel, and all the churches with their magnificent art, and public buildings, the Roman ruins. None of this majesty was in the atmosphere in the square on Easter Sunday morning, nor at Midnight Mass the previous night. Maybe I had been waiting for some image, some moment, which would illuminate the changes which were happening in Italian politics and the Church. Maybe I had even seen it and failed to recognise it. Maybe it was the strange ordinariness of the ceremonies, how much they belonged to my experience and background. Maybe that was important and instructive. I did not know.

After Mass the Pope left the altar and went on to the balcony, and he began to bless the world. He listed the names of all the countries and let people in the square who had come from those places shout up greetings and applaud. He spoke in as many languages as he could think of, including Irish. The rain had stopped now. When he had finished, he stood on the balcony waving at us, while a band played and people cheered. He remained there as though he could not decide at what moment he should leave. And then he turned and walked back into the Vatican.

16

The End of History

MY FATHER WROTE about Vinegar Hill, which we could see across the valley from the front windows of our house. 'It is a landmark that symbolises the spirit of the historic past, a monument to the grim and gallant struggle of 1798,' he wrote in an essay on the town and its past. I knew from childhood certain things – I hesitate to say facts – about the 1798 Rising in Enniscorthy in which we were defeated: how the English had muskets whereas we just had pikes; how the English poured boiling tar on the scalps of the Irish, and when the tar had dried they peeled it off, whereas our side, the peasant Catholic Irish, had been noble and brave. The names of the towns and villages around us were in the history books and in the songs which we learned in school. They were the places where battles had been fought or atrocities committed.

But there was one place that I did not know had a connection with 1798 until I was in my twenties. The place is called Scullabogue. Even as I write it down now it has a strange resonance. It was where our side took a large number of Protestant men, women and children, put them in a barn and burned them to death. Our rising, sparked off by local discontent and the ideas of the French Revolution, had become sectarian. The name Scullabogue does not come up in the songs, and I have no memory of my father talking or writing about it. Its memory was erased from what a Catholic child should know about 1798. It was a complication in our glorious past.

Our glorious past included resettlement and plantation. Between 1540 and 1640 two-thirds of the long-established Irish and Old English owners in the area were removed, and replaced by English planters. The poets and adventurers Raleigh and Spenser spent time in the town. All along the fertile Slaney valley the farms were owned by Protestants; the Catholics became the dispossessed. And the two communities remained divided, the Catholics increasingly mutinous, the Protestants always loyal to the British Crown.

Enniscorthy, with its rich hinterland, became a market town. When I was growing up there was a thriving flour mill, a maltings and a bacon factory. All three were family-owned. Two of my aunts worked in the office in the mill. A large number of families in the town made their living from these industries. On certain days you could hear pigs squealing on their way into the factory. In summer there was a permanent smell of dust and grain in the vicinity of the mill and the maltings. In the 1960s, these small factories were expanding: over the hump of the railway bridge the maltings added new iron lungs, the mill built new offices beside the silos.

The owners appeared patrician figures. Old Mr Brown who owned the mill was remote and exceptionally polite. There was a kind of steely innocence about him – he was English or Scottish – and it seemed natural that he should own a mill.

The owners of the maltings had their own mystique, they had once lived in the Castle in the middle of the town. In the 1960s the owners of the bacon factory built a huge, modern house outside the town overlooking the river. No one had ever seen so much glass.

These people had inherited the earth and we had inherited our place in the world they created. But there had been changes. All around stood old stone warehouses, derelict now because transport was easier and storage of grain and other material not as important. There were remnants of an old mill in the town, a sign that technology was improving, that a mill wheel was out of date in an era of electrification.

But none of these monuments to times gone by prepared us for the changes which were to come. At first they were small changes in name, as new partners and investors joined the old ones. No one thought too much about this, it was part of the inevitable process of modernisation.

But now the bacon factory is gone and the mill and maltings have been scaled down and are as good as closed. They did not close because of falling profits, or shifts in the market, but because of takeovers; because large conglomerates, in the brave new world of the European Community, moved in to consolidate a monopoly. They closed because such small town industries are a thing of the past. They will not open again.

In the meantime, as history slowly comes to an end in Enniscorthy, the roads have improved and people keep marvelling at the new stretches of highway, the roundabouts, the new bridge, all built with the help of European money to prepare Enniscorthy for the future and allow the container trucks to trundle through; the town has become a place on the road to somewhere else.

From the new bridge you can still see the spires of the Protestant and Catholic churches. After 1798 an uneasy peace reigned until the War of Independence, when many big Protestant houses were burned, and the Civil War, when the Protestant church was occupied by the IRA. In the new state, created in 1922, the Protestant community remained strong in the Enniscorthy area. They still had farms along the valley, and some shops in the town, and they seemed settled in the new republic so that the rise of violence and sectarian hatred in Northern Ireland made little difference.

Yet the two communities remained apart to some extent. Catholic women wore permed hair and high-heeled shoes; Protestant women wore straight hair and flat shoes. The names, both Christian names and surnames, were different. Catholics and Protestants played golf and rugby together, but the Gaelic games of hurling and football were, in general, played only by Catholics. On a Sunday morning as you walked back from Mass, you would see the Protestants outside their church after service, a small, tight community oddly separate from our own.

Our cathedral was built on a larger site at the top of a hill. It was a massive towering structure. When it opened in the 1840s, it must have been the first time that people had reason to pay attention to the clock, to arrive somewhere all at the same time, to remain quiet for long periods, to stand up together, sit down together, allow others to pass, to wait their turn. It was where a certain sort of civilisation began in the town.

My parents were married in this church; I was baptised here. I watched my father's coffin being wheeled down this church, the altar boy in front of the coffin carrying the large gold-plated cross. The walls were built of rubble from a medieval Franciscan friary. 'Many of the facing stones', wrote one local historian, a priest who was a friend of my father's, 'are no bigger than the palm of one's hand, and it would be difficult to find a piece of facing showing more than one square foot of surface. Yet the stones, running in shades from grey-blue to deep green, are beautifully laid, and the whole work is a wonderful tribute to the tradesmen who built the church.'

By 1994, however, it was clear that the cathedral was in need of serious restoration. Collections were made to fund the work and it was decided that after Easter the cathedral would have to close. Mass would now be said in the local convent and in the large hall owned by the Gaelic Athletic Association. But the local Church of Ireland offered the use of their church as well. I had never been inside the Protestant church in Enniscorthy, nor had most people in the town. For many years until the Second Vatican Council, there was a complete ban on Catholics entering a Protestant church, even for the funeral of a friend.

On Saturday, 16 April 1994, then, evening Mass was said to a packed congregation in the Protestant church in Enniscorthy. On the way into the church groups of people were photographed to mark what the priest called 'this historic occasion'. The Protestant church was much smaller than ours, and more square in shape. There was a beautiful marble pulpit with an eagle's head on the lectern. Some stained glass showed Jesus in a red tunic holding a lamb, but other long windows were made of light green glass. There were only two or three memorial plaques.

It was strange to be in the Protestant church seeing familiar Catholic faces. We looked around until the Mass began. It was announced that there would be no sermon. There must have been some old ghosts on both sides of what was once a sectarian divide hovering around us, wondering what the hell was going on. My eye wandered to the plaque on the wall to my left. It was to the memory of Archibald Hamilton Jacob, Late Captain of the Loyal Vinegar Hill Rangers, Who Departed This Life, December 1836, Aged 66 Years: 'As a Magistrate, He Was Impartial, As a Subject Loyal, As a Soldier Generous and Brave'.

He must have been up there on Vinegar Hill during the battle in 1798, and he must have been around for the slaughter afterwards, which I heard so much about when I was a child. We were in his church now; we had been invited. Protestant service as well as Mass would be said here in the morning. No one else was very interested in this plaque, or the sectarian legacy. The plaque was a memorial to a past which we would not repeat. History had come to an end in Enniscorthy.

Acknowledgments

I am grateful to Aengus Fanning and Anne Harris at the *Sunday Independent* in Dublin, where shorter versions of some of these chapters appeared. I would also like to thank Angela Rohan, Antony Farrell, Catriona Crowe, Imogen Parker, Fintan O'Toole, Aidan Dunne, Andrew O'Hagan, June Levine, Ivor Browne, Marie Donnelly, David McKenna, Vivienne Guinness and Muireann Ní Bhrollcháin who read various chapters of the book as I worked on it; and Marie Hayes, Dympna Hayes, Paddy Agnew, Sean Finnegan, Joseph O'Connor, Tim Hulse, Jim Cantwell, Helen Shaw, Andrew Noble, Mark Brennock, Yetti Redmond, Nuala Stack, Bairbre Tóibín and Michael Stack who offered shelter or support. I am also grateful to Dermot Bolger and Leo Duffy for introducing me to modern technology; to Jenny Cottom at Jonathan Cape for her painstaking and loving attention to me and my book; and to Neil Belton, my publisher, for his constant encouragement and his committed interest and involvement.